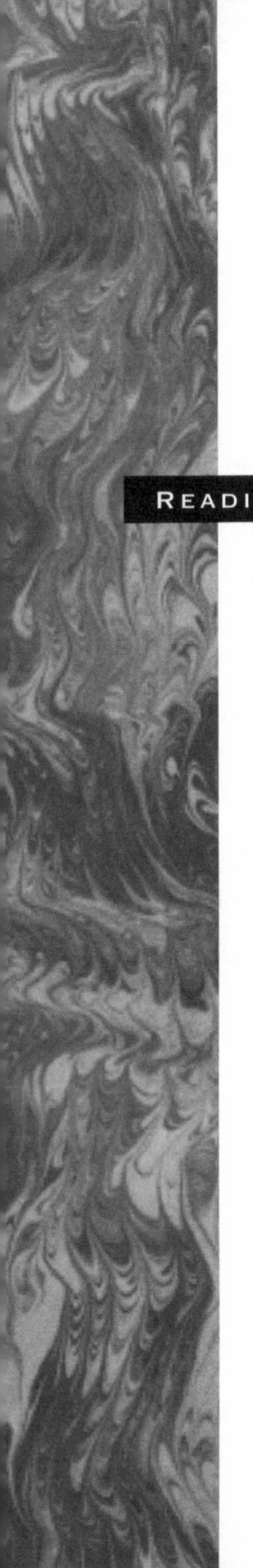

READINGS ON

THE ADVENTURES OF HUCKLEBERRY FINN

Other titles in the Greenhaven Press Literary Companion Series:

American Authors

Maya Angelou
Stephen Crane
Emily Dickinson
William Faulkner
F. Scott Fitzgerald
Nathaniel Hawthorne
Ernest Hemingway
Herman Melville
Arthur Miller
Eugene O'Neill
Edgar Allan Poe
John Steinbeck
Mark Twain
Thornton Wilder

British Authors

Jane Austen
Joseph Conrad
Charles Dickens

World Authors

Fyodor Dostoyevsky
Homer
Sophocles

American Literature

The Catcher in the Rye
The Glass Menagerie
The Great Gatsby
Of Mice and Men
The Scarlet Letter

British Literature

Animal Farm
Beowulf
The Canterbury Tales
Lord of the Flies
Romeo and Juliet
Shakespeare: The Comedies
Shakespeare: The Histories
Shakespeare: The Sonnets
Shakespeare: The Tragedies
A Tale of Two Cities

World Literature

The Diary of a Young Girl

THE GREENHAVEN PRESS

TO AMERICAN LITERATURE

READINGS ON

THE ADVENTURES OF HUCKLEBERRY FINN

David L. Bender, *Publisher*
Bruno Leone, *Executive Editor*
Brenda Stalcup, *Managing Editor*
Bonnie Szumski, *Series Editor*
Katie de Koster, *Book Editor*

Greenhaven Press, San Diego, CA

Library of Congress Cataloging-in-Publication Data

Readings on the Adventures of Huckleberry Finn / Katie de Koster, book editor.
p. cm. — (The Greenhaven Press literary companion to American literature)
ISBN 1-56510-819-1 (lib. : alk. paper). —
ISBN 1-56510-818-3 (pbk. : alk. paper)
1. Twain, Mark, 1835–1910. Adventures of Huckleberry Finn. 2. Adventure stories, American—History and criticism. 3. Mississippi River—In literature. 4. Boys in literature. I. de Koster, Katie, 1948– . II. Series.
PS1305.R42 1998
813'.4—dc21 97-43630
CIP

Cover photo: Library of Congress

PO Box 289009
San Diego, CA 92198-9009
Printed in the U.S.A.

"I've just finished writing a book, and modesty compels me to say it's a rattling good one, too."

Mark Twain, in an 1883 letter to his London publisher Andrew Chatto, on completing the manuscript for The Adventures of Huckleberry Finn

Contents

Chapter 2: Images of America in *Huckleberry Finn*

Chapter 3: Issues of Race in *Huckleberry Finn*

FOREWORD

"'Tis the good reader that makes the good book."

Ralph Waldo Emerson

The story's bare facts are simple: The captain, an old and scarred seafarer, walks with a peg leg made of whale ivory. He relentlessly drives his crew to hunt the world's oceans for the great white whale that crippled him. After a long search, the ship encounters the whale and a fierce battle ensues. Finally the captain drives his harpoon into the whale, but the harpoon line catches the captain about the neck and drags him to his death.

A simple story, a straightforward plot—yet, since the 1851 publication of Herman Melville's *Moby-Dick*, readers and critics have found many meanings in the struggle between Captain Ahab and the whale. To some, the novel is a cautionary tale that depicts how Ahab's obsession with revenge leads to his insanity and death. Others believe that the whale represents the unknowable secrets of the universe and that Ahab is a tragic hero who dares to challenge fate by attempting to discover this knowledge. Perhaps Melville intended Ahab as a criticism of Americans' tendency to become involved in well-intentioned but irrational causes. Or did Melville model Ahab after himself, letting his fictional character express his anger at what he perceived as a cruel and distant god?

Although literary critics disagree over the meaning of *Moby-Dick*, readers do not need to choose one particular interpretation in order to gain an understanding of Melville's novel. Instead, by examining various analyses, they can gain numerous insights into the issues that lie under the surface of the basic plot. Studying the writings of literary critics can also aid readers in making their own assessments of *Moby-Dick* and other literary works and in developing analytical thinking skills.

The Greenhaven Literary Companion Series was created with these goals in mind. Designed for young adults, this unique anthology series provides an engaging and comprehensive introduction to literary analysis and criticism. The essays included in the Literary Companion Series are chosen for their accessibility to a young adult audience and are expertly edited in consideration of both the reading and comprehension levels of this audience. In addition, each essay is introduced by a concise summation that presents the contributing writer's main themes and insights. Every anthology in the Literary Companion Series contains a varied selection of critical essays that cover a wide time span and express diverse views. Wherever possible, primary sources are represented through excerpts from authors' notebooks, letters, and journals and through contemporary criticism.

Each title in the Literary Companion Series pays careful consideration to the historical context of the particular author or literary work. In-depth biographies and detailed chronologies reveal important aspects of authors' lives and emphasize the historical events and social milieu that influenced their writings. To facilitate further research, every anthology includes primary and secondary source bibliographies of articles and/or books selected for their suitability for young adults. These engaging features make the Greenhaven Literary Companion series ideal for introducing students to literary analysis in the classroom or as a library resource for young adults researching the world's great authors and literature.

Exceptional in its focus on young adults, the Greenhaven Literary Companion Series strives to present literary criticism in a compelling and accessible format. Every title in the series is intended to spark readers' interest in leading American and world authors, to help them broaden their understanding of literature, and to encourage them to formulate their own analyses of the literary works that they read. It is the editors' hope that young adult readers will find these anthologies to be true companions in their study of literature.

Introduction

Since *The Adventures of Huckleberry Finn* hit the shelves in 1885, adults have found it unsuitable fare for impressionable young minds. Nineteenth-century keepers of the public morals feared the effect such an uncivilized protagonist would have on young readers. They might "follow Huck's example," in the words of Mark Twain Library editor Walter Blair, "and use faulty grammar, play hookey, steal, lie, and run away."

More than a century later, some parents, educators, and public officials still say that students should not be required—or perhaps even allowed—to read the book. But today they have an entirely different reason: racism. Some find the book's failure to condemn slavery explicitly (as Harriet Beecher Stowe did in *Uncle Tom's Cabin*, for example) to be racist. A few object to the portrayal of Jim, claiming that this runaway slave seems more childlike than adult at times, especially at the end of the book, when he submits to Tom Sawyer's wild schemes to "free" him. The most vocal objections center on just one word, which appears over and over: *nigger.*

Exposing a Racist Society

Mark Twain was raised with slaves. He was taught that slavery was good, approved by both God and man. As he wrote in his *Autobiography*, "The wise and the good and the holy were unanimous in their conviction that slavery was right, righteous, sacred, the peculiar pet of the Deity and a condition which the slave himself ought to be daily and nightly thankful for." He went on to note that

> there was nothing about the slavery of the Hannibal region [in Missouri, where he grew up] to rouse one's dozing humane instincts to activity. It was the mild domestic slavery, not the brutal plantation article. Cruelties were very rare and exceedingly and wholesomely unpopular. . . . It is commonly believed that an infallible effect of slavery was to make such as lived in its midst hard-hearted. I think it had no such effect—speaking in general terms. I think it stupefied everybody's humanity as regarded the slave, but stopped there.

This was Missouri (a slave state) during the 1840s and 1850s. It was Mark Twain's childhood world—and Huck Finn's world, too. The book presents what Blair calls Twain's "personal panoramic survey of an antebellum society." But it is Twain's adult understanding of the evils and horrors of slavery that guides Huck when a crisis of conscience leads him to defy all the rules, to reject what he has been taught is the law of God as well as of man. Huck believes he will go to hell for eternity because he decides to help Jim.

The Adventures of Huckleberry Finn is clearly antislavery. The reader is supposed to believe Huck made the right choice when he helped an escaped slave. But this does not clearly address the issue of racism, the idea that one person is better than another simply because the colors of their skin differ.

Twain was raised in a racist society, and the language he used accurately reflects the attitudes of that society. In order for Huck's sacrifice—his immortal soul—to have meaning, he must believe he is doing wrong and yet do it anyway. He is stealing a woman's property, her "nigger," and stealing is wrong. Yet Huck, without using big words like *abolition* or *emancipation*, cuts through the law to see humanity in Jim. He may not be able to articulate his rejection of racism, but in trading his soul for Jim's freedom, he has clearly rejected racist values.

The Portrayal of Jim

A few writers have objected to Twain's portrayal of Jim as being somehow less than a man, submissively going along with the boys' schemes, being easily fooled by their mischief and full of superstitious beliefs. But Jim is a true-to-life portrait of a generous and patient man, as Twain made clear when talking about his childhood in his *Autobiography:*

> We had a faithful and affectionate good friend, ally and adviser in "Uncle Dan'l," a middle-aged slave whose head was the best one in the negro quarter, whose sympathies were wide and warm and whose heart was honest and simple and knew no guile. He has served me well these many, many years. I have not seen him for more than half a century and yet spiritually I have had his welcome company a good part of that time and have staged him in books under his own name and as "Jim," and carted him all around—to Hannibal, down the Mississippi on a raft and even across the Desert of Sahara in a balloon—and he has endured it all with the patience and friendliness and loyalty which were his birthright. It was on [Twain's uncle's] farm that I got my strong liking for his race

> and my appreciation of certain of its fine qualities. This feeling and this estimate have stood the test of sixty years and more and have suffered no impairment. The black face is as welcome to me now as it was then.

In dealing with the objections to Jim's resignation, especially to Tom Sawyer's wild schemes at the end of the book, a theory put forth by Twain scholar Myra Jehlen is illuminating. She notes that while the novel was set in the period before the Civil War, it was written during Reconstruction. While the slaves had been emancipated legally, she writes,

> Reconstruction failed to establish the conditions that would realize this emancipation, so that the former slaves returned to a servitude from which it would require a different sort of intervention to free them from any declaration. . . . *Huckleberry Finn* is not only about slavery and the nation's compromised past but also, and in my view principally, about the contemporary dilemma of Reconstruction.

Twain was not merely addressing the wickedness of slavery; he was using it to reveal the problems of racism that the abolition of slavery had not solved.

The "N" Word

Even if the book and its author are absolved of all charges of racism, the problem of the "n" word remains.

Today the word *nigger* can be offensive, disrespectful, and hurtful. It appears hundreds of times in *Huckleberry Finn.* Some parents have said that their children have been hurt, humiliated, and made emotionally distraught by reading the book.

Most writers and educators agree that it is important to understand the context of the novel—the era in which it was written, the era it portrayed, and Twain's deep-seated beliefs. As Walter Blair states, "The book fiercely advocates (as its author did) tolerance and civil rights." In that context one may come to a deeper understanding of the historical facts of both slavery and racism; and in a world where neither evil has been stamped out, a sense of shock or revulsion at the reality of this part of our history is probably beneficial. But no reader should feel personally targeted by the use of the word *nigger*. Instead, one might even take comfort from the fact that a word used so casually a hundred years ago has gone through many different levels of meaning and degrees of acceptance since—all of them marking progress toward the tolerant society Twain was hoping to help create.

Mark Twain: A Biography

A word of warning is in order for those who wish to know the truth about Mark Twain: He wrote autobiographical fiction and fictional autobiography—and he is the primary source of information about his own life. The life of Mark Twain is a story told by Samuel Langhorne Clemens, and his accounts, dates, and embellishment are all, so to speak, subject to verification and clarification. When Twain was writing his autobiography, he made it plain: "I don't believe these details are right but I don't care a rap. They will do just as well as the facts."

Fortunately for those who value facts over a more artistic truth, Twain wrote prolifically in notebooks and in letters to family and friends, and many of these writings have survived. Researchers have painstakingly studied these private manuscripts for indications of "what really happened," combining them with reminiscences of his family, friends, and business associates to set the record straight.

Florida, Missouri

> I was born the 30th of November, 1835, in the almost invisible village of Florida, Monroe County, Missouri. . . . The village contained a hundred people and I increased the population by 1 per cent. It is more than many of the best men in history could have done for a town. It may not be modest in me to refer to this but it is true.

The baby who would grow up to write the preceding in *The Autobiography of Mark Twain* was christened Samuel Langhorne Clemens when he was born in that tiny hamlet in Missouri. His parents, John Marshall and Jane Lampton Clemens, both originally of Virginia families, had met in Kentucky. When they married in Lexington in 1823, Jane was twenty and John twenty-four or -five, and "neither of them had an overplus of property. She brought him two or three negroes but nothing else, I think," reported Sam. Although they were not wealthy, they were considered "gentry." The couple moved to Tennessee, where they tried to make a living in several small towns, but a steady decline in their fortunes led them to look for better opportunities farther west. The family sold nearly all they had (except for thousands of acres of undeveloped Tennessee land and their one remaining slave) and began the hard journey to Florida, Missouri, in the spring of 1835.

The two-room frame house with a lean-to kitchen in Florida must have been crowded; when they moved in, the Clemens family already included Orion (born 1825; the family pronounced his name with the accent on the first syllable), Pamela (born 1827), Margaret (1830), and Benjamin (1832). There would be one more son after Sam—Henry, born in 1838. (Pamela remembered another son, Pleasants Hannibal, who had died in Tennessee at the age of three months.)

Florida was a town with prospects. Founded on the Salt River, surrounded by rich land, already the location of flour mills, a sawmill, and distilleries, it seemed to need only vision and development to make it a bustling commercial center. But the U.S. economy suffered a crash in 1837, and the envisioned improvements for Florida never happened. John Clemens was always a better visionary than businessman; his own business—a store—was failing. In the fall of 1839, soon after Sam's sister Margaret died from "bilious fever," John traded his holdings in Florida for land and buildings in nearby Hannibal, Missouri, on the Mississippi River, and moved his household again.

Hannibal, Missouri

Although the family's fortunes continued to decline, the next few years gave young Sam the childhood he would later chronicle (with a few changes, of course) in *The Adventures of Tom Sawyer* and *The Adventures of Huckleberry Finn.* The Clemenses had moved to Missouri to be near Jane's sister, Patsy, and her family. Patsy's husband, John Quarles, was a successful farmer, respected and popular, and—unlike Sam's rather austere father—genial and generously good-natured. "I have not come across a better man than he was," wrote Sam many years later. Sam began spending the summers at the Quarles farm, and his memories of that time as recorded in his autobiography are splendid:

> It was a heavenly place for a boy, that farm of my uncle John's. The house was a double log one, with a spacious floor (roofed in) connecting it with the kitchen. In the summer the table was set in the middle of that shady and breezy floor, and the sumptuous meals—well, it makes me cry to think of them. Fried chicken, roast pig; wild and tame turkeys, ducks and geese;

> venison just killed; squirrels, rabbits, pheasants, partridges, prairie-chickens; biscuits, hot batter cakes, hot buckwheat cakes, hot "wheat bread," hot rolls, hot corn pone; fresh corn boiled on the ear, succotash, butter-beans, string-beans, tomatoes, peas, Irish potatoes, sweet potatoes; buttermilk, sweet milk, "clabber"; watermelons, muskmelons, cantaloupes—all fresh from the garden; apple pie, peach pie, pumpkin pie, apple dumplings, peach cobbler—I can't remember the rest.

The farm, with its orchards, barns, stables, wandering brook with forbidden (and therefore irresistible) swimming pools, and slave quarters (where Sam became friends with several of the slaves), played a role in the later literature of Mark Twain: "In *Huck Finn* and in *Tom Sawyer, Detective*, I moved [the farm] down to Arkansas," he recalled. "It was all of six hundred miles but it was no trouble; it was not a very large farm—five hundred acres, perhaps—but I could have done it if it had been twice as large."

The generous summer lifestyle, which probably began when Sam was seven or eight, may have contributed to his survival. He had been a sickly child and said he "lived mainly on allopathic medicines during the first seven years" of his life. As Twain biographer John Lauber points out, "Merely to live was an accomplishment for such a child, demonstrating unexpected toughness at a time when, according to a Hannibal paper, 'one quarter of the children born die before they are one year old; one half die before they are twenty-one.'" The Clemenses had already lost Margaret at the age of nine and the infant Pleasants Hannibal; Benjamin would die when he was ten, in 1842.

But Sam seemed to survive against all odds, even when he made the odds longer against himself. In 1845 Hannibal was hit with an epidemic of measles that killed many of its children. "There was a funeral almost daily and the mothers of the town were nearly demented with fright," he recalled. Jane Clemens went to extraordinary lengths to keep Pamela, Henry, and Sam away from contagion, with the result that Sam, now about the age at which Margaret and Benjamin died, constantly feared he had caught the deadly disease. He finally decided he could live in suspense no longer, and snuck into bed with a seriously ill friend, Will Bowen. It took two tries—he was caught the first time and hustled out of the sickroom—but he managed to get "a good case of measles" that took him "within a shade of death's door."

An energetic and mischievous boy, Sam attended school reluctantly. He excelled in the weekly competitive spelling bees, but did not otherwise distinguish himself, especially not in deportment, his brother Henry's forte. He later wrote, "My mother had a good deal of trouble with me but I think she enjoyed it. She had none at all with my brother Henry, who was two years younger than I, and I think that the unbroken monotony of his goodness and truthfulness and obedience would have been a burden to her but for the relief and variety which I furnished in the other direction."

A Darker Side of Hannibal

Although Missouri would officially side with the North during the Civil War (1861–1865), it had entered the Union as a slave state under the terms of the Missouri Compromise of 1820 (an attempt to prevent the issue of slavery from tearing the nation apart). Sam Clemens thus grew up with slaves. His family's decline could be charted by the sale of their slaves over the years; finally, having none of their own, they rented slaves by the year from neighbors. He later recalled:

> In my schoolboy days I had no aversion to slavery. I was not aware that there was anything wrong with it. No one arraigned it in my hearing; the local papers said nothing against it; the local pulpit taught us that God approved it, that it was a holy thing and that the doubter need only look in the Bible if he wished to settle his mind—and then the texts were read aloud to us to make the matter sure.

Sam Clemens would be an adult before he came to an understanding of slavery as "a bald, grotesque and unwarrantable usurpation." But he did relate to the slaves he knew as people: "All the negroes were friends of ours, and with those of our own age we were in effect comrades. I say in effect, using the phrase as a modification. We were comrades and yet not comrades; color and condition interposed a subtle line which both parties were conscious of and which rendered complete fusion impossible."

The subtle line maintained by a slaveholding society remained, but his empathy for his slave friends was awakened by his mother:

> We had a little slave boy whom we had hired from some one, there in Hannibal. He was from the eastern shore of Maryland and had been brought away from his family and his friends halfway across the American continent and sold. He was a cheery spirit, innocent and gentle, and the noisiest creature that ever was, perhaps. All day long he was singing, whistling, yelling, whooping, laughing—it was maddening, devastating, unendurable. At last, one day, I lost all my temper and went raging to my mother and said Sandy had been singing for an

> hour without a single break and I couldn't stand it and *wouldn't* she please shut him up. The tears came into her eyes and her lip trembled and she said something like this:
>
> "Poor thing, when he sings it shows that he is not remembering and that comforts me; but when he is still I am afraid he is thinking and I cannot bear it. He will never see his mother again; if he can sing I must not hinder it, but be thankful for it. If you were older you would understand me; then that friendless child's noise would make you glad."
>
> It was a simple speech and made up of small words but it went home, and Sandy's noise was not a trouble to me any more.

In Hannibal, separating and selling the members of a slave family "was a thing not well liked by the people and so it was not often done, except in the settling of estates," he remembered. But the rare sight of a dozen black women and men chained together, awaiting shipment to the southern slave market, left him with a memory of "the saddest faces I have ever seen." Another memory was seeing a Negro man killed by a white man "for a trifling little offence"; everyone seemed indifferent to the slave's fate, sympathizing only with the owner who had lost valuable property.

Violent death was a danger not only for slaves in that nearly frontier town. Sam suffered nightmares after witnessing several other tragedies: the shooting of an old man "in the main street at noonday" by a wealthy businessman who just walked away, unmolested, after taking this revenge for a slight; the stabbing of a young California emigrant by a drunken comrade; attempted murder by two brothers who held down their uncle and tried to shoot him with a revolver that would not fire; the death of another California emigrant who threatened a widow and her daughter and was answered by a chestful of slugs from an old musket.

The Depths of Poverty

Meanwhile, John Clemens's lifelong pattern of steady decline in fortunes, interrupted by brief flashes of prosperity, continued. John Lauber writes that "things went badly for the Clemenses in Hannibal. Creditors pressed them hard, they moved frequently, there was a sheriff's sale in 1843 and another ordered in December 1846—but the sheriff found nothing left to seize. . . . Orion was apprenticed to a printer in St. Louis—much against his will, for he felt that he was a gentleman's son and deserved a profession." In 1846 the Clemenses were reduced to sharing quarters with another family, for whom Jane cooked.

According to the family tradition, the 1846 calamity was the result of John's "going security for" (cosigning) a large note for a man named Ira Stout, who then declared bankruptcy and left the Clemenses ruined by the liability to pay the entire note. Their fortunes were about to turn around again the next year, they believed, when the ultimate disaster hit:

> When my father died, in 1847, the disaster happened—as is the customary way with such things—just at the very moment when our fortunes had changed and we were about to be comfortable once more after several years of grinding poverty and privation. . . . My father had just been elected clerk of the Surrogate Court. . . . He went to Palmyra, the county-seat, to be sworn in about the end of February. In returning home horseback twelve miles[,] a storm of sleet and rain assailed him and he arrived at the house in a half-frozen condition. Pleurisy followed and he died on the 24th of March.
>
> Thus our splendid new fortune was snatched from us and we were in the depths of poverty again.

Perhaps John Clemens's most valuable legacy to his son was his precise and careful use of the English language. John and Sam also shared a strong intellect and a deep integrity; dreams of wealth and a desire for success; independent thinking, shaded by a strain of pessimism; involvement in the affairs of their communities (which, for Sam, would become the world community); and an abiding sense of justice.

Samuel Charles Webster, a grandson of Sam's sister Pamela, wrote that "Mark Twain inherited his humor, his temperament, and his red hair from his mother's side. His accuracy in workmanship he got from his father. His accuracy in facts he never got from anybody."

"Newspaper College"

Although he later said he had been taken from school immediately upon his father's death, recent research has shown that Sam continued to attend school at least part-time for two more years. But in his fourteenth year, he was apprenticed to Joseph Ament, publisher of the weekly Hannibal *Courier*. He was to board with his master, learn the printing trade, and receive two suits of clothing a year (he got just one—Ament's oversized castoff). He soon graduated to setting type, and to making mischief with his fellows.

In the nineteenth century, printing was "the poor man's college." Newspapers were consciously "literary," offering poems and essays from both classical and contemporary authors, and liberally borrowing the best pieces from one another. Although Sam had been an unenthusiastic schoolboy, he now became an eager reader, and began the self-education that would continue throughout his life.

After the discovery of gold in California in 1848, the editor of the Hannibal *Journal* joined the gold rush, and Orion decided the time was ripe to start his own paper in Hannibal. He began the weekly *Western Union*, and offered his brother Sam $3.50 a week plus board to join him. As that was $3.50 more than the *Courier* paid, Sam accepted.

Like their father, Orion was a lousy businessman, and the promised pay failed to materialize more often than not. But Orion did offer Sam something the *Courier* had not: an opportunity to get his own work into print.

The First Newspaper Writings

Sam's first published work was "A Gallant Fireman," a one-paragraph anecdote in the January 16, 1851, *Western Union*, describing the antics of the paper's "printer's devil," Jim Wolf, when a fire broke out in the grocery store next door to the newspaper office. In May of the following year, Sam's work gained a much larger audience. "The Dandy Frightening the Squatter," a humorous tale, appeared in the Boston *Carpet-Bag* on May 1, 1852. Exactly a week later, the Philadelphia *American Courier* printed Sam's description of the town he would later make famous as Tom Sawyer and Huck Finn's St. Petersburg: "Hannibal, Missouri."

By fall 1852, Sam was on a roll. "A Family Muss," a report on a drunken man's assault on family and friends livened by the use of a comic Irish dialect, appeared with Sam's pseudonymous byline "W. Epaminondas Adrastus Perkins" on September 9 in the Hannibal *Journal*. (Orion had purchased a second paper and merged them; the publication was now known by this name.) The following week, on September 16, Sam entered his first journalistic feud, with the editor of the rival Hannibal *Tri-Weekly*, who had responded sarcastically to one of Orion's editorials.

By May 1853 the *Journal* was struggling to survive, and Sam decided to try to do better elsewhere. In late May or early June he set out for New York (although he told his family he was headed for St. Louis, to keep them from worrying—or perhaps from trying to stop him).

Breaking Away

An accomplished typesetter could find work in almost any town. Sam did stop in St. Louis for a few weeks to earn money for the rest of his journey; then he headed for New York City. Arriving in late August 1853, he was soon employed by a printing house and writing long letters home. His family had apparently heard lurid tales of what could happen to a young man alone in the big city; in one of his letters, Sam wrote: "You ask me where I spend my evenings. Where would you suppose with a free printer's library containing more than 4,000 volumes within a quarter of a mile of me, and nobody at home to talk to?" (Free public libraries were still relatively rare; most libraries were founded for a defined group of people—printers, sailors, merchants—or were subscription libraries, charging a fee.)

The free reading was about all Sam could afford. His pay was poor, so in October he moved to Philadelphia, where he worked for the *Inquirer*. His hours were odd but the pay was better, allowing him to enjoy his spare time seeing the sights, and even take a quick trip to Washington, D.C. But the novelty of the city was wearing off.

In late summer 1854, he briefly rejoined his brothers Orion and Henry and his mother, who were now living in Muscatine, Iowa, then returned to St. Louis for a few months, working as a printer but wishing he could be a riverboat pilot. When Orion married and moved to Keokuk, Iowa, to open a printing shop with Henry, Sam joined them for about a year and a half. He was reading voraciously but apparently not writing for publication, although he discovered he had a talent for public speaking, a talent that would save him financially more than once.

On November 1, 1876, in response to a letter from an old friend, J.H. Burrough, Sam recalled himself at that time:

> As you describe me I can picture myself as I was 22 years ago. The portrait is correct. You think I have grown some; upon my word there was room for it. You have described a callow fool, a self-sufficient ass, a mere human tumble-bug, stern in air, heaving at his bit of dung and imagining he is re-molding the world and is entirely capable of doing it right. Ignorance, intolerance, egotism, self-assertion, opaque perception, dense and pitiful chuckle-headedness—and an almost pathetic unconsciousness of it all. That is what I was at 19–20.

Making His Fortune, Part I

As usual, Orion's business was doing poorly. He made Sam a partner, who would share the "profits" instead of drawing his promised five-dollar weekly salary. Sam, who had failed to persuade a wealthy relative to help him finance his dream of becoming a riverboat pilot, now had a new scheme for making his fortune: "I had been reading Lieutenant Herndon's account of his explorations of the Amazon and had been mightily attracted by what he said of coca," he reported in his autobiography. "I made up my mind that I would go to the headwaters of the Amazon and collect coca and trade in it and make a fortune." (The addictive and destructive powers of cocaine were little recognized then.)

Sam spent the winter of 1856–1857 in Cincinnati, Ohio, working at the printing office of Wrightson and Company to earn money for his passage to South America. Perhaps the most noteworthy aspect of this period was a friendship he struck up with a fellow boarder, a Scotsman named Macfarlane. Little is known about him—not his occupation, not even his first name—but he said he was a self-educated man, and he had developed his own philosophy, which impressed the young typesetter who was half his age. Sam spent many evenings with Macfarlane that winter, listening to him explain his reasoning. His theory of evolution, propounded some fifteen years before Charles Darwin published *The Descent of Man,* made a particularly strong impact on Sam:

> Macfarlane considered that the animal life in the world was developed in the course of eons of time from a few microscopic seed germs, or perhaps one microscopic seed germ, . . . and that this development was progressive upon an ascending scale toward ultimate perfection until man was reached; and that then the progressive scheme broke pitifully down and went to wreck and ruin!
>
> He said that man's heart was the only bad heart in the animal kingdom; that man was the only animal capable of feeling malice, envy, vindictiveness, revengefulness, hatred, selfishness . . . the sole animal in whom was developed the base instinct called *patriotism,* the sole animal that robs, persecutes, oppresses and kills members of his own immediate tribe, the sole animal that steals and enslaves the members of any *tribe.*

Whether Macfarlane planted seeds that blossomed later in Mark Twain or simply found a soul already compatible with his philosophy, those who read the writings of Mark Twain's last years will recognize in them the same bitter pessimism expressed in the Scot's ideas.

By springtime, Sam had saved enough to pay his way to New Orleans on the steamer *Paul Jones.* He planned to set sail for the Amazon from that port, but on the way south he met one of the boat's pilots, Horace Bixby, whom he soon persuaded to help him become a riverboat pilot. Bixby agreed to teach Sam the Mississippi River from St. Louis to New Orleans for five hundred dollars—one hundred dollars in advance. Sam borrowed the advance from William Moffett, who had married his sister Pamela, and began to learn the snags, curves, and hidden obstacles of the great river.

Mark Twain wrote of his life on the Mississippi, with a certain amount of literary license, in the book called, appropriately, *Life on the Mississippi.* Being a pilot was much more than adventure and travel. Riverboat pilots were respected, almost revered. Once the boat left shore, they were in supreme command, not even subject to orders from the captain. Piloting required intense attention to details, which had to be committed to memory—an admirable trait for an author-to-be to develop. The job was lucrative: A master pilot could expect the same income as the vice president of the United States. The financial security, and the confidence that came from the sense of command, eventually led Sam to take over the role of head of the family from the feckless Orion. It was now Sam who found employment for their brother Henry.

Sam was a cub pilot on the *Pennsylvania* in June 1858, working under William Brown, master pilot and petty tyrant. Henry was working as third (or mud) clerk on the same boat when Brown accused him of insubordination and attacked him with a lump of coal. Sam sprang to his brother's defense, the only recorded time he resorted to physical violence.

As it turned out, this episode may have saved Sam's life, but it led to a lifelong feeling of guilt. Because of the altercation Sam left the ship in New Orleans, but Henry stayed aboard. At six o'clock on the morning of June 13, 1858, the *Pennsylvania*'s four boilers exploded. The boat had just won a race with a rival steamer and was preparing to race another; the boilers (one of which was known to leak badly) had been fired up to the limit. At least two hundred people died immediately; many others—including Henry—later succumbed to their injuries. Sam, who was traveling north as a passenger on the *A.T. Lacey*, arrived in time to be with his brother, who lived for six days. He blamed himself for Henry's having been on the *Pennsylvania.* The guilt he felt was only made worse by those who congratulated him on his luck for not having been aboard, as scheduled.

The accident did not drive Sam from the river, although he did take a month off, another lucky break during which he missed an epidemic of yellow fever in New Orleans. On April 5, 1859, he received his pilot's license.

A respected gentleman now, he decided that chewing tobacco was no longer appropriate for his new position in life, and he quit for good. He began to dress with style. He apparently made friends readily, and there was no shortage of young women to dance with at fancy parties. The slightly built man whose head seemed a little too large for his body, with red curly hair, blue-green eyes, and "a Roman nose, which greatly improves the beauty of his features" (according to his daughter Susy, in the biography she wrote when she was thirteen), had found a career he planned to follow until the end of his days.

The Civil War intervened.

The Civil War

In his autobiography, Mark Twain did not dwell on the war:

> I was in New Orleans when Louisiana went out of the Union, January 26, 1861, and I started North the next day. Every day on the trip a blockade was closed by the boat [it was the last one allowed to go through], and the batteries at Jefferson Barracks (below St. Louis) fired two shots through the chimneys the last night of the voyage. In June I joined the Confederates in Ralls County, Missouri, as a second lieutenant under General Tom Harris and came near having the distinction of being captured by Colonel Ulysses S. Grant. I resigned after two weeks' service in the field, explaining that I was "incapacitated by fatigue" through persistent retreating.

This offhand treatment does not reveal the difficulties Sam had in deciding which side to take in this conflict of brother against brother. Missouri was a border state; although it stayed in the Union, many of its citizens fought for the Confederacy. The Clemens family had owned slaves, and Sam had grown up with "the Peculiar Institution." Orion, however, was a staunch abolitionist.

"The Private History of a Campaign That Failed," written by Mark Twain in 1885, tells more about the choice Sam Clemens made. (Although the details may be fictionalized, family members' accounts and the reminiscences of other participants verify that the overall picture was accurate.) It is a story that recalls the differences between Tom Sawyer and Huckleberry Finn. Sam and several of his friends from Hannibal got together one night and formed a military company. They dubbed themselves the Marion Rangers and made almost everyone an officer; Sam was second lieutenant. Setting out on an "expedition" in a Tom Sawyer spirit of horseplay and fun, they basically went on a prolonged campout, playing at military drills on occasion. When rumor of an approaching enemy force reached them, the council of war (everyone in the troop) agreed that the main concern was that they not retreat *toward* the enemy.

A losing battle with a farmer's dogs was followed by several scares about Union troops searching for Confederates to hang. The frequent rumors soon lost their force, however, and so that one night, after another report of an approaching enemy, it was a surprise when a lone horseman did appear. Sam fired on him; when no other troops appeared, the Rangers crept out of hiding to approach their foe.

> When we got to him the moon revealed him distinctly. He was lying on his back, with his arms abroad; his mouth was open and his chest heaving with long gasps, and his white shirt-front was all splashed with blood. The thought shot through me that I was a murderer; that I had killed a man—a man who had never done me any harm. That was the coldest sensation that ever went through my marrow. I was down by him in a moment, helplessly stroking his forehead; and I would have given anything then—my own life freely—to make him again what he had been five minutes before. And all the boys seemed to be feeling in the same way. . . . They had forgotten all about the enemy; they thought only of this one forlorn unit of the foe. . . . He muttered and mumbled like a dreamer in his sleep, about his wife and child; and I thought with a new despair, "This thing that I have done does not end with him; it falls upon them too, and they never did me any harm, any more than he."
>
> In a little while the man was dead. He was killed in war; killed in fair and legitimate war; killed in battle, as you may say; and yet he was as sincerely mourned by the opposing force as if he had been their brother. . . . It soon came out that mine was not the only shot fired; there were five others,—a division of the guilt which was a grateful relief to me.

In his notes for *The Adventures of Huckleberry Finn,* Twain wrote, "A sound heart and a deformed conscience [prevailing but misguided social dictates] come into collision, and conscience suffers defeat." Like Tom Sawyer, who in *Huckleberry Finn* indulged in fantasy games to "free" Jim even though he knew he was unnecessarily risking Jim's life, the Marion Rangers were playing at the adventure of war. Like Huck, who defied his conscience and indulged his heart to help Jim escape slavery, Sam finally refused to play that popular game.

Some of the Marion Rangers went on to become efficient, effective soldiers, but Sam had had enough of war. After falling back with his fellows a few more times, he (along with about half the troop) set out for home.

Heading West

Although his sympathies were on the Union side, Orion no more wished to fight than Sam did. Orion had campaigned for

Abraham Lincoln for president, and an old friend of his, Edward Bates, was Lincoln's attorney general. This fortunate combination resulted in Orion's appointment as secretary of the Nevada Territory, which had been created on February 28, 1861, from land taken from Mexico. Like California with its gold, Nevada with its Comstock lode of silver (discovered in June 1859) was considered vital to the Union, so officials were dispatched to the new territory quickly. Orion could not afford the fare, but Sam (who had been supporting Orion and his family since he began earning a pilot's wages) had an idea: He would become the unofficial secretary to the new secretary and pay the way for both of them. (Orion's wife, Mollie, and daughter, Jennie, were to remain in Iowa temporarily.) The brothers went up the Missouri River to St. Joseph and, on July 26, 1861, they were off by stagecoach to Carson City. They reached that new capital of the Nevada Territory on August 14, after a journey evocatively described in Twain's *Roughing It.*

Making His Fortune, Part II

Before long Sam ventured out of Carson City. He and a friend staked a timber claim in the nearby countryside (the silver mines needed timber to shore up tunnels), but their campfire got out of control and burned down their prospective profits. He turned to mining for a while, the prospect of unlimited riches being irresistible, but found it a hard life, again with no profit. He was still writing letters home, some of which were published in a Keokuk paper, and he began sending humorous letters (signed "Josh") to the Virginia City *Territorial Enterprise,* Nevada's leading newspaper. Just as he was beginning to feel desperate about his financial situation, the *Enterprise* offered him a job as a full-time reporter for twenty-five dollars a week. It was not the millions he had been planning to make, but he accepted and set out for Virginia City.

With its new millionaires, its rough population struggling to become the *next* millionaires, and its frontier conditions, Virginia City seemed a model of the wild and woolly West. In its anything-goes atmosphere, Sam's extravagant style found plenty of room to grow. For the first time, writing was a vocation for Sam. Here he found colleagues whose examples helped develop his talent, especially the *Enterprise*'s Dan De Quille (called "Dandy Quille" by his friends, his real name was William Wright) and Clement T. Rice of the rival Virginia City *Union,* whom Sam dubbed "the Unreliable" and with whom he carried on a wild and friendly literary rivalry.

It was here, on February 2, 1863, that Mark Twain was born. This new pseudonym was clearly taken from Sam's steamboat days. "Mark twain" is the cry of the leadsman announcing that the boat is in two fathoms (twelve feet—the minimum for safety) of water.

Sam—now becoming known as Mark Twain—had restless feet, so it is unlikely that he would have remained in Nevada for long. By the spring of 1864, he wrote in *Roughing It,* "I wanted to see San Francisco. I wanted to go somewhere. I wanted—I did not know what I wanted. I had spring fever and wanted a change, principally, no doubt." Perhaps his spring fever made him more reckless in writing than usual; he managed to annoy and insult quite a few people, among them James Laird, publisher of the *Union.* Egged on by colleagues at their respective papers, Laird and Twain soon found themselves committed to a duel. Dueling was illegal, and some of those he had insulted were threatening to bring other charges against him. On May 29 prudence (and restlessness) prevailed; he took the stagecoach to San Francisco.

California

Mark Twain had been a good-sized frog in a smallish pond in Nevada and, judging from his reports of his activities there, the *Enterprise* did not overwork him. In these respects California was a letdown. He complained, "After leaving Nevada I was a reporter on the *Morning Call* of San Francisco. I was more than that—I was the reporter. There was no other. There was enough work for one and a little over, but not enough for two—according to Mr. Barnes's idea, and he was the proprietor and therefore better situated to know about it than other people." The workday began at nine with an hour at the police court and ended at eleven at night after visits to "the six theaters, one after the other: seven nights in the week, three hundred and sixty-five nights in the year. We remained in each of those places five minutes," he said, and then tried "to find something to say about those performances which we had not said a couple of hundred times before."

Although he was not signing his pieces for the *Call,* he was also writing bylined contributions as Mark Twain for the San Francisco *Californian.* The *Californian* had a knowing, sophisticated tone, and Twain's writing was becoming more consistently satirical and less crude. When he left the *Call,* he had much less money but more time to meet his fellow writers at the *Californian,* including Bret Harte, who thought

Twain's work was comparable to the best of Charles Dickens's sketches. In his connection with Harte and the other writers for the *Californian,* Twain began to see himself as an author rather than a journalist.

Finding himself somewhat at odds with the local authorities (he had posted bail for a friend who then skipped town), Twain went with a friend to an old mining camp on Jackass Hill in Tuolumne, California. To pass the time in the frequently bad weather, Twain began keeping a notebook, making notes on local characters and on the stories they told. One of those stories, with a few Twain embellishments, would later become "The Celebrated Jumping Frog of Calaveras County."

On February 20, 1865, Twain headed out of camp and back toward San Francisco on foot, arriving on February 26. Orion had lost his position in Nevada (from an overabundance of integrity, according to his brother). Will Moffett, their sister Pamela's husband, died that year, leaving her with two children. Thus Twain's self-imposed family responsibilities made his poverty seem even more desperate. He had once told Orion that he would never return home until he had made his fortune; it seemed that would never happen. He considered going back to the river as a military pilot. But even as he was touching bottom, his efforts were slowly beginning to pay off. East Coast journals picked up his writings from western papers, and began to notice this bright new humorist called Mark Twain. In September, the New York *Round Table* called him "the foremost among the merry gentlemen of the California press"; in November, the New York *Weekly Review,* a prestigious journal, said he was "one of the cleverest of the San Francisco writers." These responses heartened the humorist, and he threw himself into his work once again, writing daily letters for the Virginia City *Enterprise* and reviews for the San Francisco *Chronicle,* making enough to begin to get out of debt.

Artemus Ward, a famous western humorist he had met in Nevada, asked Twain for a story for his new book. Twain sent along the story of "Jim Smiley and His Jumping Frog" (Celebrated in a later title as being from Calaveras County). It arrived too late for inclusion in the book, so Ward sent it to the New York *Saturday Press.* Its appearance in that paper's issue of November 18, 1865, wrote the San Francisco *Alta California's* eastern correspondent, "set all New York in a roar." Widely reprinted, it made its author a minor national celebrity.

Tired of San Francisco and heartened by his growing reputation on the East Coast, Twain began planning his escape. He would write a book; he would collaborate with Bret Harte on one or another joint project; . . . he would become a travel correspondent.

In January 1866 he had been invited to join a select group of passengers on the steamer *Ajax*'s first voyage to the Sandwich Islands, as Hawaii was then called. He had declined, but soon regretted having done so, and persuaded the Sacramento *Union* to send him on the *Ajax*'s March 7 voyage to Honolulu, promising to send them "twenty or thirty letters" at twenty dollars apiece. He spent four months in the islands, writing informative, humorous, picturesque letters for the *Union*'s readers. He gave himself a fictional companion, Mr. Brown, to provide a vulgar counterpart to the genteel observations of Mark Twain—making Twain a fictional character, too.

Returning to San Francisco on August 13, he determined to head east in order to take advantage of the favorable press he was getting. But, though his finances had stabilized (and the Civil War was over), he could not afford passage to the other side of the continent. Thomas McGuire, a friend who owned several theaters, advised him: "Now was the time to make my fortune—strike while the iron was hot—break into the lecture field. I did it." His first San Francisco lecture, based on his tour of the Sandwich Islands, was a smashing success: Not only did the audience love him, but he netted nearly three months' salary for ninety minutes on the stage. He had found the medium that would, time and again, help him dig out from financial woes.

After a triumphal tour of California and Nevada towns, followed by a "farewell" tour in various venues in and around San Francisco, Twain finally had enough money and confidence to return to his family with pride intact. The *Alta California* proudly claimed him as its travel correspondent, who would tour the world and write about it for its readers. On December 15, 1866, he left for New York on the steamer *America*.

Making His Fortune, Part III

Although he was not comfortable with the "frenzied energy" of New York, he found an old California acquaintance, Charles Webb, to publish his first book, *The Celebrated Jumping Frog of Calaveras County and Other Sketches*. Then, after less than six months in New York, on June 8, 1867, he embarked on the first pleasure cruise to sail from an American port, a five-month voyage to the Mediterranean and the Holy Land on the

Quaker City, an adventure whose stories would be told in his book *The Innocents Abroad*.

On this voyage he met Charley Langdon, who showed him a picture of his sister. As Twain later wrote, "I saw her first in the form of an ivory miniature in her brother Charley's stateroom in the steamer *Quaker City* in the Bay of Smyrna, in the summer of 1867, when she was in her twenty-second year. I saw her in the flesh for the first time in New York in the following December." It had taken just that one look at her portrait, Twain said, for him to fall in love with Olivia (Livy) Langdon, daughter of a wealthy coal magnate of Elmira, New York. They were married on February 2, 1870.

By all accounts—those of their intimate friends as well as their own—the two were extremely happy with each other. It was a marriage of contrasts, and they delighted in their differences. Livy called her husband "Youth," recognizing his eternally young nature. She tried to dust him off and make him presentable, and he enjoyed her efforts to do so. He could exasperate her sense of propriety on occasion, but having her as a balance in his life seemed to help him curb (or at least keep private) many of the rash eruptions that had in the past made moving on to another place so frequently a wise decision.

The Langdons' wedding gift to the couple (a complete surprise to their new son-in-law) was a large house, fully furnished and staffed, in Buffalo, New York, where Twain had purchased a one-third share in the Buffalo *Express*. (Jervis Langdon, Livy's father, had advanced him the twenty-five-thousand-dollar purchase price.) The income from Livy's funds would be about forty thousand dollars a year; along with Twain's income, which was growing respectably, the newlyweds were able to live very handsomely.

But while they were happy in each other, their marriage withstood griefs and tragedies almost from the beginning. Jervis Langdon, Livy's beloved father, died of cancer just months after the wedding. Livy, who had spent weeks nursing him, suffered a nervous collapse when he died. She nearly miscarried in October; the baby, a son named Langdon, born on November 7, was frail, sickly, and at least a month premature. He died on June 2, 1872.

Buffalo was not proving a happy home, so the Clemenses sold the house and moved to Hartford, Connecticut. Their second child, Olivia Susan (Susy), was born there on March 19, 1872, followed by Clara (June 8, 1874) and Jean (July 26, 1880).

Making His Fortune, Part IV

The quarter-century after his marriage was a prolific period for Mark Twain. He coauthored with Charles Dudley Warner the book that would give the period its name: *The Gilded Age.* Several books of sketches were interspersed among *Tom Sawyer, A Tramp Abroad, The Prince and the Pauper,* and *A Connecticut Yankee in King Arthur's Court.* When Twain revisited his old haunts for *Life on the Mississippi,* he also found the settings and the memories for what is generally considered his greatest book—although *Huckleberry Finn* was originally just, as the subtitle has it, *Tom Sawyer's Comrade.*

But books were not Twain's only plan for profit. He was an inventor, and was perennially interested in new technology. Unfortunately, he seemed to have inherited the Clemens style of investment: buy high, sell low. He was an easy touch for almost any inventor with a new way to make things work.

One such inventor was James W. Paige, creator of a new typesetting machine. Twain felt confident in assessing the value of the new contraption, since he had been a typesetter, but it was to prove a catastrophic investment. By 1885, he had poured $190,000 into the machine and its inventor.

While he was spending himself into a hole with the typesetter, another investment, Webster & Company publishing house, was costing considerably more than it made—a grave annoyance, since it was counted on to provide income by publishing Twain's work. Along with other bad investments and a financial downturn that wiped out Livy's yearly income from coal stocks, Mark Twain was eventually brought to the point of bankruptcy. Ironically—since his father had been left holding the bag by a bankrupt man—he did not take advantage of the bankruptcy laws that would have allowed him to pay his creditors pennies on the dollar. In July 1895, at the age of fifty-nine, Mark Twain embarked on a world lecture tour; it took him five years to make enough money to repay all his creditors in full.

A Darker Side of Mark Twain

Many critics and biographers have speculated on the cause of Mark Twain's increasingly bitter pessimism in the last decade or so of his life. Although he lived very well in some years, he never was able to feel secure, and he had the Clemens dreams of great wealth. The Tennessee land bought by John Clemens gradually changed hands in transactions that seemed to bring no profit to the family; once Orion scuttled a potentially lucrative sale of part of it because the buyer wanted to plant vineyards there, and that day Orion was a teetotaler. (An untimely new dedication to abstinence from alcohol was also blamed for helping him lose his position in Nevada.) The legacy of land, which John Clemens had confidently expected would make his children wealthy, was instead a curse to Mark Twain:

> With the very kindest of intentions in the world toward us he laid the heavy curse of prospective wealth upon our shoulders. He went to his grave in the full belief that he had done us a kindness. It was a woeful mistake but fortunately he never knew it. . . .
>
> It kept us hoping and hoping during forty years and forsook us at last. It put our energies to sleep and made visionaries of us—dreamers and indolent. We were always going to be rich next year—no occasion to work. It is good to begin life poor; it is good to begin life rich—these are wholesome; but to begin it poor and *prospectively* rich! The man who has not experienced it cannot imagine the curse of it.

Twain had expected to make millions from the Paige typesetter; instead, it helped bankrupt him while he supported its inventor for years. Paige, like Orion, seemed to have a penchant for snatching defeat from the jaws of victory: At least once when the machine seemed to be working well and customers were ready to buy, he decided it must have another embellishment—which never worked.

Twain's bitterness was always entwined with a sense of guilt he could occasionally shake but never completely escape. The Calvinist beliefs of his family and boyhood neighbors—he was raised a Presbyterian—were harsh indictments of sinful man. Although he did not subscribe to the religion of his family, its stern pronouncements delivered while he was young had a strong effect in nurturing his perpetual sense of guilt. He blamed himself for the deaths of his brother Henry for whom he had found employment; his son, Langdon, whom he had taken for a carriage ride on a cold day; his daughter Susy, who became ill in Connecticut while he and Livy were in Europe (trying to recoup their fortune) and died before they could reach her. He does not seem to have blamed himself for Livy's death—she had been a near-invalid for years before he met her. But the fact that during the many months of her final illness his presence was considered so disturbing that he was not allowed to see her at all for weeks at a time, and only for a few minutes when he was allowed into the sickroom, could not have made a guilt-prone man happy.

A free spirit who disliked authority, he nevertheless accepted the burden of responsibility for his mother, brothers, and sister, supporting them more or less consistently throughout his life. That sense of responsibility made his bankruptcy and its disruptive effects on their lives as well as on his wife and daughters' lives even more crushing a blow. On their silver wedding anniversary, after twenty-five years of marriage, he had nothing to offer Livy but a silver five-franc piece. The bankruptcy, of course, would have threatened the confidence of most people; Twain felt special anger because he believed that many people—inventors and publishers headed the list—had been cheating or otherwise taking advantage of him.

The theft of his works by foreign publishers fed his bitterness. He often had to go to England to attend the publication of his books, since an author had to be in the country at the time of publication in order to receive any copyright protection. Nevertheless, many publishers around the world made money selling the works of Mark Twain without paying him a penny in royalties. (He fought for copyright reform in the United States to prevent similar unfairness for foreign authors; he hoped, of course, that the law would become international.)

He had traveled the world and found much to disturb him in the global community as well as in the personal one. He found war abhorrent, tyranny unforgivable, imperialism unjustified. The more he saw of the world, the more the pessimistic philosophizing of the Scotsman Macfarlane seemed borne out. And in his role as an international celebrity, he saw more of the world's problems—and frauds—than most of his fellows did, because people frequently asked for his support for one cause or another, presenting their pleas with the direst evidence of need.

Mark Twain had seen plenty of death all his life, but as he grew older, so did his friends and family. Jane Clemens died in 1890; so did Livy's mother. Pamela's son-in-law, Charles L. Webster (who had run the Webster publishing house) died in 1891. Pamela died in 1894, as did Orion's wife, Mollie. Susy died in 1896. Orion died in 1897. Livy died in 1904, and his life was thrown out of balance forever. Pamela's son, Samuel (named after his uncle), died in 1908. In September 1909 Clara married and moved to Europe, and Twain settled down with his third daughter, Jean, in Redding, Connecticut. On Christmas Eve, Jean suffered an epileptic seizure and drowned in her bath.

Mark Twain's frequent bouts of pessimism do not seem to present an unsolvable mystery.

Halley's Comet

Although much has been made of Twain's pessimism, his dark view of human nature in his later years, there was still evidence of sanguine Sam. His writings tended to be dark, but his sense of humor was irrepressible. He was still "Youth," and still loved cats and children. He corresponded with and occasionally entertained a coterie of girls, whom he called his "angelfish." He enjoyed their fresh views on life, their innocence, their sense of fun, and they brought back to him his happy days with his own young daughters. He was not perpetually miserable, but he was tired and his life was running out.

When Sam was born in 1835, Halley's comet was visible on its regular return visit toward the sun. He had often said he expected to die when the comet made its next appearance—in 1910. In 1909 he told his official biographer, Albert Bigelow Paine:

> I came in with Halley's comet in 1835. It is coming again next year, and I expect to go out with it. It will be the greatest disappointment in my life if I don't go out with Halley's comet. The Almighty has said, no doubt: "Now here are these two unaccountable freaks; they came in together, they must go out together."

On April 20, Halley's comet reached its perihelion—its closest approach to the sun—and then began its journey back out into the solar system. On April 21, 1910, at about midday he told his daughter Clara, "Goodbye dear, if we meet," and then fell into a doze. Around sunset, he died.

Chapter 1

The Storyteller's Art

Huckleberry Finn Is Art Drawn from Life

Brander Matthews

Mark Twain was already famous as a humorist, a travel writer, and author of *Tom Sawyer* when *Huckleberry Finn* was published in the United States in 1885. Brander Matthews, author of this unsigned review in the January 31, 1885, issue of *Saturday Review*, was one of the first to recognize that Twain had reached a new level of artistic excellence in *Huckleberry Finn*. Matthews applauds Twain's use of Huck's voice not only to create a vibrant character but also to present social issues without the moralizing in which other authors often indulged. Matthews, a prolific author, editor, and critic, wrote short stories and essays on drama and fiction as well as essays on, reviews of, and introductions to Twain's works.

The boy of to-day is fortunate indeed, and, of a truth, he is to be congratulated. While the boy of yesterday had to stay his stomach with the unconscious humour of *Sandford and Merton*, the boy of to-day may get his fill of fun and of romance and of adventure in *Treasure Island* and in *Tom Brown* and in *Tom Sawyer*, and now in a sequel to *Tom Sawyer*, wherein Tom himself appears in the very nick of time, like a young god from the machine.

Sequels of stories which have been widely popular are not a little risky. *Huckleberry Finn* is a sharp exception to this general rule. Although it is a sequel, it is quite as worthy of wide popularity as *Tom Sawyer*. An American critic once neatly declared that the late G.P.R. James hit the bull's-eye of success with his first shot, and that for ever thereafter he went on firing through the same hole. Now this is just what Mark Twain has not done.

Huckleberry Finn is not an attempt to do *Tom Sawyer* over

Reprinted from Brander Matthews, review of *Huckleberry Finn*, *Saturday Review*, January 31, 1885.

again. It is a story quite as unlike its predecessor as it is like. Although Huck Finn appeared first in the earlier book, and although Tom Sawyer reappears in the later, the scenes and the characters are otherwise wholly different. Above all, the atmosphere of the story is different. *Tom Sawyer* was a tale of boyish adventure in a village in Missouri, on the Mississippi river, and it was told by the author. *Huckleberry Finn* is autobiographic; it is a tale of boyish adventure along the Mississippi river told as it appeared to Huck Finn.

There is not in *Huckleberry Finn* any one scene quite as funny as those in which Tom Sawyer gets his friends to whitewash the fence for him, and then uses the spoils thereby acquired to attain the highest situation of the Sunday school the next morning. Nor is there any description quite as thrilling as that awful moment in the cave when the boy and the girl are lost in the darkness, and when Tom Sawyer suddenly sees a human hand bearing a light, and then finds that the hand is the hand of Indian Joe, his one mortal enemy; we have always thought that the vision of the hand in the cave in *Tom Sawyer* is one of the very finest things in the literature of adventure since Robinson Crusoe first saw a single footprint in the sand of the seashore.

But though *Huckleberry Finn* may not quite reach these two highest points of *Tom Sawyer,* we incline to the opinion that the general level of the later story is perhaps higher than that of the earlier. For one thing, the skill with which the character of Huck Finn is maintained is marvelous. We see everything through his eyes—they are his eyes and not a pair of Mark Twain's spectacles. And the comments on what he sees are his comments—the comments of an ignorant, superstitious, sharp, healthy boy, brought up as Huck Finn had been brought up; they are not speeches put into his mouth by the author.

One of the most artistic things in the book—and that Mark Twain is a literary artist of a very high order all who have considered his later writings critically cannot but confess—one of the most artistic things in *Huckleberry Finn* is the sober self-restraint with which Mr. Clemens lets Huck Finn set down, without any comment at all, scenes which would have afforded the ordinary writer matter for endless moral and political and sociological disquisition. We refer particularly to the account of the Grangerford-Shepherdson feud, and of the shooting of Boggs by Colonel Sherburn. Here are two incidents of the rough old life of the South-Western States, and of the Mississippi Valley forty or fifty years ago, of the old life which is now rapidly passing away under the influence of advancing civilization and increasing commercial prosperity, but which has not wholly disappeared even yet, although a slow revolution in public sentiment is taking place.

The Grangerford-Shepherdson feud is a vendetta as deadly as any Corsican could wish, yet the parties to it were honest, brave, sincere, good Christian people, probably people of deep religious sentiment. Not the less we see them taking their guns to church, and, when occasion serves, joining in what is little better than a general massacre. The killing of Boggs by Colonel Sherburn is told with equal sobriety and truth; and the later scene in which Colonel Sherburn cows and lashes the mob which has set out to lynch him is one of the most vigorous bits of writing Mark Twain has done.

In *Tom Sawyer* we saw Huckleberry Finn from the outside; in the present volume we see him from the inside. He is almost as much a delight to any one who has been a boy as was Tom Sawyer. But only he or she who has been a boy can truly enjoy this record of his adventures, and of his sentiments and of his sayings. Old maids of either sex will wholly fail to understand him or to like him, or to see his significance and his value. Like Tom Sawyer, Huck Finn is a genuine boy; he is neither a girl in boy's clothes like many of the modern heroes of juvenile fiction, nor is he a 'little man,' a full-grown man cut down; he is a boy, just a boy, only a boy. And his ways and modes of thought are boyish. As Mr. F. Anstey understands the English boy, and especially the English boy of the middle classes, so Mark Twain understands the American boy, and especially the American boy of the Mississippi Valley of forty or fifty years ago.

The contrast between Tom Sawyer, who is the child of respectable parents, decently brought up, and Huckleberry Finn, who is the child of the town drunkard, not brought up at all, is made distinct by a hundred artistic touches, not the least natural of which is Huck's constant reference to Tom as his ideal of what a boy should be. When Huck escapes from the cabin where his drunken and worthless father had confined him, carefully manufacturing a mass of very circumstantial evidence to prove his own murder by robbers, he cannot help saying, 'I did wish Tom Sawyer was there. I knowed he would take an interest in this kind of business, and throw in the fancy touches. Nobody could spread himself like Tom Sawyer in such a thing as that.'

Both boys have their full share of boyish imagination; and Tom Sawyer, being given to books, lets his imagination run on robbers and pirates and genies, with a perfect understanding with himself that, if you want to get fun out of this life, you must never hesitate to make believe very hard; and, with Tom's youth and health, he never finds it hard to make believe and to be a pirate at will, or to summon an attendant spirit, or to rescue a prisoner from the deepest dungeon 'neath the castle moat. But in Huck this imagination has turned to superstition; he is a walking repository of the juvenile folklore of the Mississippi Valley—a folklore partly traditional among the white settlers, but largely influenced by intimate association with the negroes. When Huck was in his room at night all by himself waiting for the signal Tom Sawyer was to give him at midnight, he felt so lonesome he wished he was dead:

> The stars were shining, and the leaves rustled in the woods ever so mournful; and I heard an owl, away off, who-whooing about somebody that was dead, and a whippowill and a dog crying about somebody that was going to die; and the wind was trying to whisper something to me, and I couldn't make out what it was, and so it made the cold shivers run over me. Then away out in the woods I heard that kind of a sound that a ghost makes when it wants to tell about something that's on its mind and can't make itself understood, and so can't rest easy in its grave, and has to go about that way every night grieving. I got so down-hearted and scared I did wish I had some company. Pretty soon a spider went crawling up my shoulder, and I flipped it off and it lit in the candle; and before I could budge it was all shriveled up. I didn't need anybody to tell me that that was an awful bad sign and would fetch me some bad luck, so I was scared and most shook the clothes off of me. I got up and turned around in my tracks three times and crossed my breast every time; and then I tied up a little lock of my hair with a thread to keep witches away. But I hadn't no confidence. You do that when you've lost a horseshoe that you've found, instead of nailing it up over the door, but I hadn't ever heard anybody say it was any way to keep off bad luck when you'd killed a spider.

And, again, later in the story, not at night this time, but in broad daylight, Huck walks along a road:

> When I got there it was all still and Sunday-like, and hot and sunshiny—the hands was gone to the fields; and there was

> them kind of faint dronings of bugs and flies in the air that makes it seem so lonesome and like everybody's dead and gone; and if a breeze fans along and quivers the leaves, it makes you feel mournful, because you feel like it's spirits whispering—spirits that's been dead ever so many years—and you always think they're talking about you. As a general thing it makes a body wish he was dead, too, and done with it all.

Now, none of these sentiments are appropriate to Tom Sawyer, who had none of the feeling for nature which Huck Finn had caught during his numberless days and nights in the open air. Nor could Tom Sawyer either have seen or set down this instantaneous photograph of a summer storm:

> It would get so dark that it looked all blue-black outside, and lovely; and the rain would thrash along by so thick that the trees off a little ways looked dim and spider-webby; and here would come a blast of wind that would bend the trees down and turn up the pale under-side of the leaves; and then a perfect ripper of a gust would follow along and set the branches to tossing their arms as if they was just wild; and next, when it was just about the bluest and blackest—*fst!* it was as bright as glory, and you'd have a little glimpse of tree-tops aplunging about away off yonder in the storm, hundreds of yards further than you could see before; dark as sin again in a second, and now you'd hear the thunder let go with an awful crash, and then go rumbling, grumbling, tumbling, down the sky towards the under side of the world, like rolling empty barrels down stairs—where it's long stairs and they bounce a good deal, you know.

The romantic side of Tom Sawyer is shown in most delightfully humorous fashion in the account of his difficult devices to aid in the easy escape of Jim, a runaway negro. Jim is an admirably drawn character. There have been not a few fine and firm portraits of negroes in recent American fiction, of which Mr. Cable's Bras-Coupé in the *Grandissimes* is perhaps the most vigorous, and Mr. Harris's Mingo and Uncle Remus and Blue Dave are the most gentle. Jim is worthy to rank with these; and the essential simplicity and kindliness and generosity of the Southern negro have never been better shown than here by Mark Twain.

Nor are Tom Sawyer and Huck Finn and Jim the only fresh and original figures in Mr. Clemens's new book; on the contrary, there is scarcely a character of the many introduced who does not impress the reader at once as true to life—and therefore as new, for life is so varied that a portrait from life is sure to be as good as new. That Mr. Clemens draws from life, and yet lifts his work from the domain of the photograph to the region of art, is evident to any one who will give his work the honest attention which it deserves. Mr. John T. Raymond, the American comedian, who performs the character of Colonel Sellers to perfection, is wont to say that there is scarcely a town in the West and South-West where some man did not claim to be the original of the character. And as Mark Twain made Colonel Sellers, so has he made the chief players in the present drama of boyish adventure; they are taken from life, no doubt, but they are so aptly chosen and so broadly drawn that they are quite as typical as they are actual. They have one great charm, all of them they are not written about and about; they are not described and dissected and analysed; they appear and play their parts and disappear; and yet they leave a sharp impression of indubitable vitality and individuality. No one, we venture to say, who reads this book will readily forget the Duke and the King, a pair of as pleasant 'confidence operators' as one may meet in a day's journey, who leave the story in the most appropriate fashion, being clothed in tar and feathers and ridden on a rail.

Of the more broadly humorous passages—and they abound—we have not left ourselves space to speak; they are to the full as funny as in any of Mark Twain's other books; and, perhaps, in no other book has the humourist shown so much artistic restraint, for there is in *Huckleberry Finn* no mere 'comic copy,' no straining after effect; one might almost say that there is no waste word in it. Nor have we left ourselves room to do more than say a good word for the illustrations, which, although slight and unpretending, are far better than those to be found in most of Mark Twain's books. For one thing, they actually illustrate—and this is a rare quality in illustrations nowadays. They give the reader a distinct idea of the Duke and the King, of Jim and of Colonel Sherburn, of the Shepherdsons and the Grangerfords. They are all by one artist, Mr. E.W. Kemble, hitherto known to us only as the illustrator of the Thompson Street Poker Chub, an amusing romance of highly-coloured life in New York.

Precisely the Right Tone of Voice

Victor A. Doyno

Author and critic Victor A. Doyno studied Twain's manuscript for *Huckleberry Finn* to learn about the author's process of revision. In the following essay, Doyno presents specific instances when Twain changed words—sometimes more than once—to make his characters' voices precisely reflect the images of them he was trying to create. Doyno spent twenty-five years studying 55 percent of the manuscript for *Huck Finn.* Just before the publication of his book *Writing* Huck Finn: *Mark Twain's Creative Process,* from which this essay was excerpted, the remaining 45 percent was found, and he is now working on a study of the entire manuscript.

Editor's note: In the quotations from Huck Finn, *material in <angle brackets> was deleted from the final manuscript; material in* ***boldface*** *was added after the first draft; and material in both* ***<boldface and angle brackets>*** *was added but later deleted.*

> . . . the difference between the *almost right word* and the *right* word is really a large matter—'tis the difference between the lightning-bug and the lightning.

If we accept the persona of Mark Twain at face value, we conceive him as an unschooled hick, a surprisingly lucky lout, a naive native genius too careless by temperament to bother about details and too casual to do anything so difficult as revise a sentence. If Sam Clemens had such a personality, he would have been an unusual typesetter; hence the pose was contrary to at least a part of Sam Clemens's personality. But such a pose created a uniquely valuable effect: it helped put the relatively unschooled writer from

Hannibal, Missouri beyond nitpicking or sophisticated criticism and potential humiliation by the literary establishment. The American literary world has been—and still is—peculiarly supportive of such a character. Many American teachers, literary critics, and ordinary citizens appear more sympathetic to democratic mixtures of illiteracy and sincerity than their British or French counterparts. Moreover, the popular traditions of regional writing permit a supposedly unsophisticated person to speak with authenticity, frequently unaware of the humor, in a deadpan fashion. . . .

With *Huck Finn* Twain accepted the apparent limitation of one definable point of view—that of a young boy—and thereby created an immense freedom and aid for himself as a novelist. . . . Huck's unique blend of innocence, practicality, spiritedness, and literalness creates a disarmingly appealing, lifelike character. And these attributes carry thematic importance and may coincide with or reflect parts of a putative national character. Twain's achievement involves the use of Huck's voice, full of freshness and eagerness, as a wistfully striking contrast to the world's bleak reality.[1] The contrast resembles that operative in a tall tale when a deadpan or naive narrator does not seem aware of his outrageously funny statements. Twain can have Huck utilize both types of contrast. . . .

Huck's Voice

Huck's voice greets us in a special way, and Twain labored over this boy's exact tone. At first Huck sounded proper, saying, "You will not know about me . . . ,"* but that was changed to, "You <will> ***do*** not know about me. . . ."* Not until Twain had again canceled and revised did Huck's friendly, vernacular way of talking live on the page:

> You <will> <***do*** not> ***don't*** know about me, without you have read a book by the name of "The Adventures of Tom Sawyer," but that ain't no matter. That book was made by Mr. Mark Twain, and he told the truth, mainly. There was things which he stretched, but mainly he told the truth. (MS.A, unnumbered first page)*

1. Among the many studies of Twain which explore the role of innocence, Tony Tanner's *The Reign of Wonder: Naivety and Reality in American Literature* and William C. Spengemann's *Mark Twain and the Backwoods Angel: The Matter of Innocence in the Works of Samuel L. Clemens* deserve special mention.

* Special mention and great gratitude go to the Mark Twain Project which, under the guidance of Dr. Robert Hirst, actually guards valuable material for the Mark Twain Foundation. I wish to be scrupulous about acknowledging this help and permission to print previously unpublished material; I have noted the protected material by an *. Moreover, I would emphatically encourage other scholars to be meticulous in respecting such literary rights.

. . . The second paragraph of *Huck* presents a summary, from Huck's point of view, of the conclusion of *Tom Sawyer.* There may be other books which similarly insist upon their special status and origin as books, but they must be rare.

Huck becomes specific about his situation, and we learn more of his "style":

> The widow she cried over me, and called me a poor lost lamb, and she called me a lot of other names, too, but she never meant no harm by it. She put me in them new clothes again, and I couldn't do nothing but sweat and sweat, and feel all cramped up. Well, then, the old thing commenced again. The widow rung a bell for supper, and you had to come to time. When you got to the table you couldn't go right to eating, but you had to wait for the widow to tuck down her head and grumble a little over the victuals, though there warn't really anything the matter with them. That is, nothing only everything was cooked by itself. In a barrel of odds and ends it is different; things get mixed up, and the juice kind of swaps around, and the things go better.

Huck's way of talking includes pleonasm, as in saying "The widow she." He seems to be relatively unresponsive to the traditional cliches of religion such as "poor lost lamb." In fact, he may at one point have been ignorant of the biblical allusions, and we may ponder with amusement his possible puzzlement when the widow called him a "lamb" since he knows himself as a boy. His literalist explanation of the ritual of grace as grumbling over the food reveals that he sees what is actually happening—but he misreads the frown of concentration for dissatisfaction—without reference to superstructures or abstract systems. He knows, as a street child would, whether a person intends harm or kindness, and he sees beneath the words. Huck does not appreciate restrictions or need boundaries. He keeps letting the reader share his situation by phrases such as "You had to come to time," and the process creates a sympathetic identification of reader with narrator. Because Huck sounds confident and trustworthy, the reader enters Huck's world confident that a mixed condition is better.

Revising Huck's Tone of Voice

With this information in mind, let us turn to the manuscript to listen and observe how Twain shaped his narrator's tone of voice. After Colonel Sherburn has shot Boggs, a mob decides to lynch the killer and tears down his fence. Huck describes the situation as the Colonel appears:

> Sherburn never said a word—just stood there, looking down. It seemed to me that the stillness was as awful, now, as the racket was before; and somehow it was more creepy and uncomfortable. Sherburn run his eye slow along the crowd; and wherever his eye struck, the people tried a little to outgaze him, but couldn't; they dropped their eyes and looked <sickish> <and> sneaky. Then pretty soon Sherburn sort of laughed; not the kind of laugh you hear at the circus, but the kind that's fitten for a funeral—the kind that makes you feel crawly. (MS, 162–63)

The voice is recognizably Huck's, but it sounds a bit too formal, a bit too measured, and the expression seems distant. Twain's revision went through at least two stages: in the manuscript he dropped "sickish and," leaving the townspeople looking furtive, but not ill. A fair amount of the revision within the manuscript is of this sort, dropping acceptable phrases. Later, when revising the book for print more significant changes were made. Twain dropped the adequate, formal second sentence; perhaps the sentence was a shade too balanced, too structured, too literary a tone for Huck. The revised way of saying it seems simple and direct. "The stillness was awful creepy and uncomfortable." The temporal comparison disappeared, but the functional words have been extracted and put in a simple asymmetrical form.

Twain changed Huck's way of describing the laugh. "Not the kind of laugh you hear at the circus, but the kind that's fitten for a funeral—the kind that makes you feel crawly" became "not the pleasant kind, but the kind that makes you feel like when you are eating bread that's got sand in it." The loss of the polar contrasts seems, at first, regrettable. Perhaps Twain thought the circus reference too artificial a foreshadowing of the immediately following incident at the circus; at any rate, the new version, "not the pleasant kind," seems functional but unexceptional. The circus-funeral contrast is suppressed and, instead, Twain has Huck speak not of opposite situations but of concrete, tactile reality: "bread that's got sand in it." Moreover, the reader is not told about feeling "crawly," but is given a vivid image of personal muscular discomfort. As a result of such revisions, Huck speaks with a tone of voice which sounds lively but without apparent literary polish. . . .

Contrasts in Characters Are Reflected in Dialogue

Variations in tonality are most easily seen in dialogue because the contrast between two characters frequently permeates their language. Accordingly, let us examine two dialogues involving the king, one comparatively private, the other quite public. After

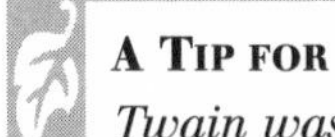

A Tip for Revising Manuscripts

Twain was generous in encouraging young writers. In this excerpt from an August 1888 letter, he gives a humorous clue about his process of revision.

When a word is so near the right one that a body can't quite tell whether it is or isn't, it's good politics to strike it out and go for the Thesaurus.

these detailed examples, we shall not have to be quite so particular again. The first situation occurs as the king, the aging confidence man, senses a possible swindle and attempts to get more information. This section leads into the important Wilks episode. When first composing this section, at the discovery draft stage, Twain probably did not know where his incident would lead. When Huck and the king pick up a country bumpkin in their canoe, the king begins casually:

> "Where you bound, young man?"
> "For the steamboat; going to Orleans."
> "Git aboard," says the king. "Hold on a minute, my servant'll help you with them bags. Jump out and help the gentleman, Adolphus". . . (MS, 218)

Twain gives the king more words than needed and thereby characterizes him as loquacious by inserting the pleonasm, "Where you bound ***for***, young man?" The growth from manuscript to printed text included several polishing changes, dropping the final "e" from "Where," and twice changing "help" to "he'p." As a result, the king's tone becomes that of a wordy, bossy master of limited pronunciation. The country bumpkin, on the other hand, seems at first unimportant and received no attention in this portion.

But after the local youth implies that a chance exists for a mistaken identity . . . the king senses a chance for money and desires information, saying:

> ". . . I'm <just> ***jest*** as able to be sorry for Mr. Wilks for not arriving in time, all the same, if he***'s*** <has> missed anything by it,—which I hope ***he*** hasn't."

The country jake replies:

> "Well, he don't miss any property by it, because he'll get that, all right; but he's missed seeing his brother Peter die—which he mayn't mind, nobody ***can*** tell as to that—" (MS, 220)

Some revisions are required by sense, probably because Twain, in his excitement, skipped ordinary, necessary words like ***he*** and ***can***. And Twain also works to keep the king's informal dialect voice.

At this point in the manuscript Twain may have become more concerned with the country fellow as a storyteller, the key informant for the king's possible plot. The bumpkin at first says:

> . . . He left a letter behind, for Harvey, and said he had told in it where his money was and how he wanted the rest of the property divided up so that George's gals would be all right—for George didn't leave anything. (MS, 223)

Clearly this passage sounds like straightforward, tedious yet proper, prose. Twain revised "where his money was ***hid***," making explicit a possible future plot complication.[2] He later changed, for print, the ordinary "gals" to "g'yrls," thereby creating the voice of a rural dialect, and developed the speaker's characterization by canceling "anything" and using a double negative, "didn't leave nothing."

The king continues to pump for information, "Why do you reckon Harvey don't come? Where does he live?" But Twain canceled the final letter from "Where," carefully, consistently, maintaining the king's dialect.

Furthermore, we can observe Twain experimenting with the precise sounds for the voices. In the top margin of MS, 227, he jotted "young fel'r" and "wid'r," oral versions, but then canceled these spellings. Similarly Twain adjusts the country bumpkin's "I was afraid" to ". . . afeard." Many revisions, in fact, shift away from proper diction toward regional, colloquial pronunciation. "Yellow boys," meaning gold pieces, occurs twice, and both are changed to "yeller boys"; "foreign" becomes "furrin." Many changes of this sort provide compelling evidence of the attention Twain lavished on minor details, putting the sounds of local color and the dialect on paper, as he had for many years.[3]

2. This section of the novel, like several others where an episode is beginning, needed many clarifying revisions. Twain had to change the temporal scheme to allow sufficient time for a transatlantic message and for the Wilks brothers' voyage. And Twain also revised for simple clarity; the king inquires, "Did they send them word?" and Twain canceled "they" and substituted "anybody" (MS, 206). 3. It was occasionally difficult for Twain to capture some of the voices and phrasing accurately. For example, later in the episode Twain first had the king say, "Good land, duke, lemme hug you! It's the most gorj'" but then Twain struck out "gorj'" and wrote in "gorgue," clearly an alternative method of spelling, then crossed out "gorgue" and substituted "gorjis," an apparently acceptable version of "gorgeous" (MS, 251). However, by the time the novel appears in print the word has become "dazzling." Perhaps "gorjis" seemed too hard to recognize, and the change to "dazzling" is an example of revision of voice toward clarity and readability. Throughout the novel Twain was concerned with voice, tone, and dialect. He even tinkered with the voice of the very minor character Sister Hotchkiss, working on the short words to get her dialect precisely to his liking by changing "heard" to "hearn" (MS, 723). See also David Carkeet's "The Dialects in *Huckleberry Finn*" for an intelligent analysis of the evidence. See also Twain's comments about revising "A True Story" in a letter to Howells of 20 September 1874 (*Mark Twain–Howells Letters: The Correspondence of Samuel L. Clemens and William D. Howells, 1872–1910*).

The voice of the king also received a great deal of attention in another, more public scene. Twain seems to have been intrigued enough to lavish care upon the creation of the personality of this aging confidence man.[4] When the king impersonates the bereaved Rev. Harvey Wilks, he must have the right tone of voice as he manipulates the crowd while he dramatically debates in public with the iron-jawed Dr. Robinson, who attempts but fails to unmask the impostor. The king ingratiates himself with the townspeople by making the correct invitations, saying:

> "—They being partickler friends of ***the*** diseased. That's why they're invited here this evenin'; but to-morrer we want all to come—everybody; for he respected everybody, he liked everybody, and so it's fitten that his funeral orgies should be public." (MS, 256–57)

Many readers have not perceived how cleverly Twain has constructed this paragraph, beginning and ending with the king's outrageous malapropisms which characterize him as ignorant. Most readers catch the mistake of "orgies," but the opening error of the king's usual "diseased" for "deceased" is scarcely observed. Hence the readers duplicate the Doctor's situation, perceiving error, but not the full extent of the error.

The king repeats "orgies" several times and receives a corrective note from the duke, but continues:

> "I use the word orgies, not because it's the common term, because it ain't—obsequies is the common term—but because it's the right term." (MS, 258)

Twain revised this passage in an enormously subtle way; the modified manuscript version reads: "obsequies ***bein'*** the common term—but because ***orgies is*** the right term." The insertion of "***bein'***" subordinates the correct phrase, makes it more parenthetical, more under the breath, as if less time has elapsed in the saying. On the other hand, the change from the less definite "It's the right term" to "***orgies is*** the right term" shifts the definite verb to assert boldly the grotesquely incorrect word. The entire paragraph becomes paradoxically more subtle and more bold. The king's voice seems to be absolutely in command of the situation as he explains:

> "Obsequies ain't used in England no more, now—it's gone out. We say orgies, now, in England. Orgies is better, because it means the thing you are after, more exact. It's a word that's

4. The king's character has, of course, certain traits required both of a novelist and of Huck, including fluency, fabulating skill, deceptiveness, and the ability to make a rapid, shrewd analysis of character. It is worth mentioning that Twain was later called, ironically enough, "the King" by Miss Lyon, his secretary from 1902 to 1907; Livy's nickname for her husband was "Youth."

> made up out of the Greek *orgo*, outside, open, abroad; and the Hebrew *jeesum*, to plant, cover up: hence *inter*. So, as you see, funeral orgies is an open or public funeral." (MS, 258–59)

Twain's later change in the printed version from "out of" to "out'n" and from "or" to "er" simply improves the dialect and thus gives greater emphasis to the humorous incongruity between pedantic-sounding derivations and wildly non-standard usage. The king's tone of voice—imperious and imperative—conveys his pretentious, ignorant arrogance.

Contrasting the Doctor's Voice and the King's Pretentiousness

All of this minute attention to the king's language prepares for the stark contrast of the Doctor's speech denouncing the king as a fraud. After Doctor Robinson laughs at the king's speech and refuses the impostor's hand, he criticizes the king's imitation of an Englishman. The Doctor then turns to the girls and says:

> "I was your father's friend, and I'm your friend; and I warn you *as* a friend, and an honest one, that wants to protect you and keep you out of harm and trouble, to turn your backs on that scoundrel, and have nothing to do with him, the ignorant hog, with his putrid and idiotic Greek and Hebrew as he calls it. He is the thinnest of thin imposters. . . ." (MS, 262)

Twain moderated the Doctor's contempt in the printed version by changing "the ignorant hog" comparison to "the ignorant tramp" and by omitting the malodorous "putrid"; as a result the description is less pungent but the Doctor is more dignified in tone. The meaningless intensive, "thinnest of thin imposters," becomes simply "the thinnest kind of an impostor." The Doctor states that the rascal:

> "has come here with a lot of empty names and facts which he has picked up somewhere, and you weakly take them for *proofs*, and are assisted in deceiving yourselves by these thoughtless unreasoning friends here, who ought to know better." (MS, 262–63)

The Doctor's language becomes less elevated, less polysyllabic, and his tone less melodramatic as "weakly" disappears and as "assisted in deceiving yourselves" becomes "helped to fool yourselves." The Doctor's characterization of the townspeople changes somewhat by changing "thoughtless unreasoning" to the more ordinary word "foolish" (218). The Doctor, in obvious contrast to the king, seems less pretentious in his word choice.

Originally, the Doctor's impassioned pleas had been melodramatic in tone:

> "Mary Jane Wilks, you know me for your friend, and your honest and unselfish friend. Now listen to me: cast this paltry villain out—I beg you, I beseech you to do it. Will you?" (MS, 263)

While preparing for the printed version, Twain dropped the repetition of "honest" as a self-characterization. The phrase "cast this paltry villain out" sounds so melodramatic that a standard gesture, a pose, and a tableau spring immediately to mind; the printed "turn this pitiful rascal out" seems slightly less melodramatic, but more contemptuous. "I beseech you" was dropped, but the request, in printed form, gains some emphasis because "beg" became italicized. The Doctor's voice becomes more genuine, less pedantic, and the contrast between the pretentious rascal and the correct, blunt, honest country doctor is heard more clearly in the finished text. Such attention to voice and tone contributes both to the sense of realistic conflict and to the allocation of sympathy among the characters.

'Hearing' the Characters Speak

Just how important the imagination of the human voice was to Twain in those actual moments of composition cannot be over-emphasized. A case in point occurs quite a bit later in the novel, after the boys have engineered Jim's escape, when Huck talks to Jim, and Jim answers. The unrevised, first manuscript version reads:

> "Now, old Jim, you're a free man again, and I bet you won't ever be a slave anymore."
>
> "En a mighty good job it was, too, Huck. It was planned beautiful, en it was done beautiful; en <day> dey ain't nobody kin git up a plan dat's mo' mixed up <XXX a' fine> den what dat one wuz." (MS, 707)

This fascinating revision occurs when Twain works on Jim's voice. At this point in the novel, after the chase and shooting on the Phelps's farm, Jim has been silent for a considerable time, and Twain therefore had not 'heard' Jim speak in his imagination for quite a while. The change of "day" to "dey" occurred in the process of the original composition, and thereafter Twain makes no apparent dialect changes in the rest of the speech, because then he was 'hearing' Jim. But once Jim's voice was 'heard' accurately, Twain had to go back in his manuscript to change the earlier "was" to "wuz" and "'uz," precisely capturing Jim's speech.

One of Huck's remarks about Tom Sawyer may serve as an emblem of Twain's actual practice. The original version read:

> In them circumstances he could always throw in an amount of style that was suitable. (MS, 500)

But Twain crossed out "he could always throw" and wrote in above the cancellation so that the revised version reads:

> In them circumstances ***it warn't no trouble to him to throw*** in an amount of style that was suitable.

The revision presents a brilliantly paradoxical metafictional statement. Although there is little substantive difference between the versions, Twain has himself taken the trouble to create a revision which emphasizes the ease of appropriate style. Genetic criticism reveals that effort was exerted to create a sense of effortlessness.

The Use of Humor Helps Point Up Huck's Moral Dilemma

James M. Cox

By the use of "low vernacular" dialect, Mark Twain implies conventional language, notes James M. Cox: the mind automatically recognizes the "errors" in the characters' speech. In much the same way, he writes, when Huck commits the "sin" of trying to free a slave, the mind realizes the error in Huck's belief that he is wrong to help Jim. This inversion of conventional reasoning makes Twain's point more powerfully than straightforward argument would. Yet at the end of the novel Twain maintains the humorous touch, Cox argues, by making Huck choose the moral path not because it is right, but because it is expedient. Cox, an English professor at Dartmouth College, is the author of *Mark Twain: The Fate of Humor.*

The triumph of Mark Twain's art is, as everybody knows, *The Adventures of Huckleberry Finn.* It is his masterpiece, and in encountering its strengths we implicitly deal with Mark Twain's weaknesses, for it, like *Moby-Dick, The Scarlet Letter,* and *Walden,* is the kind of achievement which, revealing the author's wholeness in one economic stroke, exposes all the other works by the same author as somehow partial.

A Book to Read at Least Four Times

Now the first thing to emphasize about *Huckleberry Finn* is that it is a book for everyone—for children, for young adults, for the middle-aged, and for the old. Because it is, everyone can read it at least four times in life, and each time it will be a different book. For the child it will be pure adventure; for the young adult it will be a somber exposure of the evils of slavery; for the middle-aged it will begin to reveal more and more of its humor; and for the man deep in life it will, I hope, become an act of total humor—a pure pleasure wherein even the ending, which is such a problem for us from youth into the middle years, will no longer be dismaying. At that late time, perhaps Tom Sawyer, so long rejected in favor of Huck, will at last regain his dominion as the necessary, the inevitable companion of Huck.

Now of course this does not mean that the book will be one long guffaw; it does mean that the maturing consciousness will see more and more humor as the adventure of childhood dies into the emerging conscience of the man, and as the conscience itself dies into, or at least is deeply tempered by, the irony of experience. Whatever the outcome, we know that *Huckleberry Finn* will be part of our future as much as it will have been a part of our past. It will always be waiting for us to grow into it even as we have a little sadly grown out of it. There is really no other American book like it—there is probably no book in the world's literature like it. Its capacity to meet us throughout our lives is what makes it a book for everybody, whether educated or uneducated, rich or poor, old or young, sophisticated or plain—and it reminds us that, beyond all his expressed attitudes, his wealth, his resentment, and his ambition, Mark Twain was completely democratic. That seems to me the first and last fact about his achievement. No one can ever quite get over *Huckleberry Finn* any more than anyone can ever quite get beyond it.

The Inversion of Moral Feelings

That first and last truth about the book brings us irrevocably to the language, the character, and the action of the book. For what Mark Twain was able to do at the height of his career was to let the "low vernacular" of his culture thrust him aside in the person of Huckleberry Finn. Thus, instead of being framed by conventional language, Huck's vernacular implies it; his errors, characterized by his excessive double negative and his ignorance of tense distinctions, evoke as much as they deny the norm from which they deviate. This "bad" language is the expression of a "bad" boy doing a "bad" thing—freeing a slave in the Old South, a triply reinforced vision which secures total audience approval. For Huck, though fictively freeing a slave in the Old South, is acquiring all his virtue from an implied post–Civil War morality. It is just this crucial implication which constantly transforms Huck's bad actions into good ones. The process of inversion embodies what can best be called the moral sentiment sustaining the action of the book.

The moral sentiment is nothing less than the powerful and indulgent wish which Huck's great language and his great journey arouse and which the ending of the novel frustrates. For in those last ten chapters, the novel changes its direction from its seeming high purpose to mere burlesque. Those are the chapters in which Tom Sawyer returns to stage-manage the action of freeing Jim from slavery. It is indeed mere theatricality, for Tom knows what Huck does not know—that Jim is already free. It is Tom's domination of the action which has brought him forever under moral fire just as it has brought Mark Twain under critical fire. Yet if Tom is secretly relying on his knowledge that Jim is legally free, what is every reader of the novel doing but relying on the unquestioned moral security that Jim ought to be free. That security of the moral sentiment makes the reader as safe as, to borrow a line from Mark Twain, a Christian holding four aces. And in scapegoating Tom Sawyer and Mark Twain because of the ending of the novel, the reader is somehow evading the moment when the novel turned against the moral sentiment.

That moment was none other than the very climax of the action—the high-water mark in the novel and surely the high-water mark in Mark Twain's whole career—the moment when Huck utters his grandest line, "All right, then, I'll go to hell." Just then, the moral sentiment drowns Huck in applause and sends him to the heart of heaven. Now the only hell there is for Huck to go to in this novel which makes fun of the whole notion of superstitious hereafters is the hell of adult society, and he is there in five minutes of reading time after his grand assertion. For that grand assertion is itself the moment when what had been Huck's instinct becomes his conscience. The very accent and rhythm of the line reveals Huck in the act of beginning to play Tom Sawyer—for he proclaims the fact that he is acting on principle.

Northern vs. Southern Society: Both Are Hell

That principle is in reality his Northern or inner conscience in the act of displacing his Southern or social conscience. The Southern conscience had put him in flight from his society; his Northern conscience welcomes him into ours. And either society is hell. Surely that is why we feel that it is so right for Huck to reject civilization at the end of the novel. His rejection is the radically nihilistic action which his doubly negative grammar has been leading toward. Yet if the book is nihilistic—and it surely is—it is humorously nihilistic, which means that it must neither fulminate, satirize, nor complain, but continue to be acted out under the reader's indulgence, affection, and approval. But with Huck's fatal choice, Mark Twain had reached, though he probably could not afford to know how completely he had reached, the limits of his humor: that point at which humor's necessity to gain indulgent and affectionate approval mortally threatened the very identity and character of his humor. Yet even here the form of his masterpiece saved him. For even as Huck elects the Northern conscience, there is a dimension, an inescapable dimension, of his character which chooses to act not heroically because it is the best and right course of action, but *helplessly* because it is the easiest thing to do in a tight place. The good life for Huck has been, and remains, life based not on principle but on comfort, and he leaves civilization not because it is a sham but because it is cramped, smothery, and uncomfortable. Tom and the adult reader are the ones who have all the principle. Moreover, Huck goes into the territory not as an apostle of freedom but as a boy to play. This is not all. The ending leaves all adult readers still in the throes of the moral sentiment, if not in approval of the action, in a state of greater self-approval than at any point in the novel—complacently superior to the author's "failure" and obtusely scornful of their own sentimental surrogate, Tom Sawyer. If it is not a perfect ending it is as good as one can easily imagine for this complete novel of reconstruction which brought not the Old South but an entirely new South back into the union, converting in the process the tragic issues of slavery and Civil War into the very sentiment which would so please the mind that the novel's radical disclosure that the adult conscience is the true tyranny of civilization would pass the rapt censor. That disclosure nakedly seen would be no joke. Yet the book shows that it is under the sign of the conscience that civilized man gains the self-approval to justify the atrocities of adult civilization. And thus man's cruelty is finally his pleasure.

It is just that bleak vision which Mark Twain faced for the rest of his life. It was not that he wanted to reform man and

Huck Finn Forced Mark Twain to Become a Master Novelist

Alfred Kazin

The Adventures of Huckleberry Finn was intended as a sequel to Twain's first novel, *The Adventures of Tom Sawyer*, points out literary critic Alfred Kazin. But in changing from a third-person to a first-person narrative for Huck Finn, Twain created a character whose voice took over the story. In assuming Huck's character, says Kazin, Twain was pulled deep into his quest for freedom; and by presenting an image of society as seen through Huck's naive eyes, Twain constructed a powerful social satire. Kazin is the author of the influential critical work *On Native Grounds: An Interpretation of Modern Prose Literature.*

When Mark Twain turned to *The Adventures of Huckleberry Finn* after finishing *The Adventures of Tom Sawyer* in 1876, he clearly meant to write another "boy's book" in the light comic tone that for the most part had carried Tom and his friends in St. Petersburg from one escapade to another. Despite the dread, the fear-soaked superstitions, and the violent deaths described in *Tom Sawyer*, the book is a comedy and in tone benign and more than a shade condescending to boys who, when all is said and done, are merely . . . boys. Mark Twain had become a wealthy and ultrarespectable member of the best society in Hartford when he sat down to re-create his own boyhood in *Tom Sawyer*—minus his religious fear and loneliness. "Part of my plan has been to try to pleasantly remind adults of what they once were themselves, and of how they felt and thought and talked, and what queer enterprises they sometimes engaged in."

The benevolence of this toward childhood and boyhood is more than a little smug. Mark Twain undertook more than he could have anticipated when he now turned to *Huckleberry Finn.* By an instinct that opened the book to greatness, he wrote Huck's story in the first person and so at many crucial places in the book *became* Huck. Yet the facetious "Notice" facing the opening page is only one of many indications that *Huckleberry Finn* was inferred to be just a sequel to *Tom Sawyer:* "Persons attempting to find a motive in this narrative will be prosecuted; persons attempting to find a moral in it will be banished; persons attempting to find a plot in it will be shot." Yet from the moment Mark Twain began to describe things directly as Huck would see them, and to make of Huck's immortal vernacular a language resource of the most captivating shrewdness, realism, stoical humor, Mark Twain was almost against his will forced to go deeper into his own imaginative memory than he had ever gone before. Funny as it may seem, he was "forced"—in this one book—to become a master novelist.

He had not been a novelist at all before writing *Tom Sawyer;* obviously everything having to do with his early life in Hannibal recharged him, opened not only the gates of memory but his unexpected ability to write close, sustained narrative. Writing in the first person became the deliverance of Mark Twain. Still, given his training in one vernacular style after another during his days as a frontier humorist, it was not exceptional in itself for him to impersonate a fourteen-year-old vagabond, the son of the town drunk, who hates being "adopted." "The Widow Douglas, she took me for her son, and allowed she would sivilize me; but it was rough living in the house all the time, considering how dismal regular and decent the widow was in all her ways."

The Eternal Quest for Freedom

What made the difference between this and just another humorous "oral delivery" performance was that Mark Twain fell completely into Huck's style and Huck's soul. (There were to be passages, obviously aimed at the audience, in which Huck became Mark Twain.) Smart-alecky and sometimes mechanically facetious as Mark Twain was when he first assumed Huck's voice, winking at the reader as he presented Huck's ignorance of religion, of polite language, of "sivilized" ways, Mark Twain would soon be committed to a great subject—Huck, the runaway from his father, and Jim, the slave running away from Miss Watson, go down the river hoping to find the Ohio River and freedom. Freedom from respectable ways for Huck, freedom from slavery for Jim: the quest goes on, even though they miss the Ohio River in the dark and keep going south. In the last third of the book they go back to the purely boyish world of *Tom Sawyer,* with Tom the everlasting kid, prankster, brat, forcing a Jim who was really free all the time (as only Tom knows) to be a "prisoner" on the Phelps farm.

The quest for freedom is eternal because Huck and Jim have nothing in this world but a quest. Mark Twain the ultrasuccess in Hartford had returned to what he once knew, most feared, and what always excited his imagination most—the Mississippi Valley world at its human bottom, the world of the totally powerless and unsettled. He too remained something of a vagrant, drifter, in old age he called himself a "derelict." He would never, despite appearances, be content with his celebrated position in life; like Huck at the end of this book, he wanted "to light out for the Territory ahead of the rest."

A Novel of Low Company

Huckleberry Finn is above all a novel of low company—of people who are so far down in the social scale that they can get along only by their wits. In 1885 the Concord Public Library banned *Huckleberry Finn* from its shelves. It was not altogether mistaken when it described the humor as "coarse," and said that the substance was "rough, coarse and inelegant, dealing with a series of experiences not elevating, the whole book being more suited to the slums than to intelligent, respectable people." The wonderful satire in chapter 17 on the genteel way of life in the Grangerford family would not be possible without Huck's unpreparedness for such a way of life: the hilarious Victorian sentimentality is put into true perspective by Huck, the anguished observer of the murderous feud between the Grangerfords and the Shepherdsons.

Huck has *nothing* but his wits. As he says about himself, "But I go a good deal by instinct." The society along the river is class-conscious, but the classes cannot help knowing each other and entering into each other's lives. In chapters 24–29 the awful Duke and Dauphin enter into the family of the dead Peter Wilks, pretending to be its English branch, and the fact that they do not talk "educated," but make the most ridiculous mistakes, does not alert the family until it is almost too late. From time to time Huck temporarily attaches himself to plain middle-class folks like Mrs. Judith Loftus in chapter 11, when he disguises himself as a girl; it is his sex rather than his low-class speech that gives him away.

Huck certainly gets around. He can be pals with Tom Sawyer, be taken in hand by Judge Thatcher, the Widow Douglas, and Miss Watson; he convinces Mrs. Judith Loftus that he *did* grow up in the country; in chapter 13, he steals the canoe attached to the foundering *Walter Scott* and so helps send the robbers caught on the boat to their deaths; he can play the servant to professional con men like the Duke and Dauphin, who at successive times masquerade as actors, medicine men, and Englishmen.

In every great novel of society—which *Huckleberry Finn* so wonderfully and bitterly turns out to be whenever Huck and Jim go ashore—what counts is the reality behind the appearance. That reality, though sometimes naively misinterpreted by Huck (but only for a self-deluded moment), depends always on Huck's inexperience. Nothing could be more devastating as social satire than the Victorian gingerbread and sentimental mourning described absolutely "straight" by the homeless and naively admiring Huck. All this turns into a hideous bloodbath through Huck's ingenuous help to the lovelorn couple from feuding families. To go from the Grangerford parlor to the riverbank where Huck covers the heads of the Grangerford boys slain in the insane feud is to travel a social epic. Only the classical "poor white" Huck fully knows it.

But this last scene ends on one of those recurrent escapes that make up the story line of *Huckleberry Finn*—"I tramped off in a hurry for the crick, and crowded through the willows, red-hot to jump aboard and get out of that awful country." Huck *has* to keep running off from "quality" folks like the Grangerfords, the Wilkses, the murdering "awful proud" Colonel Sherburn. He "weren't particular"; he just wants to go "somewheres." So he chooses to *stay* low company, as his father does. Vagrancy is his first freedom. He does not even choose to go traipsing down the Mississippi with Jim, who just happens to be on Jackson's Island when Huck gets there. The book is one happening after another; Huck *happens* to fall in with a runaway slave instead of living by the book with Tom Sawyer. As Pap Finn chooses the mud, so

Huck chooses the river. But didn't the river really choose him?

The Novel as a River

Thanks to the river, the everlasting river, the "monstrous big river," the always unpredictable river, Huck and Jim on their raft float into a tough American world. It is a real world full of hard characters: crooks, confidence men, kindly widows and starchy spinsters who in good Mark Twain fashion never seem to be sexually involved with anyone, slave owners and slave hunters who can never be expected to regard Jim as anything but a piece of property, pretty young girls for whom Huck's highest accolade is that they have "the most sand"—grit and courage, the power to disbelieve and defy the lying elders around them. The church is fundamental to these people, but their religion emphasizes duty to God rather than brotherhood for the outcast and the slave. They are hard in a way that D.H. Lawrence described as typical of the frontier American—"isolate, stoic, a killer."

So Huck, not yet fourteen, has to struggle for a knowledge of adult society without which he will not survive. In *Tom Sawyer* children and adults live in parallel worlds without each other; here, as in real life, children and their elders are in conflict. A middle-class boy like Tom Sawyer has to "win" a game in order to triumph over his inevitable defeats in later life. Huck has to survive right now. He has to win, to win over Pap Finn's meanness and the Widow Douglas's strictness; over Tom Sawyer's boyish silliness and Jim's constant terror that he may be caught; over the murderous robbers on the *Walter Scott* and even the protectiveness of Mrs. Judith Loftus; over the horrible arrogance of Colonel Sherburn and the lynch mob foolishly crowding Colonel Sherburn's door; over the greediness of the "King" and the cool cynicism of the Duke.

The French call an episodic, wandering novel like *Huckleberry Finn* a "roman fleuve"—the novel as a river. Nothing could be apter for describing this novel in which a great river is one of the principal characters. Huck on the river, becoming part of the river, reminds us of the genesis of *Tom Sawyer* and *Huckleberry Finn* in Mark Twain's description in "Old Times on the Mississippi" of having to learn the *whole* river in order to become a pilot. Huck has to be the unresting pilot of his life and Jim's; he must become our American

Ulysses in order to survive at all. This is why from time to time he can rest and take in the beauty and wonder of the scene, as in the glorious description of sunrise on the Mississippi that opens chapter 19. This chapter significantly has the book's meanest characters, the Duke and Dauphin, coming aboard. Think of a boy Huck's age struggling against a father who wants to keep him down, imprisons him, robs him, and who does beat him and keep him locked up. Whereupon our Ulysses contrives his own "death" and gets away with it after making as many preparations for his deception and runaway as a soldier going into battle. No wonder, as he says, he is always on "thin ice," or as he puts it in one of his best descriptions of the predicament of being always in flight—"I was kind of a hub of a wheel."

A Boy's Tale of Adventure, an Adult's Epic of Life

There, in the struggle of a boy to establish himself over the hostile powers, in the discovery of menace when you confront life on your own terms, there is the true meaning of a "boy's book" that explains why boys can read *The Adventures of Huckleberry Finn* as boys and then grow up to read it as an epic of life that adults can identify with. The great epics, the tales of the wandering hero triumphing over circumstances—this is the stuff of literature that a boy is nearest to, since every initiation into the manhood he seeks must take the form of triumphing over an obstacle. Whether he is planning to deceive his father into thinking that he is dead, or scaring off slave hunters with stories of smallpox on their craft, or in the last ten chapters submitting to Tom Sawyer's games and thus subjecting poor Jim to real imprisonment, the hero of this book is still only a boy. This proximity to both real danger and made-up danger is how life appears to a boy, who must steal from the adult world the power, but also the fun, that he needs to keep feeling like a boy. Though he must trick this world, lie to it, outwit it, he is a boy in his conventional attitudes. The Wilks girl had the most "sand" you ever did see in a girl, as the Grangerford house was the "splendidest."

Huck does not have the easy out of pretending to despise a middle-class world whose love he can use—without his seeking it. Nor does love from people he has just met mean as much to him as his own measure of people. He is attachable, but not for long; adoptable, but he will not admit liking it. You remember his boyish inexperience when you see how much he values—in the sunrise along the river and the circus into which he has sneaked—the beauty and "splendidness" the world has kept in store for him. The nature of the life experience, and the story of a boy always makes it seem central, is that we just pass through, are soon different from what we thought we were, are soon gone. Life is a series of incommensurable moments; it is wise to enjoy this; one minute the Grangerford boys are bloody dead along the river, but soon after "Two or three days and nights went by; I reckon I might say they swum by, they slid along so quiet and smooth and lovely."

Pap Finn in delirium tremens cries out to the Angel of Death—"Oh, let a poor devil alone!" This expresses the real struggle, against underlying despair, that Mark Twain admitted for the first time, here and there in *Huckleberry Finn,* before he savagely settled into despair in his old age. The river that so to speak "holds" the book in its grasp is full of menace as well as unreal floating peace. For the most part traveling the river *is* a struggle, a *wariness,* even when Huck is temporarily on land. In the marvelous and somehow central scene when Huck methodically arranges his "death" and then, all worn out, prepares to catch a few "winks," he is still a river rat who feels himself pursued at every turn.

From the very beginning of their flight, Huck and Jim are in ecstasies whenever they are safe for a while. Early in the book, when Huck watches the townspeople shooting cannon to raise his body from the bottom, he says with an audible easing of his breath—"I knowed I was all right now. Nobody else would come a-hunting after me." Just treading on a stick and breaking it "made me feel like a person had cut one of my breaths in two and I only got half, and the short half, too." A boy is up against forces bigger than himself, the greatest of which can be his inexperience. So he has to play "smart." But the smarter the boy, the more fatalistic he is; he knows who runs things. Wary about people, Huck weaves his way in and out of so many hazards and dangers that we love him for the dangers he has passed. He is our Ulysses, he has come through. Yet coming up from the bottom, he has none of Tom Sawyer's foolish pride; the "going" for this boy has become life itself, and there is eventually no place for him to go except back to Tom Sawyer's fun and games.

Trouble Everywhere

The sense of danger is the living context of the book's famous style, the matchless ease, directness, and naturalness of Huck's language. Huck and Jim are forever warding off trouble, escaping from trouble, resting from trouble—then by words putting a "spell" on trouble. Jim is always getting lost and always being found; Huck is always inventing stories and playing imaginary people to get out of scrapes before they occur. As Jim in his ignorance is made to play the fool, so Huck in the full power of his cleverness is made to play the con man. They need all the parts they can get. They live at the edge of a society that will never really accept either one; they are constantly in trouble, and it is real trouble, not "prejudice," that Jim is menaced by. Although Mark Twain often hammily plays it to the gallery when he mocks the iniquity of slavery from the complacent perspective of Connecticut, the feeling that Huck and Jim attain for each other is deservedly the most famous side of the book now. For once blacks and whites actually love each other, for they are in the same fix. "Dah you goes, de ole true Huck; de on'y white gentleman dat ever kep' his promise to old Jim."

But let us never forget what the hard American world around them is really like and why they are both in flight. For people who are penniless, harried, in real danger of death, vigilance alone gives a kind of magical power to a life over which "mudsills" and slaves have no power. The superstitions Huck and Jim share are all they have to call on against the alien forces of nature. Equally effective, a kind of superstition as well, is the spell they put on things by arranging them in strict order. Although Huck sometimes becomes Mark Twain when Mark wants to satirize old-time property "rights" in slaves, Mark sinks into Huck when, in the crucial scene preparing his getaway, Huck doggedly lists everything he has, everything he is taking with him, everything he *knows*—in order to shore himself against danger.

It must have been this scene in chapter 7 of *Huckleberry Finn* that so deeply drew Ernest Hemingway to the book. All modern American writing, he said in *Green Hills of Africa*, comes out of *Huckleberry Finn*. He called the much-disputed end of the book "cheating," but he recognized his affinity with the book as a whole. Hemingway came to his famous "plain" style, I believe, through his compulsion to say about certain objects—*only this is real, this is real, and my emotion connects them.* In Hemingway's great and perhaps most revealing story, "Big Two-Hearted River," the suffering mind of the veteran Nick Adams seeks an accustomed sense of familiarity from the stream he fished before the war. He then puts his catch away between ferns, layer by layer, with a kind of frantic deliberateness. So Huck preparing his getaway in chapter 7 tells us:

> I took the sack of corn meal and took it to where the canoe was hid and shoved the vines and branches apart and put it in; then I done the same with the side of bacon, then the whisky-jug. I took all the coffee and sugar there was and all the ammunition; I took the wadding; I took the bucket and gourd; took a dipper and a tin-cup and my old saw and two blankets and the skillet and the coffeepot. I took fish-lines and matches and other things—everything that was worth a cent. I cleaned out the place. I wanted an ax but there wasn't any, only the one out at the woodpile, and I knowed why I was going to leave that. I fetched out the gun and now I was done.

The boy without anything to his name finally has something to carry away. This inventory of his full possessions in life is a ritual that Huck goes through whenever he is in danger and about to hunt up a new place to "hide." This element of necessity is the moving side of the book to me. It "explains" the unique freshness of the style as much as anything can. A writer finds his needed style, his true style, in the discovery of the book's hidden subject, its "figure in the carpet." Here is a book which is an absolute marvel of style, but in which, by a greater marvel, life is not reduced to style and is certainly not confused with style. Huck Finn's voice has many sides to it, but fundamentally it is the voice of a boy-man up to his ears in life, tumbling from danger to danger, negotiating with people and fighting back at things as necessity commands. The sense of necessity that only bottom dogs know is what gives such unmediated, unintellectualized beauty to the style. Mark Twain, fully for the first time, knew how to let life carry its own rhythms.

Games: A Key to Understanding *Huckleberry Finn*

Ralph Cohen

The "games, disguises, tricks, superstitions" that permeate *Huckleberry Finn* seem at first to be simply boys' fun, writes Ralph Cohen. But the adults indulge in games, too, and the reader gradually realizes that games are not just play but explorations of life and quests for truth. Cohen asserts that examining the games played by all of the characters in *Huckleberry Finn* provides a framework for understanding life. What Huck discovers through games, Cohen declares, is how to protect what one loves. Cohen compiled the anthologies *The Future of Literary Theory* and *New Directions in Literary History.*

The form of a book is the way it is told—the ideas and actions expressed in a particular order. To understand the form of a story means to understand *how* it is told as well as *what* it tells. No one who reads *Huckleberry Finn* can fail to see that it is dominated by games, disguises, tricks, superstitions. At first the reader sees them as a boy's way of having fun. However, the work deals with adults, too; they also play games, accept superstitions, carry on feuds, adhere to beliefs and traditions that often prove to be vicious and inhumane. From all of these activities the novel derives, at some times, an exuberant, comic gaiety; at others, a violent and threatening somberness.

What are the implications of these games and disguises? They are ways of exploring life and of discovering the truths that are worth preserving. To confront another or oneself, to understand and confess what games and disguises mean and why one engages in them—these are the ways, in *Huckleberry Finn,* by which the characters arrive at the most profound moral decisions.

Mark Twain himself plays games with the reader even before the narrative begins. In the "Notice" he posts, he warns that his book is not to be taken seriously: "Persons attempting to find a motive in this narrative will be prosecuted; persons attempting to find a moral in it will be banished; persons attempting to find a plot in it will be shot." This is clearly a joke because it is followed by "Explanatory," a notice to take the language variations seriously: "The shadings have not been done in a haphazard fashion, or by guesswork; but painstakingly, and with the trustworthy guidance and support of personal familiarity with these several forms of speech." Why does Mark Twain provide contradictory signposts? Because the book itself is a form of play that has been constructed carefully and seriously. It is a game that should be enjoyed, but it should also be understood. Along with the fun—or, rather, through it—the book comes to terms with serious human issues.

The Game as Child's Play

Huckleberry Finn can be divided into three main sections, each of which begins and ends with a kind of make-believe or play. The novel opens with Huck joining Tom's gang of "robbers" and the first section concludes with Huck's elaborate scheme for planting clues to his own fictitious murder, followed by his escape. Explaining this to Tom, he says, "I warn't even murdered at all. I played it on them." The second section begins with Huck's ruse for escaping the searchers and his accidental discovery of Jim. It concludes with the trick the Duke plays on Huck and Jim by revealing Jim to the Phelpses. This "trick" is no longer play; it has the dangerous and vicious consequences of betrayal. The last section of the novel begins with Huck accepting the identity of "Tom Sawyer" given to him by Aunt Sally, goes on to the elaborate game of digging Jim out, and concludes with Huck about to follow Tom's suggestion for some "howling adventures among the Injuns, over in the territory."

The games that Huck plays in the first section can be considered childish games about random killing, and with these Huck quickly gets bored: "We hadn't robbed anybody, hadn't killed any people, but only just pretended." Huck is not against "pretending," only aimless pretending. When he stages his own murder, this is a purposeful pretense. It leads to his escape. In rebelling against his father and departing from the Widow Douglas, Huck leaves behind him the only family he has; and by "abandoning" his life, he begins a search for a new identity.

THE GAME AS A DISGUISE

On Jackson Island. When Huck escapes, he meets Jim on Jackson Island, and, in order to survive, the two fugitives have to conceal their identity from all others. In the union of the Negro slave and the "murdered" Huck there is established an open and full understanding. This "nonexistent" boy and the nonexistent black man—for the slave was not considered a "person"—need to hide from the world to protect themselves; in doing so they discover and preserve their true feelings. For a few weeks Huck and Jim live on Jackson Island in a kind of primitive paradise: "Jim, this is nice," Huck says. "I wouldn't want to be nowhere else but here." But the choice of remaining on the island is finally shown to be neither Huck's nor Jim's. For the pursuit of Jim continues, and the pleasure of the happy island is disturbed by forces that are beyond their control.

The understanding that develops between the boy and the man derives from an intimacy that is essentially democratic: the boy is the son of a member of the lowest white class in the South—his father is an illiterate drunkard, with the most violent anti-Negro prejudices. When "Pap" hears about an educated, free Negro who can vote, he declares, "What is this country coming to? . . . when they told me there was a state in this country where they'd let that nigger vote, I drawed out. I says I'll never vote ag'in." Voting, the exercise of democracy, is considered by "Pap" as a kind of game in which only whites can play; it is an ironic commentary on the political meaning of "democratic" voting.

Pap's prejudice may be compared with Jim's foolish superstitions. Superstitions are fictitious personal or social beliefs that belong in the category of games because they too are a kind of "make-believe." When Huck puts Jim's hat on a limb causing Jim to believe he has been ridden by witches, Huck knows that this notion is ridiculous. The basis, however, for the love that Jim and Huck begin to feel for each other comes not from old superstitions, but from their isolation. By facing each other without the surroundings of an inherited culture, they are free to reject what society has taught them.

On Jackson Island Huck and Jim play the game of primitive innocence. For the first time, they can honestly confess their feelings; they begin to look after one another. What this game does for them is to make them treat each other as persons, and democracy becomes, in their relationship, a love and respect for persons regardless of color or knowledge or beliefs. It is a love that grows from need and from the sharing of experiences without the desire to assert authority. But Twain finally shows, in the flight of Huck and Jim from Jackson Island, the impossibility of maintaining a decent relationship in a vacuum. Society in the form of its laws and its members cannot long be escaped. And the ideal society created by a runaway white boy and a runaway slave can only defend itself by creating its own false devices—by lies, by tricks, by disguises—but such protection is inevitably temporary.

Life on the Mississippi. During the period on the raft, floating down the Mississippi, Huck discovers the adult world into which he has been born, and he discovers how, in this world, boys' games are converted into the realities enacted by men. Huck learns, too, through his relation with Jim that there is a difference between considerate and inconsiderate pranks. When Huck and Jim get separated, then reunited, Huck tries to fool Jim into thinking the separation was all a dream (like the witch superstition). But Jim has been heartbroken at Huck's disappearance, and he exposes his naked feelings. When Huck tries to ridicule him, to make fun of his love and his suffering, Jim calls Huck "trash": "Trash is what people is dat puts dirt on de head er dey fren's en makes 'em ashamed." "Trash" in this context is not a reference to Huck's background, but a reference to his loss of human decency. And Huck understands this when he humbles himself and apologizes; he understands this difference between innocent fun and brutal jokes that ridicule a man's humanity: "I didn't do him no more mean tricks and I wouldn't done that one if I'd 'a' knowed it would make him feel that way."

When Huck and Jim leave their hiding place on Jackson Island, their trip down the Mississippi unfolds as a series of threats from the river and the land, as a struggle between restraint and liberty. The very disguises that Huck adopts involve restraints, for he must try to act consistently with each new character. Yet each "disguise" permits him the liberty of behavior he would not have if he revealed himself. The disguises permit him to explore the world in which he becomes involved. First he becomes "Sarah Williams," then in succession he becomes "George Peters," "son of a family who knows Miss Hooker," "son of a father with smallpox," the orphan owner of a slave, "George Jackson," "the servant Adolphus," "an English valet" and, finally, "Tom Sawyer." Thus there is a distinction between imposed restraints and those one chooses to accept, like Huck's disguises, or Jim's refusal to leave Tom and seek his liberty. Chosen restraints are, in the novel, the basis for ideal human relationships. But the restraints enforced upon Huck by his father, by the Duke and Dauphin—these are threats to a person's character and identity.

Feuding—the Game That Kills. When Huck swims for shore after the raft is smashed, his liberty is again threatened by the behavior of men, for the Grangerfords who take Huck in are "feuding" with the Shepherdsons. Now the feud, the cause of which the participants no longer know, is an adult game played to the death of those involved. The Grangerfords are aristocrats; a family with a mixture of sentiment and violence: "Col. Grangerford was a gentleman, you see. He was a gentleman all over, and so was his family." But this gentlemanly family lives by an outdated code that formalizes murder and, in its feud, is no respecter of human life or decent behavior. In this game, for the feud is a form of murderous play, their actions no longer have any connection with the immediate moral experience of the families. Unaristocratic Huck feels the moral cruelty of this game more deeply than any of the aristocratic participants. When he comes to the Grangerfords he has only "pretended" killing. Seeing dead Buck Grangerford, a boy his own age, he begins to grasp what killing is, and he is sick, shocked by the irresponsible and brutal consequences: "I wished I hadn't ever come ashore that night to see such things. I ain't ever going to get shut of them—lots of times I dream about them."

The World's a Stage. When Huck escapes from the old aristocracy and gets back to the raft, he and Jim are beset by the arrival of "new aristocrats"—the Duke and Dauphin. These fraudulent claimants are exploiters of human weakness, just as the Grangerfords show no regard for it. Twain suggests that there is little to choose between false and true nobility; Huck knows that the Dauphin and Duke are not a real King and Duke, but he adds, "you couldn't tell them from the real kind." True or false kings are no ideal, but neither are the common river-town inhabitants. If the Duke and Dauphin represent the vulgar "culture" because they are actors and "preachers," the people who come to see them are equally vulgar. The loafers in the Arkansas town, for example, play vicious games that involve the torture of living things. "There couldn't anything wake them up all over, and make them happy all over, like a dog-fight—unless it might be putting turpentine on a stray dog and setting fire to him, or tying a tin can to his tail and see him run himself to death."

Into this town comes the harmless, boastful drunkard, Boggs, who, as one of the men says, "never hurt nobody, drunk nor sober." But his insulting remarks offend the third aristocrat whom Huck observes, Colonel Sherburn. Boggs, a drunken fool, arrives playing the role of the hero; he is shot down coldly and inhumanly by the Colonel, who is neither a fraud nor a feudist, but a man who despises the people. When the townsmen come to lynch him, he humiliates them, ridiculing their cowardice and their corruption: "If any real lynching's going to be done it will be done in the dark, Southern fashion; and when they come they'll bring their masks."

The Colonel derides the so-called great tradition of Southern honor and decency, especially the use of disguise to execute "justice." As the true feudal aristocrat, he offers personal, tyrannical exercise of the law. If disguise is a form of cowardice, aristocratic assertion of individual privilege is a form of despotism. Where, then, is one to look for the democratic exercise of power? Certainly not in the games the townspeople play reenacting the murder of Boggs.

When Huck sees the mob disperse, he goes to a circus where another drunkard scene is enacted. This is now the third such incident, for Huck has told of his drunkard father, the unfortunate Boggs, and finally the circus drunkard who stumbles into the ring, stopping the show and belligerently insisting upon riding a horse. Here again is the drunkard blindly shoving his way into a situation that can prove fatal. But the ringmaster permits the drunkard to ride the horse, to suffer the consequences of his folly and his desire. As Huck watches, he says, "It warn't funny to me though; I was all a tremble to see his danger." But the drunkard suddenly begins to act sober, controls the horse, sheds his false suits and stands revealed as a slim, handsome, heroic figure. Huck believes that the ringmaster was completely fooled by one of his own men, but the point of the circus game is that drunkenness was a disguise; the rider was in full control all

Not Just Twain's Characters Play

These excerpts from a 1905 New York Times *interview with Mark Twain may help explain why his characters are always playing games.*

"Not a day's work in all my life. What I have done I have done because it has been play. If it had been work I shouldn't have done it. . . . When we talk about the great workers of the world we really mean the great players of the world."

the time. The game amused those who came to see it, and the drunkard, permitted to pursue the consequences of his actions, achieves a triumph of discipline and restraint.

The circus show is followed by the show of the Duke and Dauphin. The Shakespeare they offer is no Shakespeare; the audience, however, is interested neither in Shakespeare nor in their version of him. But when they advertise "The Royal Nonesuch" and include a line, "Ladies and Children not Admitted," the Duke says, "If that line don't fetch them, I don't know Arkansaw!" It fetches them; the audience are cheated; and feeling cheated, are only too ready to have their townsmen cheated: "What we want is to go out of here quiet, and talk this show up, and sell the rest of the town! Then we'll all be in the same boat."

There exists no sense of the decent community, no sense of love and affection such as Huck and Jim share, no sense of refusing to go along with a cheat when it will injure others. And it is the "judge" who makes the corrupting suggestion.

At the end of the section Jim is sold back into slavery by the Duke in an ironic repayment for all the assistance received. Thus the love and trust that had been established between Huck and Jim seem no longer operable. The union that they formed at Jackson Island is now destroyed, and destroyed, as was their "paradise," by forces beyond their control.

The reasons for such destruction, the inability of men and boys to steer their lives as they see fit—is the consequence of a world that is full of conflicting interests, dominated by traditional injustices or by personal despotism. Caught in this net, the young boy and the decent man are surrounded either by corrupt people who are lawless, by people who insist on "playing the game" by the given rules like Tom or Aunt Polly, or by aristocratic tyrants who make their own rules, or by helpless innocents who don't know what the world is like.

With such choices, the decent man can only do what Huck does: loving Jim, and placing his trust in this love rather than in proper laws, he prepares to break the laws and "go to hell." In one of the most moving passages in the book, he makes the choice between human values and legal values, with the full awareness of the consequences. He chooses "wickedness," and he chooses the consequences of it.

The Game Becomes Life

The disguises of Huck and Jim have served to give order and significance to the second section of the novel, the journey down river; in it, the incidents have an interrelatedness that prevents them from being mere chance encounters. The concluding section of the novel returns to a single place, the Phelps's farm, and deals, as does the first section, with a game devised by Tom Sawyer. It is a return to a boy's view of playing, but too much has happened to Huck for him to consider this a mere "adventure." In Tom's "gang of robbers" nothing was at stake; in this "game," Jim's freedom is, and Huck is knowingly opposing the laws of society. Huck has understood that deliberate attacks on adult behavior, like that of Boggs or even the vulgar tricks of the Duke and Dauphin, can have dangerous consequences, but he is prepared to free Jim even at the cost of "going to hell."

Tom has not undergone Huck's "education." He is playing a game that he believes to be a respectable "adventure" because he knows Jim is free. Huck, not knowing this, is aghast at Tom's apparent loss of respectability: "Here was a boy that was respectable and well brung up; and had a character to lose . . . I couldn't understand it no way at all." But Tom's game does not include confiding in Huck so that these boys do not duplicate the shared union of Huck and Jim on the raft. Tom's make-believe rules and romantic notions lead, without his awareness, to an attack upon society. He warns the adults of his intention to steal Jim because warnings are part of the game. But he discovers, at the time of Jim's escape, that although he set up imaginary rules, the adults find real bullets. When the doctor asks Huck how Tom was shot, Huck replies, "He had a dream . . . and it shot him."

The statement implies a clash between play or dream and reality, and this is how the last section treats the game of escape. The romantic rules are set up by Tom and followed by Huck, but the adult world is made part of the game without knowing about it. To them the warnings and messages are real. Going down the river Huck used disguises and tricks to delude the adult world into believing him. By this connivance Huck and Jim avoided clashes with society and created firm ties between them by being true to each other. Tom has no personal involvement with or love for Jim, and the plan for freedom becomes formalized, unrelated to moral values. Tom offers Jim fake freedom, since Jim is already free. He has his fun at the expense of another's suffering and danger. When Huck hurt Jim's feelings, he apologized; Tom does not. Although Tom is the victim of his own game, his wound does not teach him the meaning of his game.

The adult world triumphs; it is more powerful and it "plays" with real weapons. It is one thing to avoid antagonizing the adult world; another to challenge it and attack it without understanding the risks involved. Huck understands these risks; he has come to understand the ironic meaning of "civilized" behavior, and he wishes none of it. The only way for a boy to avoid this behavior is to escape, as Huck escaped before. And at the end of the novel Huck is about to head for "Injun" country: "Aunt Sally she's going to adopt me and sivilize me, and I can't stand it. I been there before."

Critics have objected to the fact that Jim is freed and that Twain does not face the likelihood that Jim would be returned and punished. But this objection seems to miss the point of the game. By substituting formal rules for personal love, "civilized" tradition for human values, Tom converts freeing a man into a staged act. Thus a game can reduce the most noble deed to a trivial event by neglecting personal involvement. The world in its civilized ways can be sentimental, mean, and brutal, but games can make it possible for a youth to explore this world without succumbing to its dangers. The most significant function of games, as Huck comes to realize, is to protect what one loves—all else is just "pretending."

Chapter 2

Images of America in *Huckleberry Finn*

Extraordinary Characters Among Provincial Country Folk

Horace Spencer Fiske

Himself a prime example of the American citizen, as judged by his contemporary Horace Spencer Fiske, Mark Twain was able to paint a true picture of provincial life in the states along the Mississippi River. Fiske presents excerpts from *Huckleberry Finn* that encapsulate the characters of uncommon members of the cast, and contrasts them with such true provincial types as Colonel Sherburn. Fiske was an extension lecturer in English literature at the University of Chicago.

In his sense of duty and of honor, his abounding humor, his energy and dauntless pluck, his simplicity and sympathy and fidelity, Mr. Clemens is justly regarded as a high type of an American citizen. He naturally enough comprehends pretty fully the salient characteristics of American types, and has, besides, the literary art to embody them in entertaining and convincing form. The impression of artistry in his work, however, is likely to be lost in a laugh,—the truth and power and dramatic quality in his characterizations are often overlooked in the effects of his humor. As Mr. [William Dean] Howells suggests, "Mark Twain portrays and interprets real types, not only with exquisite appreciation and sympathy, but with a force and truth of drawing that makes them permanent." And the especial praise of the literary critics is given to *Huckleberry Finn* for its essential truthfulness to certain aspects of provincial life and character along the Mississippi and the borders of adjoining states. . . .

Mr. Clemens's own boyhood life at Hannibal, Missouri, on the Mississippi River, and his years as a pilot on the same river, gave him a vivid background and a close familiarity

Reprinted from Horace Spencer Fiske, *Provincial Types in American Fiction* (New York: Chautauqua Press, 1903).

with various Southwestern types that proved invaluable in the production of such a book as *Huckleberry Finn.*

Huckleberry Finn first became known to the reading world as the companion of Tom Sawyer, of whose *Adventures* he was a part. Their good luck in finding the money hidden by the robbers in a cave left Huck in such affluent circumstances that he was getting a dollar a day in interest—"more than a body could tell what to do with." He had been adopted by the Widow Douglas, who was bent on civilizing him; but he found it rough living in the house all the time, considering how "dismal regular and decent the widow was in all her ways.". . .

Huck's Father

The unexpected appearance of Huck's drunken and vagabond father in the boy's room at the widow's had, for a moment, a terrifying effect on Huck. After looking his son all over, the father said, with a critical and injured air: "Starchy clothes—very. You think you're a good deal of a big-bug, *don't* you?" To which Huck was non-committal; and the father continued: "You've put on considerable many frills since I been away. I'll take you down a peg before I get done with you. You're educated, too, they say—can read and write. You think you're better'n your father, now, don't you, because he can't? *I'll* take it out of you. Who told you you might meddle with such hifalut'n foolishness, hey?" On Huck's reply that it was the widow, the father threatened to "learn her how to meddle," and then added, ominously: "And looky here—you drop that school, you hear? I'll learn people to bring up a boy to put on airs over his own father, and let on to be better'n what *he* is. You lemme catch you fooling around that school again, you hear? Your mother couldn't read, and she couldn't write, nuther, before she died. None of the family couldn't write before *they* died. I can't; and here you're a-swelling yourself up like this. I ain't the man to stand it—you hear?" Asked by his father to read a little, as an example of what he could do, Huck read something about General Washington and the wars; when suddenly the father struck the book from his son's hand and cried out angrily: "It's so. You can do it. I had my doubts when you told me. Now, looky here; you stop that putting on frills. I won't have it. I'll lay for you, my smarty; and if I catch you about that school, I'll tan you good. First you know you'll get religion. I never see such a son."

To show his superiority to the widow who had adopted Huck, his father carried him off up the river to an old log hut he had made the headquarters for his vagrant life. The intolerable monotony of a respectable life with the widow was thus done away with; but Huck soon found that his father's restraint, ugly temper, and drunkenness, finally culminating in a night of delirium tremens, were as hard to bear as the widow's respectability, and he escaped down the river to Jackson's Island. The next morning after his arrival he lay and listened to the booming of the cannon by which they were endeavoring to find his dead body. . . .

Jim

It was on this island that he discovered Miss Watson's runaway "nigger," Jim, just as he was waking at dawn by the side of his camp-fire. Jim, in his amazement at seeing Huck, who had been reported murdered, suddenly sprang up, and then dropped upon his knees and put his hands together, crying superstitiously; "Doan' hurt me—don't! I hain't ever done no harm to a ghos'. I awluz liked dead people, en done all I could for 'em. Yo go en git in de river agin, whah you b'longs, en doan' do nuffin' to Ole Jim, 'at uz awluz yo' fr'en'." But Jim was soon so much reassured that he told Huck all the details of his own escape. He even grew confidential and told Huck about his past speculation in stock,—a cow, and in a bank set up by "Misto Bradish's nigger,"—at the end of which Jim had only ten cents left. "Well, I 'uz gwyne to spen' it, but I had a dream, 'en de dream tole me to give it to a nigger name' Balum—Balum's Ass dey call him for short; he's one er dem chuckleheads, you know. But he's lucky, dey say, en I see I warn't lucky. De dream say let Balum inves' de ten cents en he'd make a raise for me. Well, Balum he tuck de money, en when he wuz in church he hear de preacher say dat whoever give to de po' len' to de Lord, en boun' to git his money back a hund'd times. So Balum he tuck en give de ten cents to de po', en laid low to see what wuz gwyne to come of it." To Huck's inquiry as to what did come of it, the darky replied: "Nuffin never come of it. I couldn' manage to k'leck dat money no way; en Balum he couldn'. I ain' gwyne to lea' no mo' money 'dout I see de security. Boun' to git yo' money back a hund'd times, de preacher says! Ef I could git de ten *cents* back, I'd call it squah, en be glad er de chanst." Huck's hopeful suggestion that Jim was going to be rich sometime or other—according to Jim's own prophecy—

called to the negro's mind the happy thought that he was already rich. "I owns myse'f, en I's wuth eight hund'd dollars. I wisht I had de money, I wouldn' want no mo'."

Huck's discovery—in the guise of a girl—that there was a reward out for the capture of Jim and that Jackson's Island was a dangerous place, was the signal for their hurried departure from the island by night. The second night—they concealed themselves in a "towhead" of cottonwoods during the day—the raft they were on ran between seven and eight hours, with a current that carried them along over four miles an hour. . . .

The Feuding Grangerfords and Shepherdsons

Huck's escape from the wreck of the raft that had been smashed by a steamboat in the night brought him to the big old-fashioned double log house of Colonel Grangerford, whose dogs refused to let the dripping Huck go by. After a very warlike examination of Huck, he was gradually admitted to the house; and when it was learned that he was in no way connected with the rival house of the Shepherdsons,—between whom and the Grangerfords there was a deadly feud,—Huck was very hospitably received and compassionately entertained on the strength of his trumped-up story. In the admiring words of Huck: "It was a mighty nice family, and a mighty nice house, too. I hadn't seen no house out in the country before that was so nice and had so much style. It didn't have an iron latch on the front door, nor a wooden one with a buckskin string, but a brass knob to turn, the same as houses in a town. There warn't no bed in the parlor, nor a sign of a bed; but heaps of parlors in towns has beds in them. There was a big fireplace that was bricked on the bottom, and the bricks was kept clean and red by pouring water on them and scrubbing them with another brick. . . . They had big brass dog-irons that could hold up a saw-log." There was also a wonderful clock ("it was beautiful to hear that clock tick"), and some books piled up with perfect exactness on each corner of the table. "One was a big family Bible full of pictures. One was *Pilgrim's Progress,* about a man that left his family, it didn't say why. I read considerable in it now and then. The statements was interesting but tough. Another was *Friendship's Offering,* full of beautiful stuff and poetry; but I didn't read the poetry. Another was Henry Clay's Speeches, and another was Dr. Gunn's *Family Medicine,* which told you all about what to do if a body was sick or dead.". . .

In the eyes of Huck the proprietor of the place was a gentleman—"a gentleman all over." Colonel Grangerford . . . was "very tall and very slim, and had a darkish-paly complexion, not a sign of red in it anywheres; he was clean shaved every morning all over his thin face, and he had the thinnest kind of lips, and the thinnest kind of nostrils, and a high nose, and heavy eyebrows, and the blackest kind of eyes, sunk so deep back that they seemed like they was looking out of caverns at you, as you may say. His forehead was high, and his hair was black and straight and hung to his shoulders. His hands was long and thin, and every day of his life he put on a clean shirt and a full suit from head to foot made out of linen so white it hurt your eyes to look at it; and on Sundays he wore a blue tail-coat with brass buttons on it." He had a personal dignity that Huck was impressed by, and a pervasive kindliness, and his smile was good to see. In his presence manners were instinctively good, and there was a genial sunshine about the man that every one liked; "but when he straightened himself up like a liberty-pole, and the lightning began to flicker out from under his eyebrows, you wanted to climb a tree first, and find out what the matter was afterwards."

The tall, handsome older sons, Tom and Bob, dressed, like their father, in white linen from head to foot, and wore broad Panama hats; and in their home life they had been reared to show especial courtesy to the parents. On the latter's arrival in the dining room the sons always rose from their chairs and remained standing till their parents were seated; and after mixing at the sideboard a glass of bitters for their father and then for themselves, they would bow and say, "Our duty to you, sir and madam."

But this Southern family, so chivalrous and courtly toward one another, were in deadly feud with their neighbors, the rival family of the Shepherdsons. Huck's ignorance of a feud was somewhat lessened by Buck Grangerford's definition: "Well, a feud is this way: A man has a quarrel with another man, and kills him; then that other man's brother kills *him*; then the other brothers, on both sides, goes for one another; then the *cousins* chip in—and by and by everybody's killed off, and there ain't no more feud. But it's kind of slow, and takes a long time." Buck also informed Huck that their own feud started some thirty years before, when there was "trouble 'bout something," a lawsuit, and a shooting of the man who won the suit by the man who lost. Buck was entirely ignorant of the cause of the trouble and whether it was a Grangerford or a Shepherdson that did the shooting; but he thought that perhaps his father knew. To Huck's question as to whether many had been killed in the feud, Buck cheerfully replied: "Yes; right smart chance of funerals. But they don't always kill. Pa's got a few buckshot in him; but he don't mind it 'cuz he don't weigh much, anyway. Bob's been carved up some with a bowie, and Tom's been hurt once or twice." "Has anybody been killed this year, Buck"? inquired Huck. "Yes; we got one and they got one."

Buck, in a truly chivalrous spirit, insisted that there wasn't a coward among "them Shepherdsons," even if they were inveterate enemies. "Why, that old man [Shepherdson] kep' up his end in a fight one day for half an hour against three Grangerfords, and come out winner. They was all a-horseback; he lit off of his horse and got behind a little woodpile, and kep' his horse before him to stop the bullets; but the Grangerfords stayed on their horses and capered around the old man, and peppered away at him, and he peppered away at them. Him and his horse both went home pretty leaky and crippled, but the Grangerfords had to be *fetched* home, and one of 'em was dead, and another died the next day. No, sir; if a body's out hunting for cowards, he don't want to fool away any time amongst them Shepherdsons, becuz they don't breed any of that *kind*."

And Huck himself, from his lookout in a tree, was to see Buck Grangerford and another young man shot to death by the merciless Shepherdsons, one of whose number had run off in the night with Colonel Grangerford's younger daughter. . . .

The Duke and the King: Professional Humbugs

Two sublime types of professional humbugs, such as must now and then visit gullible small towns along the Mississippi in the Southwest, are the "Duke of Bridgewater" and the "King," whom Huck, under mental protest, rescued from an outraged community. The King was about seventy, with a bald head and very gray whiskers. He wore an old battered-up slouch hat, a greasy blue woolen shirt, and ragged old blue jeans breeches stuffed into his boot-tops, and home-knit "galluses,"—or rather only one; and when rescued he and his companion, the Duke, were each carrying a "big, fat, ratty-looking" carpet-bag.

They proved to be strangers to each other, and in explaining the cause of his trouble the Duke said to his new-found acquaintance: "Well, I'd been selling an article to take the tartar off the teeth,—and it does take it off, too, and gen-er'ly the enamel along with it,—but I stayed about one night longer than I ought to, and was just in the act of sliding out when I ran across you on the trail this side of town. . . . That's the whole yarn, what's yourn?" To which the King replied, with a little more detail: "Well, I'd ben a-runnin' a little temperance revival thar 'bout a week, and was the pet of the women-folks, big and little, for I was makin' it mighty warm for the rummies, I *tell* you, and takin' as much as five or six dollars a night—ten cents a head, children and niggers free—and business a-growin' all the time, when somehow or another a little report got around last night that I had a way of puttin' in my time with a private jug on the sly. A nigger rousted me out this mornin' and told me the people was getherin' on the quiet with their dogs and horses, and they'd be along pretty soon and give me 'bout half an hour's start, and then run me down if they could; and if they got me they'd tar and feather me and ride me on a rail, sure. I didn't wait for no breakfast—I warn't hungry."

It seemed feasible that these two "professionals" should from this time forth reënforce each other's talents, the Duke of Bridgewater (the King called it "Bilgewater") explaining first what his "line" was: "Jour printer by trade; do a little in patent medicines; theater-actor—tragedy, you know; take a turn to mesmerism and phrenology when there's a chance; teach singing—geography school for a change; sling a lecture sometimes—oh, I do lots of things—most anything that comes handy, so it ain't work." The King then explained his "lay": "I've done considerable in the doctoring way in my time. Layin' on o' hands is my best holt—for cancer and paralysis, and sich things; and I k'n tell a fortune pretty good when I've got somebody along to find out the facts for me. Preachin's my line, too, and workin' camp-meetin's and missionaryin' around."

Working the Camp-Meeting

Learning that a camp-meeting was being held in the woods some two miles back from the little river town near which the raft was tied up for the day, the King "allowed" that he would go and "work it" for all it was worth, and permitted Huck to go with him. The first shed they came to contained a preacher that was "lining" out a hymn. He lined out two lines and everybody sang them; and then he lined out two more for them to sing, and so on indefinitely. The people grew more and more animated, and sang louder and louder; and toward the end some began to groan and some to shout. The preacher was of the loud-voiced, hortatory, unctuous type. . . . In the language of Huck: "He went weaving first to one side of the platform and then the other, and then a-leaning down over the front of it, with his arms and his body going all the time, and shouting his words out with all his might; and every now and then he would hold up his Bible and spread it open and kind of pass it around this way and that, shouting, 'It's the brazen serpent in the wilderness! Look upon it and live!' and people would shout out, 'Glory!—A-a-*men!*' And so he went on, and the people groaning and crying and saying Amen: 'Oh, come to the mourners' bench! come, black with sin! (*amen!*) come, sick and sore! (*amen!*) come, lame and halt and blind! (*amen!*) come, pore and needy, sunk in shame! (*a-a-men!*) Come, all that's worn and soiled and suffering!—come with a broken spirit! come with a contrite heart! come in your rags and sin and dirt! the waters that cleanse is free, the door of heaven stands open—oh, enter in and be at rest! (*A-a-men, glory, glory hallelujah!*)'" The shouting and crying, as reported by Huck, became so great that the preacher's words could no longer be distinguished. People rose in all parts of the crowd and made their way by sheer strength to the mourners' bench, with the tears streaming down their faces; and when the mourners had filled the front benches in a throng, they sang and shouted and flung themselves down on the straw, "just crazy and wild."

By playing the part of a converted pirate who had been robbed the night before, and was now returning to the Indian Ocean to convert his brother pirates, the King was able to carry back to the raft some eighty-seven dollars and seventy-five cents which he had "gathered in" at the camp-meeting by a skillful appeal from the platform and passing the hat for a collection. He promised to say to every pirate converted, "Don't you thank me, don't you give me no credit; it all belongs to them dear people in Pokeville camp-meeting, natural brothers and benefactors of the race, and that dear preacher there, the truest friend a pirate ever had!" And the King had brought back with him, too, a three-gallon jug of whisky, which he had found under a wagon when he was starting for the raft through the woods. To use Huck's report: "The King said, take it all around, it laid over any day he'd ever put in in the missionarying line. He said it warn't no use talking, heathens don't amount to shucks alongside of pirates to work a camp-meeting with."

A True Provincial

A truly Southern provincial type is the fierce-natured, cool-headed Colonel Sherborne who shot down in cold blood the drunken, good-natured, but abusive Boggs; and when the mob threatened him with lynching, his accurate knowledge of them was shown by his sudden appearance on the porch of his home and his cool defiance, characteristically reënforced by a shot gun: "The idea of *you* lynching anybody! It's amusing. The idea of you thinking you had pluck enough to lynch a *man!*... You didn't want to come.... But if only *half*-a-man–like Buck Harkness, there—shouts 'Lynch him! lynch him!' you're afraid to back down—afraid you'll be found out to be what you are—*cowards*—and so you raise a yell, and hang yourselves on to that half-a-man's coat-tail, and come raging up here, swearing what big things you're going to do. The pitifulest thing out is a mob; that's what an army is—a mob; they don't fight with courage that's born in them, but with courage that's borrowed from their mass, and from their officers. But a mob without any *man* at the head of it is *beneath* pitifulness. Now the thing for *you* to do is droop your tails and go home and crawl in a hole. . . . Now *leave*—and take your half-a-man with you." As the Colonel tossed his gun up across his left arm and cocked it, the mob "washed back sudden," broke apart, and dashed into a wild run, with the "half-a-man" bringing up the rear.

Old Uncle Silas Phelps, the easy-going, inconsequential farmer and preacher, who had a little log church down back of the plantation and "never charged nothing for his preaching, and it was worth it, too"; the generous-souled, credulous, and motherly Aunt Sally; and the versatile, unconscionable Tom Sawyer, who insisted on freeing in formal and adventurous style the negro Jim that was already free,—these are additional types in *Huckleberry Finn* that Mr. Clemens has characterized with easy and inimitable touch. In fact, much of the characterization in the book seems wrought out of the closest familiarity with those strange, crude, virile types that belonged to life along the Mississippi half a century ago.

Huck Finn as a Symbol of Jacksonian Ideals

Andrew Jay Hoffman

Andrew Jay Hoffman calculates that the events of *Huckleberry Finn* took place during the period when Andrew Jackson became hero and symbol of his age. He uses ideas associated with Jacksonian ideals—Nature, Providence, and Will—to demonstrate that Huck Finn also serves as a symbol of the Jacksonian age. Hoffman is the author of *Inventing Mark Twain: The Lives of Samuel Langhorne Clemens.*

Twain sets the time of [*Huckleberry Finn*] at "Forty to fifty years ago." Some quick math gives us the range of possible dates. Twain began writing the novel in 1876 and published it in America in 1885. Forty to fifty years before stretches the scope to between 1826 and 1845. The latter date is the year Andrew Jackson died. The earlier is halfway between the Presidential election he should have won and the first he did: in 1824, the House of Representatives denied Andrew Jackson the Presidency, despite his plurality at the polls; but he won handily in 1828 and 1832. His top aide, Martin Van Buren, succeeded him, and the issues and ideals of Jacksonianism dominated the American scene until the question of slavery elbowed them from view in the years following Jackson's death. . . .

Huck and Jacksonian Cultural Ideals

A small leap nominates Huck as a Jacksonian ideal, by which I mean that the same ideological structure which made a symbol of Jackson makes a symbol of Huck. John William Ward's *Andrew Jackson—Symbol for an Age* articulates part of that ideology successfully by showing how the American people of the first half of the last century created a hero out of a man. Ward writes in his coda on symbolism, "The symbolic

Andrew Jackson is the creation of his time. Through the age's leading figure were projected the age's leading ideas. Of Andrew Jackson the people made a mirror for themselves." And he concludes his essay, "To describe the early nineteenth century as the age of Jackson misstates the matter. The age was not his. He was the age's.". . .

Ward argues that three more or less inseparable ideas—Nature, Providence and Will—"are the structural underpinnings of the ideology of the society of early nineteenth-century America, for which Andrew Jackson is *one* symbol." I will use Ward's ideas to point out how Huck Finn is another.

Nature

Jacksonian America's conception of Nature was, according to Ward, an uneasy compromise between the savagery of uncivilization, as identified with the Indians, and the moral decay of too much civilization, embodied in the Europeans. "The ideal of the admixture of nature and civilization was a static one. It could be achieved only in the pioneer stage when the wildness of nature had been subdued but the enervating influence of civilization had not yet been felt.". . . Ward explains, "Americans were willing to accept the idea that nature, symbolized by the forest, was the source of vitality, but their attitude was ambivalent. They celebrated nature, but not wild nature." Wild nature belonged to the Indians. . . .

Though in recent years critics have withdrawn support for the vision of Huck Finn as a child of Nature, the impression remains with readers of the novel. The initial chapters of the book encourages this interpretation, even if they do not wholly endorse it. Huck, caught between the poles of the widow's stultifying "sivilizing" and Pap's brutal uncivilizing, the second defined against the first, escapes both by plunging into the relative wilderness of the Mississippi river, then the boundary between the tamed states and the untamed territories. Huck writes of the moment just before releasing the canoe into the current, hovering on the precipice of freedom, "Everything was dead quiet, and it looked late, and *smelt* late. You know what I mean—I don't know the words to put it in." This passage points to two aspects of Huck's relationship to Nature: his rare ability to detect the minutiae of nature, like the odor of night, and the resistance such natural phenomena have to language. Once Huck achieves his independence he overcomes the resistance. Out on the Mississippi Huck becomes the mouthpiece for Nature: "The sky looks ever so deep when you lay down on your back in the moonshine; I never knowed it before. And how far a body can hear on the water such nights!" While his knowledge of Nature never seems more than adequate—when Mrs. Loftus questions him about the rising patterns of animals, for example, or in his river-mastery during the fog—Huck's ability to speak for Nature binds Huck and Nature in our imagination. Even during the terror of the fog, his sense of personal relationship to Nature impresses us more than his knowledge: "I was floating along, of course, four or five miles an hour; but you don't even think of that. No, you *feel* like you are laying dead still on the water, and if a little glimpse of a snag slips by, you don't think to yourself how fast *you're* going, but you catch your breath and think, my! how that snag's tearing along." This power of speaking for Nature becomes more apparent when periodically throughout the novel Huck takes his moments of peace to enjoy it. His description of the sunrise at the beginning of Chapter 19 is the classic passage of the type. These passages appear infrequently, as contemporary critics point out in their arguments against conceiving of Huck as Nature's child, but when they do occur they establish an alliance between Huck and Nature, better understood as a partnership than as a familial relationship. . . .

PROVIDENCE

Ward's delineation of the second concept, Providence, begins with the popular belief that God intervened on Jackson's and America's behalf in the astounding War of 1812 victory over the British at New Orleans. Though in the flurry of panegyrics after the battle Jackson was made an equal to the deity, in time he settled for a role as, in his own words, "the humble instrument of a superintending Providence." This Providence particularly superintended America. Ward writes:

> Perhaps the most durable among the many ideas that have fallen under the generic term, nationalism, is the belief that God will see to it that America will succeed. . . . Americans of the nineteenth century, preoccupied with immediate tasks, argued that a self-conscious social philosophy against which all change must \be measured was unnecessary because man, in America, would intuitively trod the path to justice.

This moral intuition is a fundamental characteristic of America's ideal relationship to divine will. God's word mostly came to Americans through the Bible and the lessons of Nature, and careful reasoning about right and wrong meant less than instinctive ethics. Even the superb reasoner Thomas Jefferson expressed the belief that in moral cases a ploughman will decide as well as or better than a professor, and Andrew Jackson, Western farmer elevated to America's moral and political leader, embodied proof of that belief for his time. In the strictly political arena Manifest Destiny strikingly shows American belief in the divinity of its leadership, a belief grounded in the conviction that we have a natural, god-given morality. The deity behind this morality is not precisely the ruler of Nature; Jacksonian America saw only the creation of Nature, and not its direction, as proof of God's power. Instead, God has a plan larger than Nature, and America and Andrew Jackson were significant parts of it.

Huck shares with Jackson this direct relationship to the divinity; that Ward and Huck use the same word for it makes this relationship easy to prove. Huck refers to two experiences of divine intervention within a few pages of each other at the story's moral climax. Finding himself in a moral corner about Jim in Chapter 31, Huck writes:

> And at last, when it hit me all of a sudden that here was the plain hand of Providence slapping me in the face and letting me know my wickedness was being watched all the time whilst from up there in heaven, whilst I was stealing a poor old woman's nigger that hadn't ever done me no harm, and now was showing me there's One that's always on the lookout, and ain't a-going to allow no such miserable doings to go only just so fur and no further, I most dropped in my tracks I was so scared.

Many critics have pointed out the verbal ambiguity of this sentence: Who hadn't done Huck any harm? Which miserable doings? Allow how, or what? Others have shown a structural irony in that this slapping God seems not only to allow these goings-on but to encourage them; in that Huck in fact rejects this God's interference; and in that Huck's subsequent cleansing of sin in fact leaves the sin and cleans out the morality. But before we can confront these ironies and ambiguities we have to grant Huck's perception that God does interfere directly in his life. The irony and ambiguity actually depend on the temporary sincerity of Huck's perception that God watched him and tried to stop his immorality. Huck later backs down from this perception, but his belief in a false case of providential interference prepares the reader for a true intervention on his behalf in the subsequent chapter. Wandering up to the Phelps house wishing for death, Huck "went right along, not fixing up any particular plan, but just trusting to Providence to put the right words in my mouth when the time come; for I'd noticed that Providence always did put the right words in my mouth, if I left it alone." Aside from this being a succinct expression of Ward's concept of innate moral divinity, it is reliable prophecy. Providence lives up to its name, providing Huck through the Phelps with an identity and words to fill it. "But if they was joyful, it warn't nothing to what I was; for it was like being born again, I was so glad to find out who I was." Huck's "chin was so tired it couldn't hardly go," so many words did Providence put in his mouth. The false Providence of Chapter 31 leads us to trust the Providence of Chapter 32. God appears to have chosen Huck.

Will

Will, Ward's last concept, removes the responsibility for differences in people's accomplishments from the larger forces of Nature or Providence and places them with the individual. "From the time of his victory in 1815 to his death in 1845, Jackson was constantly before the American imagination as the embodiment of the success that awaits the man of iron will, the man who can overcome insuperable opposition simply by determination." While this faith in the self-made man does in the extreme negate the importance of Providence and Nature, its practical danger lies in demagoguery. Against this, Ward asserts, the American ideal of Will had moderating attributes.

> A highly fluid society, such as the United States in the early years of the nineteenth century, faces the problem of insuring social conformity and establishing social direction without the aid of traditional institutions which implement such purposes. . . . What actually seems to happen is that the individual incorporates society's demands into his own consciousness and thereby is led to strive even harder because the demands of the society seem to be the demands of one's own self.

America created out of Andrew Jackson a man of indomitable will who dearly loved his wife, adopted a score of children, and had nearly impeccable scruples. This modified concept of Will—indomitable desire soft at heart—protected society from a Napoleon, the age's emblem of a harder sort of will. America watched Napoleon with great interest and reserved admiration; Jackson's own library contained five biographies of the French leader. If the internalized rules of society and native kindness were not sufficient to protect society from an iron will, America could appeal to a higher authority. "The universal stress on the fact that the man of iron will had in the end bowed to God"—Jackson turned to religion before his death—"proved that in the last analysis God ruled the universe, that the man of iron will offer no threat to society because he too had his master."

I cannot prove Huck Finn a boy of iron will without stretching the novel. Part of the novel's grievously frustrating ending is Huck's inability to make Tom Sawyer accept anything he says, to the point that Tom even changes the meanings of Huck's words while they are still in his mouth. Tom's willful "psychopathic personality, for whom all that counts are energy and charisma"[1] easily dominates Huck. But Ward's concept of Will is not merely a matter of energy and charisma; it includes self-determination and moral responsibility. These two elements have long been the central focus of appreciation of Huck Finn. Traditional interpretations of the novel, starting with those by T. S. Eliot and Lionel Trilling and continuing to the present day, stress Huck's moral development, his eventual acceptance that, in the problem of human cruelty, "The solution, simply, is human love."[2] More recent criticism, in shooting down the notion of Huck's moral enlightenment, erects yet another defense of Huck as an embodiment of Will by stressing Huck's increased skills as a maker of situations, a player of roles, a fabricator of his own life in the form of a book called *Adventures of Huckleberry Finn.* Further, Huck's inability to completely embrace Will is partially mitigated at the novel's end by his partnership with Tom, whose ability to make things happen by just saying so is proved to have no power outside the realm of fiction. Will has endless effect in the personal world each of us creates with lies, but in the reality of the novel, we are shown, Will has limits. For Huck to possess Tom's absolute will would abrogate the novel's final thrust and Huck's final lesson: That the world of history cannot be manipulated, even by Huck's heroic powers. If supernatural force cannot change history, how can Will? In this novel, Will is less subject to Providence than to whatever force creates history.

1. George Carrington, *The Dramatic Unity of "Huckleberry Finn."* Columbus: Ohio State University Press, 1976 2. Gilbert M. Rubenstein, "The Moral Structure of *Huckleberry Finn.*" *College English* 18, 1956 (Nov) 72–76

Huck and Jacksonian Socio-Political Ideals

Huck, then, shares with the popular conception of Andrew Jackson the ideological space which made Jackson a hero. The confluence of Nature, Providence, and Will—the last of these concepts modified out of Ward to suit *Huckleberry Finn*'s larger purpose—establishes a matrix of cultural beliefs which an effective Jacksonian hero will symbolize. These cultural ideals shared the Jacksonian imagination with certain socio-political ideals, ideals we might identify as even more certainly Jacksonian than Ward's cultural ones. Alexis de Tocqueville's *Democracy in America* remains the best source for abstractions about the ideals behind Jacksonian society. Tocqueville

> was less interested in describing the American actuality than in explaining the inevitable tendencies of an abstract or generalized democracy. . . . His interest was not in fact but in ideas. . . . His characteristic method was to have an extended discussion with a prominent personage, then to indulge his great powers of deduction and imagination to create a logical theoretical structure based on the idea he had extracted from the words of his informant.[3]

. . . We can see easily how Huck Finn embodies the three core ideals Tocqueville saw. The first of these—the notion of independence, of freedom, of individuality—shares ideology with the last of Ward's concepts. Those three terms, used with a bewildering interchangability in some histories of the period, all concern the same value: the right of an individual to make and follow his [pronoun employed with knowledge] own rules within territory solely his own. Tocqueville writes, "There's a general distaste for accepting any man's word as a proof for anything. . . . Each man is narrowly shut up in himself and from that basis makes the pretension to judge the world.". . . Huck fills Tocqueville's prophecy that individualism—perhaps the best term for this concept—born of democracy "isolates [men] from their contemporaries. Each man is forever thrown back on himself alone, and there is danger that he may be shut up in the solitude of his own heart."

The second socio-political ideal of Jacksonianism is democracy. In Tocqueville's view the dangers of individualism are offset by a kind of democracy of free association. The frequent exercise of voting rights means that political "direction really comes from the people, and though the form of

3. Edward Pessen, *Jacksonian America.* Homewood, Illinois: Dorsey Press, 1969

government is representative, it is clear that the opinion, prejudices, interests and even passions of the people can find no lasting obstacles preventing them from being manifest in the daily conduct of society."

The maintenance of this ideal depends on the third, equality. Tocqueville believed that the equality of condition that reigned among European colonists in New England encouraged them to do away with most aristocratic distinctions. Even Southern aristocrats conceded the virtue of rule of law, a fundamental political tenet in the ideology of equality, and laws restricting inheritance forwarded the cause of economic equality. In Tocqueville's view a belief in equality is a precondition of the universal suffrage which gave American democracy its unique and idealistic quality. "The more I studied American society," Tocqueville claims, "the more clearly I saw equality of conditions as the creative element from which each particular fact derived."

Readers of *Huckleberry Finn* need very little argument to see in Huck the particular embodiment of the abstractions of equality, democracy, and individualism. Huck regards the King and the Duke with the same indulgence he grants Silas Phelps, though the con-artists' shrewd evil matches measure for measure the farmer-preacher's simple-minded goodness. Huck treats both sorts of people with equal dishonesty, lingers illogically in their company, and still presents them to the reader with a brutal directness. For all Huck's acknowledgement of the differences in social status he leaves no doubt that moral value and community rank have nothing in common. . . .

Embodying Ward's Nature, Providence, and Will on one side and Tocqueville's individualism, democracy, and equality on the other, Huck becomes a symbol for the ideals of Jacksonian America. These elements, and minor others not here articulated, are what we believe Americans in the second quarter of the nineteenth century hoped their country was.

A Satire on American Institutions

Gladys Carmen Bellamy

Gladys Carmen Bellamy finds in Tom, Huck, and Jim depictions of three levels of civilization. Tom represents a high level, but it is romantic and artificial. Jim is prey to superstitions and taboos; he, like Tom, is bound by his "institutions." Huck is the only character, according to Bellamy, who is free of such bonds. Although he goes along with Tom and Jim when he is with them, she points out, when he is alone he has no rules to follow but the dictates of his own heart. Bellamy is the author of *Mark Twain as a Literary Artist*, from which this viewpoint is excerpted.

It is no secret that Mark Twain had difficulty in writing *Huckleberry Finn*. He described it to [William Dean] Howells as "a book I have worked at, by fits and starts, during the past five or six years." Actually, it was seven years; yet the finished whole seems easy, simple, natural. Huck, the unifying thread tying everything together, gains in stature by having no taller rivals near him—only the river tramps who impose on his generosity and the hunted Negro whom he befriends.

Three Thematic Units

In spite of its episodic nature, the book falls naturally into three thematic units. In the first sixteen chapters the theme has to do with what is of and from St. Petersburg: Huck, Tom, Nigger Jim, and Pap. The second thematic unit includes the most strongly satiric, the most powerful part of the book, bringing Huck and Jim into contact with the outside world. In the cross-section of the South through which they journey, Huck witnesses the Grangerford-Shepherdson feud, the chicanery of the king and the duke, the killing of

Boggs, Colonel Sherburn's quelling of the mob, and finally the village funeral. The characters of the king and the duke add to the thematic unity of this section. The third thematic unit is short, a sort of coda to the rest, covering the period at the Phelps farm in which Tom re-enters the story. It repeats the romanticized motif of the first part, bringing the book full circle before its close.

The art of characterization is the one most important to a novelist, and Mark Twain's characters are his greatest literary achievement. Something of his method in characterization may be learned from a passage he wrote in 1907:

> Every man is in his own person the whole human race, with not a detail lacking. I am the whole human race without a detail lacking; I have studied the human race with diligence and strong interest all these years in my own person; in myself I find in big or little proportion every quality and every defect that is findable in the mass of the race.

This suggests that when he had need of a certain trait, his habit was to dig for it within himself, to isolate and study it, then to enlarge it to the proportion proper to the character in question. This suggestion is borne out by a marginal note in one of his books: "If Byron—if any man—draws 50 characters, they are all himself—50 shades, 50 moods, of his own character, And when the man draws them well, why do they stir my admiration? Because they are me—I recognize myself."

A careful study of *Huckleberry Finn* shows that it is the characters and their interrelationship which determine the arrangement and structure of the book. The three thematic sections subdivide into little units notable for the contrast they offer each other. The first three chapters continue, naturally enough, the vein of *Tom Sawyer*, to which this book becomes a sort of sequel. Everything is colored by the excitement of Tom's imaginary adventures; he insists on doing all things according to the books he has read, from having his Gang sign in blood their oaths of allegiance to capturing and holding people for ransom. Ben Rogers, a Gang member, wants to know what being "ransomed" means, and Tom replies:

> "I don't know. But that's what they do. I've seen it in books; and of course that's what we've got to do."
>
> "But how can we do it if we don't know what it is?"
>
> "Why, blame it all, we've *got* to do it. Don't I tell you it's in the books? Do you want to go to doing different from what's in the books and get things all muddled up?"

A Satire on Institutionalism

And here, in a simple argument among boys, Mark Twain sets the pattern for this, his greatest story, as a satire on institutionalism. The three figures, Tom, Huck, and Jim, represent three gradations of thought and three levels of civilization. Tom, pretending so intensely that it becomes so, says we can't do it except as in the books. Is this what civilization really is—merely a pretense according to a set pattern? Tom is on the highest level, in the sense of being most civilized; but he represents a mawkish, romantic, artificial civilization. Compared with him, Nigger Jim and Huck are primitives; and the closer Mark Twain gets to primitivism, the better his writing becomes. He shows us the African in Jim, imbuing him with a dark knowledge that lies in his blood and his nerve ends. Huck Finn stands between these two; he is the "natural man," suggesting Walt Whitman's dream of the great American who should be simple and free. Both Tom and Jim are in bondage to institutionalism.[1] Tom can't do anything against the rules of his books; Jim can't do anything against the rules of his taboos, his voodoo fears and charms and superstitions. Only Huck is free of institutions. Tom and Jim are always sure they are right, since each has his institution to consult and to follow; but Huck is tormented by doubts. When he is with Tom, he is willing to join Tom in following the books; when he is with Jim, he is careful not to break Jim's taboos, especially after the incident of the rattlesnake skin. But when Huck is alone, because he has no rules to go by he is guided by the voice within himself. He listens to what goes on inside him. He is free to probe within his own heart, where is to be found whatever bit of divinity man has—what we know as his soul.

If *Tom Sawyer* is accepted as a satire against the moralizing Sunday school tales, *Huckleberry Finn* has a much broader field as a satire against institutionalism in general. The institution of slavery is basic in this book. . . .

Within each of the thematic units in *Huckleberry Finn* there is a subtle variation of character and atmosphere. After the idyllic, romantic atmosphere which permeates the first three chapters, in the next four the story veers sharply from the

1. I am indebted to Professor Floyd Stovall, formerly of North Texas State Teachers College and now of the University of North Carolina, for the suggestion that *Huckleberry Finn* is a satire on institutionalism, as well as for some suggestions pertaining to the structure of the book.

mood of *Tom Sawyer,* and Pap takes the stage, drunken and disreputable, feeling himself the victim of sundry social ills. Into this satiric portrait went Mark Twain's years of observation of mountain whites, piney-woods people, and river rats. Pap is completely revealed through his oration on the "guv'ment." This unit ends when Huck flees because he fears his father will kill him in a fit of delirium tremens.

After so much violence, Jackson's Island gives him a feeling of peace. He explores the island, and just as he begins to feel lonely he discovers Jim, a Negro who has run away from home because his owner is planning to sell him "down to Orleans"—the Negro's equivalent of hell. Thereafter the runaway slave and the outcast waif share the island and comfort each other. This small unit of four chapters, the interlude on Jackson's Island, ends once more in the threat of violence and fear. Men are approaching the island to search for Jim.

Strong Characters

Mark Twain's prefatory note warns the reader that seven different dialects are used in the book; the shadings among them are so fine that not every reader can perceive them, and he does not want readers to think that "all these characters were trying to talk alike and not succeeding." His sensitivity to speech enabled him to say, "The shadings have not been done in haphazard fashion, or by guesswork, but painstakingly." But the artistry of such shadings in dialect fades before his skill in employing the vernacular of Huck Finn for a book-length narrative. Huck has a strong, vivid, natural imagination—not an artificial one, such as Tom's, or a superstitious one, such as Jim's. He describes, with memorable effect, a summer storm which he and Jim watched from the security of their cave on the island:

> . . . it looked all blue-black outside, and lovely; and the rain would thrash along by so thick that the trees off a little ways looked dim and spiderwebby; and here would come a blast of wind that would bend the trees down and turn up the pale underside of the leaves; and then a perfect ripper of a gust would follow along and set the branches to tossing their arms as if they was just wild; and next, when it was just about the bluest and blackest–*fst!* it was as bright as glory, and you'd have a little glimpse of tree-tops a-plunging about a way off yonder in the storm, hundreds of yards further than you could see before; dark as sin again in a second, and now you'd hear the thunder let go with an awful crash, and then go rumbling, grumbling, tumbling, down the sky towards the under side of the world,

> like rolling empty barrels down stairs—where it's long stairs and they bounce a good deal, you know.

Mark Twain's elemental imagination lends vigor and freshness to many passages. As Huck and Jim lie on their backs at night looking up at the stars, while the raft slips silently down the river, they argue about whether the stars "was made or only just happened": "Jim said the moon could 'a' *laid* them; well, that looked kind of reasonable . . . because I've seen a frog lay most as many." Huck describes Pap as having hair that was "long and tangled and greasy, and hung down, and you could see his eyes shining through like he was behind vines," while his face was white—"not like another man's white, but a white to make a body sick . . . a fish-belly white." At the parlor funeral of Peter Wilks, "the undertaker he slid around in his black gloves with his softy soothering ways, . . . making no more sound than a cat. . . . He was the softest, glidingest, stealthiest man I ever see." When the old king got a sudden shock, he "squshed down like a bluff bank that the river has cut under, it took him so sudden." Huck's language is equal to any effect demanded of it.

Part of the power of this book lies in Mark Twain's drawing of the character of Nigger Jim. From the time Jim first appears, a "big nigger" silhouetted in the kitchen door with the light behind him, he is a figure of dignity. In the famous syllogism in which Jim argues that since a Frenchman is a man, he should talk like a man, Mark Twain shows Jim's slow, purposeful reasoning. But in other moods Jim's spirit opens out to a wider horizon. Like Huck, he senses the beauty of the river. In his interpretation of a dream, Jim lets "the big, clear river" symbolize "the free States"—in other words, freedom. If "The Enchanted Village" might serve as a subtitle for *Tom Sawyer*, so "The Road to Freedom" might serve the same purpose for *Huckleberry Finn*. Jim has two big scenes in the book. One occurs when he relates the tragic moment of his discovery that his little girl was "plumb deef en dumb, Huck, plumb deef en dumb." His second big scene comes when he risks capture to help the doctor care for the wounded Tom Sawyer.

Developing Huck's Character

Whatever may be said of Tom Sawyer, Huck Finn is a developing character. Much of his development is due to his association with Jim and his increasing respect for the black man. In *Tom Sawyer*, Huck apologized to Tom for eating with a Negro, the Rogerses' Uncle Jake, who had given him food: "A body's got to do things when he's awful hungry he wouldn't . . . do as a steady thing." When he first finds Jim on the island, he is glad simply because he wants companionship; but as the two share the peace of the place, Huck comes to regard Jim as a human being rather than a faithful dog. When he hears there is a reward for Jim, the money offers no temptation to him; but under attack by his conscience, he fears he may have done wrong in helping a slave to escape. His traditions and environment pull him one way; what he feels in his heart pulls him the other way. Finally, he goes so far as to write a note to Miss Watson, Jim's owner, telling her where Jim is to be found. At first, he feels better for writing the note:

> . . . thinking how near I come to being lost and going to hell. . . . [Then I] got to thinking over our trip down the river; and I see Jim before me all the time: in the day and in the night-time, . . . and we a-floating along, talking and singing and laughing. But somehow I couldn't seem to strike no places to harden me against him, but only the other kind . . . and then I happened to look around and see that paper.
>
> It was a close place. I took it up and held it in my hand. I was a-trembling, because I'd got to decide, forever, betwixt two things, and I knowed it. I studied a minute, sort of holding my breath, and then says to myself:
>
> "All right, then, I'll *go* to hell"—and tore it up.

A part of Huck's development came when he apologized to Jim for fooling him about a dream. Jim very properly resented Huck's deceit, and Huck was abashed before Jim's stately indignation. When Huck waked in the night to find Jim mourning for his children—"Po' little 'Lizabeth! po' little Johnny!"—a new realization was borne in upon the boy: "I do believe he cared just as much for his people as white folks does for their'n. It don't seem natural, but I reckon it's so." Although the doctor and others seemed amazed at Jim's risking capture to aid the wounded Tom, Huck felt no surprise at all: "I knowed he was white inside."

The beautiful stretches of the river had power over Huck's spirit, as is shown in his own words: "It was kind of solemn, drifting down the big, still river . . . looking up at the stars, and we didn't ever feel like talking loud, and it warn't often we laughed." He has learned to read early in the story, and he reads at the Grangerford home; of *Pilgrim's Progress*, his verdict is, "The statements was interesting, but tough." He feels that somebody should write a poetical tribute to the dead Emmeline Grangerford, "so I tried to sweat out a verse or two myself, but I couldn't seem to make it go somehow." Such a sentiment would have seemed out of character for Huck in the beginning, but not now. He describes Colonel Grangerford as an aristocrat, and his own sensitive nature responds to the Colonel's fine-wire temperament: "everybody was always good-mannered where he was."

The first thematic unit ends with the smashing of the raft by a steamboat. This incident also ended the writing of *Huckleberry Finn* for an indefinite period. Mark Twain had written thus far in the summer of 1876; he apparently had no further plan, and when the raft was smashed, he stopped working on the book for a time. Two years after he had shelved *Huckleberry Finn,* he wrote the 1878 letter to Howells, explaining that he felt unable to write successful satire because to do so calls for "calm, judicial good humor." His trip down the river in 1882 to get material for *Life on the Mississippi* naturally was related to the other river story in his mind. Somehow, after this trip, he arrived at the design which made the book a masterpiece. All the meannesses of Mark Twain's "damned human race" are seen through the eyes and presented through the lips of Huck Finn. Mark Twain was enabled, at last, to attain the calm detachment with which satire should be presented.

The Art of Restraint

The second thematic unit begins when Huck stops at the Grangerford mansion after the wreck of the raft. The Grangerford-Shepherdson feud is one of the most tragic things in the book, but nothing is told with greater restraint. This restraint is art; but Mark Twain, as John Erskine observed, makes it seem the work of nature. Beginning his account of the climax of the feud, Huck says, "I don't want to talk much about the next day." All that blood and dying was nauseating to the boy, and "it would make him sick again" if he should tell about the killings. He tries not to remember the details, because those memories spoil his sleep at night. To measure Mark Twain's growth in artistry, one has only to compare this restraint with the early sketches in which the reformer purposefully emphasized blood and violence for their shock value in directing attention to situations he deplored. Now, to get back to the raft and to Jim is, for Huck, like going home; and his soul expands in the healing peace of the quiet river "We said there warn't no home like a raft. . . . Other places do seem so cramped up and smothery."

After the episode of the feud, the king and the duke board the raft and begin to dominate the lives of Huck and Jim. The loafers of Bricksville, Arkansas, lean and whittle; around noon, they all laugh and look glad, for old man Boggs comes riding into town drunk and begins to blackguard Colonel Sherburn. Finally Sherburn's outraged honor demands that he stop this blackguarding with a bullet, and Boggs dies in a little drugstore, with a heavy Bible on his chest.

All these wrongs are condemned through the mere fact of their presentation. With the exception of one scene, Mark Twain is invisible, inaudible, lost in the artistry of Huck's particular kind of communication. In that scene Colonel Sherburn appears on his veranda to pour his withering scorn down upon the mob and send them scurrying like whipped curs. "I know you clear through. I was born and raised in the South, and I've lived in the North." It is Mark Twain speaking:

> So I know the average all around. The average man's a coward. . . . Your mistake is that you didn't bring a man with you; that's one mistake, and the other is that you didn't come in the dark and fetch your masks. . . . The pitifulest thing out is a mob. . . . But a mob without any *man* at the head of it is *beneath* pitifulness. Now the thing for *you* to do is to droop your tails and go home and crawl in a hole.

Mark Twain's voice rings out, clear and unmistakable, in the hit at militarism: "an army is—a mob; they don't fight with courage that's born in them, but with courage that's borrowed from their mass." If a "Colonel" had talked like that, would Huck have reported him like that? No matter; the force of the book is so strong at this point that the illusion is not shattered; but the utter objectivity of the scene immediately preceding ranks it far above this one.

There, we see the innate cruelty of the dead-alive loafers. "There couldn't anything wake them up all over, and make them happy all over, like . . . putting turpentine on a stray dog and setting fire to him, or tying a tin pan to his tail and see him run himself to death." Then old Boggs rides in "on the waw-path," a pitiful figure who "throwed his hat down in the mud and rode over it, and . . . went a-raging down the street again, with his gray hair a-flying" while the loafers, at first "listening and laughing and going on," are quickly sobered by the ultimatum of Colonel Sherburn. "Everybody that seen the shooting was telling how it happened," and one "long, lanky man, with long hair and a big white fur stovepipe hat" enacted the scene in its entirety. Huck's comment is, "The people that had seen the thing said he done it perfect." And Mr. [Bernard] DeVoto adds that the long lanky man records this society "with an unemotional certainty beside which either Mr. Lewis's anger or Mr. Anderson's misery" seem merely hysterical. Those who understand Mark Twain can only guess how much of that calm detachment, that "unemotional certainty," was sheer artistry, a triumph of technique.

With each of these scenes, Huck's character develops as his experience is widened. He perceives the manly qualities of Jim and scales correctly the duke and the king; he knows that the duke is not so low as the king, and yet he is tolerant of the "poor old king" when he sees him in "a little low doggery, very tight, and a lot of loafers bullyragging him for sport." When Huck finds himself stranded on the *Walter Scott* with some murderers, his sympathy, broad and beautiful, makes him realize "how dreadful it was, even for murderers, to be in such a fix. I says to myself, there ain't no telling but I might come to be a murderer myself yet, and then how would I like it?" In his last glimpse of the king and the duke, tarred and feathered so that they "just looked like a couple of monstrous big soldier-plumes," he was "sorry for them poor pitiful rascals," and it made him sick to see it: "Human beings *can* be awful cruel to one another."

A Hint of Determinism

There is an occasional hint of determinism in *Huckleberry Finn.* Early in the story Huck backslides under the power of environment while living with Pap: "I was used to being where I was, and liked it." If fear of his drunken father had not driven him forth, Mark Twain seems to say, Huck might have become another Pap. When his conscience troubles him over not giving up the runaway slave, he excuses himself on the ground of early environment and its effects:

> I knowed very well I had done wrong, and I see it warn't no use for me to try to learn to do right; a body that don't get *started* right when he's little ain't got no show—when the pinch comes there ain't nothing to back him up. . . . Then I . . . says to myself, hold on; s'pose you'd a done right and give Jim up, would you felt better than what you do now? No, I says, I'd feel bad—I'd feel just the same way I do now. Well, then, says I, what's the use you learning to do right when it's trouble-

> some to do right and ain't no trouble to do wrong, and the wages is the same?

Huck's questioning of himself recalls Ernest Hemingway's definition of morality, which appears early in *Death in the Afternoon:* "I know only that what is moral is what you feel good after." Unquestionably, Mark Twain and Hemingway are akin in their preoccupation with death and in the care and skill with which they write the idiom of their people; but it seems to me that Hemingway's nearest approach to the earlier writer lies in the moral tests his characters apply inwardly. Having no moral code to go by, they test an action by the way they feel after it.[2]

Huck usually looks into his own heart for guidance. He "goes to studying things out" whenever he feels himself "in a tight place." He learns from experience, but his environment determines him only as his experiences develop what is within. Moral intuition is the basis on which his character rests. But if a man is not responsible to God or to society, and Mark Twain's determinism holds that he is not, why should he be responsible to himself? The inner voice of conscience, the voice of God, always holds him morally responsible. In this way *Huckleberry Finn* is a wise book, as all great books are wise.

In the final thematic unit, the story lags for most readers. Tom re-enters the plot to free Jim according to all the time-worn devices of literature, thus resuming his perpetual game of make-believe. Tom's imagined adventures are merely cheap after the real ones which Huck and Jim have experienced together. Is this anticlimax altogether accidental? Was Mark Twain perhaps comparing the genuine experience of life with the fanciful, secondhand one? If the book is viewed as a satire on institutionalism, Tom's silly insistence on "going by the books" has more point. Or, remembering Jim's use of the "big, clear river" to symbolize freedom, is there an even deeper symbolism here? the fact that, living in a civilization, we can keep our freedom only by conforming to its patterns?

2. Joseph Warren Beach said, "In certain ways, contemporary American fiction opens with Ernest Hemingway." In the first chapter of *Green Hills of Africa,* Hemingway himself said: "All modern American literature comes from one book by Mark Twain called *Huckleberry Finn.* . . . It's the best book we've had. All American writing comes from that. There was nothing before. There has been nothing as good since."

American Civilization Threatens to Destroy Huck

Jay Martin

Huck Finn sacrifices his innocence, writes Jay Martin, when Tom Sawyer, the Widow Douglas, and Miss Watson all impose on him their versions of American civilization. Martin notes that it is only through his relationship with Jim that Huck is able to break free of stereotyped social patterns—patterns that would urge him to betray his friend. In the end, Martin concludes, Huck's only salvation is to escape civilization altogether. Martin has written books on several authors, including Henry Miller, Nathanael West, and Paul Laurence Dunbar.

Toward the end of *Life on the Mississippi* Twain found in Hannibal [Missouri] a striking symbol of the simultaneity of past and present. "I woke up every morning," he writes, "with the impression that I was a boy—for in my dreams the faces were all young again, and looked as they had looked in the old times." Stimulated momentarily into a blissful dream of youth—and so declaring the continued possibility of a free existence—he daily watched his dream dissolve in reality. "But I went to bed," he immediately adds, "a hundred years old, every night—for meantime I had been seeing those faces as they are now." In Hannibal he found realized his own diverse allegiances: to youth and adulthood, to nature and technocracy, to the free creature as well as to the astute businessman, to the loving husband and father and to the professional scribbler of books—to the Huck Finn that he admired and to the Tom Sawyer whom he resembled.

The hero of *The Adventures of Huckleberry Finn* (1885) shares with Twain his richly ambiguous personality, even in name. While Huck's surname was derived, appropriately,

Reprinted by permission of the author from Jay Martin, *Harvests of Change: American Literature, 1865–1914* (Englewood Cliffs, NJ: Prentice-Hall, 1967).

from the actual Hannibal town drunkard, Jimmy Finn, "Huckleberry" is the name of a fruit strictly New England in origin, one Twain had not seen in the West.[1] Like Twain himself, Huck is both the anarchical Westerner and the conservative New Englander. In the fictive time which elapsed between *Tom Sawyer* and this novel, Huck's character has shifted. Under the supervision of the widow Douglas and Miss Watson, he has begun to absorb and assume the conventions of his society. He has become his own Tom Sawyer. No longer "conscience-free," he finds, in the course of the novel, that his conscience follows him like a "yaller dog," as theirs had earlier pursued Tom and Joe. Drawn into acquisitive society by his accidental acquisition of wealth at the end of *Tom Sawyer*, his problem is how to reachieve and retain his earlier Adamic state.

Shaped by the Pressures of Society

In this novel, then, the pressure of society is all the more imperative. Huck learns both Presbyterian and Methodist versions of Heaven and Hell; in a slaveholding house he absorbs the assumptions of slavery. In school he learns to spell, read, and write; he wears new clothes and sleeps in a bed. In short, after three or four months, Huck finds that although

> I liked the old ways best, . . . I was getting so I liked the new ones, too, a little bit. The widow said I was coming along slow but sure, and doing very satisfactory. She said she wasn't ashamed of me.

Tom, too—now even more obsessed than earlier with chivalric fancies—initiates Huck into the rituals of romance. As slavishly as others follow the formal rules of Christian culture, Tom relies upon his "pirate books . . . and robber books" for their unimpeachable (though frequently incomprehensible) codes of behavior. Still being shaped by this environment, Huck begins to be affected by both Christianity and romance: on the one hand he prays; on the other, he attempts to raise a genie by rubbing an old tin lamp. But when, shortly, Pap arrives and forces Huck to live with him, he soon reverts, ostensibly, to his conscience-free existence.

1. Rose Terry Cooke, who was intimate with the Twichell family and whose stories—particularly "Freedom Wheeler's Controversy with Providence"—Twain admired, named her last collection of tales *Huckleberries: Gathered from New England Hills*, explaining: "I have called this latest collection of New England stories by the name of a wild berry that has always seemed to me typical of the New England character."

Nevertheless, the impressions exerted on him by culture, however briefly, have altered the state of his mind. Now that he is no longer the innocent his only alternative to social acquiescence, we are made to realize, is to become bestial and brutal like Pap. Unless he is innocent he cannot escape society without degradation. His father, for instance, although alienated from society, a vagrant and a hopeless drunk, still carries with him a guilt-ridden conscience and a full measure of social prejudices. His delirious hallucination of the Angel of Death and his disquisition on the free Negro able to vote show him to be, in his ignorance, not free from society, but merely the lowest, most vicious form of it. Now tainted with convention like Pap, and invested with a conscience, Huck, the innocent of *Tom Sawyer,* threatens to sink into barbarianism in *Huckleberry Finn.* In *Roughing It* and *Following the Equator* Twain described how, touched by the knowledge of good and evil—the civilizing effect of Christian missionaries—the noble Hawaiian islanders soon disintegrated into a shiftless, diseased, ignoble, rapidly dying race. Huck stands perilously on the edge of a similar transformation.

Saved by a Slave

His salvation comes, of course, through Jim. A slave, and therefore never a part of the dominant conventional society, Jim revives in Huck an immediacy of response to nature—a response outer and inner—undistorted by stereotyped social patterns of belief or action. Terrorized in slavery by the vagaries of the white society over which he has no control—his ultimate terror is of being sold down the river—Jim is, in society, merely the grotesque darky who tells tall tales for psychic self-protection. But when he is free upon the river, Jim becomes, as Daniel G. Hoffman has written, "a magus, . . . a magician in sympathetic converse with the spirits that govern—often by malice or caprice—the world of things and men."[2] Helplessly impotent as magician and prophet in the slave huts, he becomes an infallible guide in the natural world. For the brutal, half-civilized father Huck has lost, he is given a surrogate in Jim. (It is Jim, significantly, who finds and conceals Pap's body.) Continuing the theme of initiation from the first part of *Life on the Mississippi,* in his novel

2. *Form and Fable in American Fiction* (New York, 1961), p. 332

Twain removed all traces of the technology that threatened joyous life in the second part of that book by substituting, in this new fable, a raft for the steamboat, Jim for the riverwise pilot, and Huck for the cub who has run away from home. The child and savage drive through the adult, civilized mask. By the conclusion of the novel Twain has understood society through Huck and Jim in ways that he could not understand it in his own person in *Life on the Mississippi*. And in this respect *Huckleberry Finn* is a more nearly perfect *Life on the Mississippi*.

But their river remains an Eden infested with serpents. Ever touched and invaded by the life of the shore, it provides only moments of true freedom. Tricked by nature, Huck and Jim drift past Cairo, Illinois, in a fog and so lose their opportunity to mount the Ohio to freedom. Once their chance for freedom is lost, they are immediately beset by the serpents of civilization. The troublesome conscience which Huck has acquired now asserts itself. At Jim's joy over the likelihood of literal freedom, Huck meditates:

> He *was* most free—and who was to blame for it? Why, *me*. I couldn't get that out of my conscience, no how nor no way. . . . It hadn't ever come home to me before, what this thing was that I was doing. But now it did; and it staid with me, and scorched me more and more. I tried to make out to myself *I* warn't to blame . . . but it warn't no use.

Driven by conscience, Huck prepares to betray Jim by paddling ashore. He fails because, he says significantly, "I warn't man enough." Rather, he is child enough to follow his natural impulses.

Immediately thereafter civilization reenters upon the river even more ominously: a steamboat runs over their raft and drives Huck to shore. The Shepherdson-Grangerford feud that Huck witnesses there and, later, Colonel Sherburne's murder of Boggs and the deception of the Wilks girls present Huck with testaments concerning the essential brutality of a society that pretends to be chivalric, law-abiding, and Christian. Jim, shaman of nature, is subjugated and replaced by the Duke and Dauphin, who, assuming a sequence of disguises, duping an ignorant and degraded populace, are the magicians of civilization. Pretending to be exiled royalty, repeating the chivalric formulas, playing heroic scenes from Shakespeare, disguising Jim as an Arab, or playing a multiplicity of other fantastic roles, these two are adult versions of Tom Sawyer, refashioning his romantic fantasies as devices in their confidence game.

Isolation Fantasies Protect Against Society

Huck, too, assumes disguises, chiefly of a protective variety, the natural expression of his fear of discovery by society. Nowhere are his psychic fears better demonstrated than in the roles he spontaneously assumes. In all of his deceptions he imagines his isolation. As "Sarah Williams" ("my father and mother was dead, and the law had bound me out to a mean old farmer, . . . so I . . . cleared out"); in his tale of the shipwreck and disaster of the *Walter Scott* to the ferryboat-man; in the account of his family tragedy to the Grangerfords ("my sister Mary Ann run off and got married and never was heard of no more, and Bill went to hunt them and he warn't heard of no more, and Tom and Mort died, and then there warn't nobody but just me and Pap left, and he was just trimmed down to nothing . . . so when he died I took what there was left, . . . started up the river, . . . and fell overboard, and that was how I come to be here"); with the King and the Duke ("my folks was living in Pike County, in Missouri, . . . and they all died off but me and pa and my brother")—in all of these he naturally hints, in the kind of masks he assumes, at his fears about his own alienation and death. Unlike the deceptions of the confidence men, these guises are the spontaneous, unconscious expression of his essential being. Of the tales he tells, he himself says: "I went right along . . . just trusting to Providence [i.e., intuition] to put the right words in my mouth, . . . for I'd noticed that Providence always did put the right words in my mouth, if I let it alone."

Returning—Temporarily—to the Conventions of Society

Thus conceiving of himself as a spy in society, he can pierce the ultimate guise of conventional society itself—the notion of slavery and the mask of color that veneer Jim's essential manhood. Thus he can learn that Jim is "white inside." Surrendering only for a moment to his social conscience in his ultimate moral self-confrontation, Huck finally decides: "All right, then, I'll *go* to hell," and sets out to free Jim. Heroically accepting the alienation from society that he so deeply fears, he resolves to follow the impulses of intuition. W.H. Auden well calls this a pure act of "moral improvisation."[3] But in returning to the shore Huck is once more immersed in social convention. Although he has resolved to be an outlaw in a literal sense, he is mistaken by Aunt Sally, in the book's sternest irony, for Tom Sawyer. True to his final identity, he plays out the mannered "Evasion" of setting Jim free according to the conventional plot of romantic escape. He identifies as wholly with his new role as with his earlier ones, and reassumes the mores of the shore. Explaining to Aunt Sally why he is late, for instance, he says:

> ". . . We blowed out a cylinder-head."
> "Good gracious! Anybody hurt?"
> "No'm. Killed a nigger."
> "Well, it's lucky; because sometimes people do get hurt."

Up to the end of the book he remains Tom Sawyer. Only at the very end, with the Evasion concluded happily within social convention, is he free from this role and able to "light out for the territory ahead of the rest," where he hopes thenceforth to be free from civilization. On the river or in the territory, we know, Huck can never return into the Eden of innocence; even if the Tom Sawyers of the world did not pursue him, he carries his sense of them within him. It is appropriate, then, that the numbers of *The Century* that serialized *Huckleberry Finn* also carried Thomas Nelson Page's idealization of the slaveholding Old Dominion, "Marse Chan."

3. "Huck and Oliver" in *Mark Twain: A Collection of Critical Essays*, ed. Henry Nash Smith (Englewood Cliffs, N.J., 1963), pp. 113–14

CHAPTER 3

Issues of Race in *Huckleberry Finn*

Huckleberry Finn Is Racist Trash

John H. Wallace

John H. Wallace has long fought to keep *Huckleberry Finn* out of schools below the college level on the grounds that the use of the word *nigger* in the book is offensive, racist, and harmful to black students. In this essay Wallace argues that even the best teachers cannot keep the novel from harming students, and requiring or even allowing it to be taught in intermediate or high schools violates black students' constitutional rights. Wallace, a consultant for Chicago public schools, has produced an expurgated version of *Huckleberry Finn* with the words *nigger* and *hell* removed, which he holds is appropriate for school use.

The Adventures of Huckleberry Finn, by Mark Twain, is the most grotesque example of racist trash ever written. During the 1981–82 school year, the media carried reports that it was challenged in Davenport, Iowa; Houston, Texas; Bucks County, Pennsylvania; and, of all places, Mark Twain Intermediate School in Fairfax County, Virginia. Parents in Waukegan, Illinois, in 1983 and in Springfield, Illinois, in 1984 asked that the book be removed from the classroom—and there are many challenges to this book that go unnoticed by the press. All of these are coming from black parents and teachers after complaints from their children or students, and frequently they are supported by white teachers, as in the case of Mark Twain Intermediate School.

For the past forty years, black families have trekked to schools in numerous districts throughout the country to say, "This book is not good for our children," only to be turned away by insensitive and often unwittingly racist teachers and administrators who respond, "This book is a classic."

Reprinted by permission of the publisher from John H. Wallace, "The Case Against *Huck Finn,*" in *Satire or Evasion? Black Perspectives on "Huckleberry Finn,"* edited by James S. Leonard, Thomas A. Tenney, and Thadious M. Davis, pp. 16–24. Copyright 1992, Duke University Press.

Classic or not, it should not be allowed to continue to cause our children embarrassment about their heritage.

Louisa May Alcott, the Concord Public Library, and others condemned the book as trash when it was published in 1885. The NAACP and the National Urban League successfully collaborated to have *Huckleberry Finn* removed from the classrooms of the public schools of New York City in 1957 because it uses the term "nigger." In 1969 Miami-Dade Junior College removed the book from its classrooms because the administration believed that the book creates an emotional block for black students which inhibits learning. It was excluded from the classrooms of the New Trier High School in Winnetka, Illinois, and removed from the required reading list in the state of Illinois in 1976.

My own research indicates that the assignment and reading aloud of *Huckleberry Finn* in our classrooms is humiliating and insulting to black students. It contributes to their feelings of low self-esteem and to the white students' disrespect for black people. It constitutes mental cruelty, harassment, and outright racial intimidation to force black students to sit in the classroom with their white peers and read *Huckleberry Finn.* The attitudes developed by the reading of such literature can lead to tensions, discontent, and even fighting. If this book is removed from the required reading lists of our schools, there should be improved student-to-student, student-to-teacher, and teacher-to-teacher relationships.

"Nigger" Is an Offensive Word

According to *Webster's Dictionary,* the word "nigger" means a Negro or a member of any dark-skinned race of people and is *offensive.* Black people have never accepted "nigger" as a proper term—not in George Washington's time, Mark Twain's time, or William Faulkner's time. A few white authors, thriving on making blacks objects of ridicule and scorn by having blacks use this word as they, the white authors, were writing and speaking for blacks in a dialect they perceived to be peculiar to black people, may have given the impression that blacks accepted the term. Nothing could be further from the truth.

Some black authors have used "nigger," but not in literature to be consumed by children in the classroom. Black authors know as well as whites that there is money to be made selling books that ridicule black people. As a matter of fact, the white child learns early in life that his or her black peer makes a good butt for a joke. Much of what goes on in the classroom reinforces this behavior. Often the last word uttered before a fight is "nigger." Educators must discourage the ridicule of "different" children.

Effects on Children in the Classroom

Russell Baker, of the *New York Times* (14 April 1982), has said (and Jonathan Yardley, of the *Washington Post* [10 May 1982], concurred),

> Kids are often exposed to books long before they are ready for them or exposed to them in a manner that seems almost calculated to evaporate whatever enthusiasm the students may bring to them. . . . Very few youngsters of high school age are ready for *Huckleberry Finn.* Leaving aside its subtle depiction of racial attitudes and its complex view of American society, the book is written in a language that will seem baroque, obscure and antiquated to many young people today. The vastly sunnier *Tom Sawyer* is a book for kids, but *Huckleberry Finn most emphatically is not.*

The milieu of the classroom is highly charged with emotions. There are twenty to thirty unique personalities with hundreds of needs to be met simultaneously. Each student wants to be accepted and to be like the white, middle-class child whom he perceives to be favored by the teacher. Since students do not want their differences highlighted, it is best to accentuate their similarities; but the reading of *Huck Finn* in class accentuates the one difference that is always apparent—color.

My research suggests that the black child is offended by the use of the word "nigger" anywhere, no matter what rationale the teacher may use to justify it. If the teacher permits its use, the black child tends to reject the teacher because the student is confident that the teacher is prejudiced. Communications are effectively severed, thwarting the child's education. Pejorative terms should not be granted any legitimacy by their use in the classroom under the guise of teaching books of great literary merit, nor for any other reason.

To paraphrase Irwin Katz,[1] the use of the word "nigger" by a prestigious adult like a teacher poses a strong *social* threat to the black child. Any expression by a white or black teacher of dislike or devaluation, whether through harsh, indifferent, or patronizing behavior, would tend to have an un-

1. Martin Deutsch, Irwin Katz, and Arthur R. Jensen, *Social Class, Race, and Psychological Development* (New York: Holt, Rinehart, and Winston, 1968): 256–57.

favorable effect on the performance of black children in their school work. This is so because *various psychological theories suggest that the black students' covert reactions to the social threat would constitute an important source of intellectual impairment.*

Dorothy Gilliam, writing in the *Washington Post* of 12 April 1982, said, "First Amendment rights are crucial to a healthy society. No less crucial is the Fourteenth Amendment and its guarantee of equal protection under the law." *The use of the word "nigger" in the classroom does not provide black students with equal protection and is in violation of their constitutional rights. Without equal protection, they have neither equal access nor equal opportunity for an education.*

One group of citizens deeply committed to effecting change and to retaining certain religious beliefs sacred to themselves are members of the Jewish religion. In a publication issued by the Jewish Community Council (November 1981), the following guidelines were enunciated regarding the role of religious practices in public schools: "In no event should any student, teacher, or public school staff member feel that his or her own beliefs or practices are being questioned, infringed upon, or compromised by programs taking place in or sponsored by the public school." Further, "schools should avoid practices which operate to single out and isolate 'different' pupils and thereby [cause] embarrassment."[2]

I endorse these statements without reservation, for I believe the rationale of the Jewish Community Council is consistent with my position. I find it incongruent to contend that it is fitting and proper to shelter children from isolation, embarrassment, and ridicule due to their religious beliefs and then deny the same protection to other children because of the color of their skin. The basic issue is the same. It is our purpose to spare children from scorn, to increase personal pride, and to foster the American belief of acceptance on merit, not color, sex, religion, or origin.

The Teacher's Extraordinary Responsibility

Many "authorities" say *Huckleberry Finn* can be used in our intermediate and high school classrooms. They consistently put stipulations on its use like the following: It must be used with appropriate planning. It is the responsibility of the

2. Jewish Community Council of Greater Washington, *Guidelines on Religion and the Public School* (Washington, D.C., 1981).

Changing Meanings

Mark Twain wrote about reading works that were a century old in the December 1909 issue of Harper's Bazaar.

Naturally, we are apt to clothe a word with its present-day meaning—the meaning we are used to, the meaning we are familiar with; and so—well, you get the idea: some words that are giants today were very small dwarfs a century ago, and if we are not careful to take that vast enlargement into account when we run across them in the literatures of the past, they are apt to convey to us a distinctly wrong impression.

teacher to assist students in the understanding of the historical setting of the novel, the characters being depicted, the social context, including prejudice, which existed at the time depicted in the book. Balanced judgment on the part of the classroom teacher must be used prior to making a decision to utilize this book in an intermediate or high school program. Such judgment would include taking into account the age and maturity of the students, their ability to comprehend abstract concepts, and the methodology of presentation.

Any material that requires such conditions could be dangerous racist propaganda in the hands of even our best teachers. And "some, not all, teachers are hostile, racist, vindictive, inept, or even neurotic," though "many are compassionate and skillful."[3] Teacher attitudes are important to students. Some teachers are marginal at best, yet many school administrators are willing to trust them with a book that maligns blacks. *Huckleberry Finn* would have been out of the classroom ages ago if it used "dago," "wop," or "spic."

When "authorities" mention the "historical setting" of *Huckleberry Finn,* they suggest that it is an accurate, factual portrayal of the way things were in slavery days. In fact, the book is the outgrowth of Mark Twain's memory and imagination, written twenty years after the end of slavery. Of the two main characters depicted, one is a thief, a liar, a sacrilegious corn-cob-pipe-smoking truant; the other is a self-deprecating slave. No one would want his children to emulate this pair. Yet some "authorities" speak of Huck as a boyhood hero. Twain warns us in the beginning of *Huckleberry Finn,* "Persons attempting to find a motive in this narrative will be prosecuted;

3. Robert D. Strom, *The Innercity Classroom* (Columbus, Ohio: Charles E. Merrill, 1966): 104.

persons attempting to find a moral in it will be banished; persons attempting to find a plot in it will be shot." I think we ought to listen to Twain and stop feeding this trash to our children. It does absolutely nothing to enhance racial harmony. The prejudice that existed then is still very much apparent today. Racism against blacks is deeply rooted in the American culture and is continually reinforced by the schools, by concern for socioeconomic gain, and by the vicarious ego enhancement it brings to those who manifest it.

Huckleberry Finn Is a Racist Book

Huckleberry Finn is racist, whether its author intended it to be or not. The book implies that black people are not honest. For example, Huck says about Jim: "It most froze me to hear such talk. He wouldn't ever dared to talk such talk in his life before. Just see what a difference it made in him the minute he judged he was about free. It was according to the old saying, 'give a nigger an inch and he'll take an ell.' Thinks I, this is what comes of my not thinking" (chap. 16). And in another section of the book, the Duke, in reply to a question from the King, says: "Mary Jane'll be in mourning from this out; and the first you know the nigger that does up the rooms will get an order to box these duds up and put 'em away; and do you reckon a nigger can run across money and not borrow some of it?" (chap. 26).

Huckleberry Finn also insinuates that black people are less intelligent than whites. In a passage where Huck and Tom are trying to get the chains off Jim, Tom says: "They couldn't get the chain off; so they just cut their hand off and shoved. And a leg would be better still. But we got to let that go. There ain't necessity enough in this case; and, besides, Jim's a nigger, and wouldn't understand the reason for it" (chap. 35). On another occasion, when Tom and Huck are making plans to get Jim out of the barn where he is held captive, Huck says: "He told him everything. Jim, he couldn't see no sense in most of it, but he allowed we was white folks and knowed better than him; so he was satisfied, and said he would do it all just as Tom said" (chap. 36).

Twain said in *Huckleberry Finn*, more than one hundred years ago, what Dr. W.B. Shockley and A.R. Jensen are trying to prove through empirical study today.[4] This tells us some-

4. [Wallace's reference here is to doctrines of biological determinism, especially to the notion that some racial groups are genetically superior, in certain ways, to other groups—ED. of *Satire or Evasion?*]

thing about the power of the printed word when it is taught to children by a formidable institution such as the school.

Huckleberry Finn even suggests that blacks are not human beings. When Huck arrives at Aunt Sally's house, she asks him why he is late:

> "We blowed a cylinder head."
> "Good gracious! anybody hurt?"
> "No'm. Killed a nigger."
> "Well, it's lucky; because sometimes people do get hurt."
> (chap. 32)

There are indications that the racist views and attitudes implicit in the preceding quotations are as prevalent in America today as they were over one hundred years ago. *Huckleberry Finn* has not been successful in fighting race hate and prejudice, as its proponents maintain, but has helped to retain the status quo.

The Black Student

In 1963 John Fisher, former president of Columbia Teachers College, stated:

> The black American youngster happens to be a member of a large and distinctive group that for a very long time has been the object of special political, legal, and social action. . . . To act as though any child is separable from his history is indefensible. In terms of educational planning, it is *irresponsible.*
>
> Every black child is the victim of the history of his race in this country. On the day he enters kindergarten, he carries a burden *no white child* can ever know, no matter what other handicaps or disabilities he may suffer.[5]

The primary school child learns, almost the minute he enters school, that black is associated with dirtiness, ugliness, and wickedness. Much of what teachers and students think of the black child is color based. As a result, the black pupil knows his pigmentation is an impediment to his progress.

As early as the fifth grade, the black student studies American history and must accept his ancestors in the role of slaves. This frustrating and painful experience leaves scars that very few educators, writers, and especially English teachers can understand. We compound these problems for black children when we force them to read aloud

5. Harry A. Passow, *Education in Depressed Areas* (New York: Teachers College Press [Columbia U], 1963): 265.

the message of *Huckleberry Finn.* It is so devastatingly traumatic that the student may never recover. How much pain must a black child endure to secure an education? No other child is asked to suffer so much embarrassment, humiliation, and racial intimidation at the hands of so powerful an institution as the school. The vast majority of black students have no tolerance for either "ironic" or "satirical" reminders of the insults and degradation heaped upon their ancestors in slavery and postslavery times.

Dorothy Gilliam (*Washington Post,* 12 April 1982) makes a good case for protecting the rights of students when she says, "Where rights conflict, one must sometimes supersede the other. Freedom of speech does not, for example, allow words to be deliberately used in a way that would cause someone to suffer a heart attack. By the same token, the use of words in ways that cause psychological and emotional damage is an unacceptable exercise of free speech."

Huckleberry Finn Is Supported by Racist Groups

If indeed, as *Huckleberry Finn*'s proponents claim, the book gives a positive view of blacks and has an antislavery, antiracist message, then the Nazi party, the Ku Klux Klan, and the White Citizens Council must see something different. Most of the hate mail received when a school in northern Virginia restricted the use of the book was from these groups.

It is difficult to believe that Samuel Clemens would write a book against the institution of slavery; he did, after all, join a Confederate army bent on preserving that peculiar institution. Also, he could not allow Huck to help Jim to his freedom. It seems he was a hodgepodge of contradictions.

Huckleberry Finn is an American classic for no other reason than that it ridicules blacks to a greater extent than any other book given our children to read. The book and racism feed on each other and have withstood the test of time because many Americans insist on preserving our racist heritage.

Marguerite Barnett (1982) points out:

> By ridiculing blacks, exaggerating their facial features, and denying their humanity, the popular art of the Post–Civil-War period represented the political culture's attempt to deny blacks the equal status and rights awarded them in the Emancipation Proclamation. By making blacks inhuman, American whites could destroy their claim to equal treatment. Blacks as slaves posed no problem because they were under complete domination, but blacks as free men created political problems.

> The popular culture of the day supplied the answer by dehumanizing blacks and picturing them as childlike and inferior.[6]

In this day of enlightenment, teachers should not rely on a book that teaches the subtle sickness of racism to our young and causes so much psychological damage to a large segment of our population. We are a multicultural, pluralistic nation. We must teach our young to respect all races, ethnic groups, and religious groups in the most positive terms conceivable.

Recommendations

This book should not be used with children. It is permissible to use the original *Huckleberry Finn* with students in graduate courses of history, English, and social science if one wants to study the perpetration and perpetuation of racism. The caustic, abrasive language is less likely to offend students of that age group because they tend to be mature enough to understand and discuss issues without feeling intimidated by the instructor, fellow students, or racism.

My research relating to *Huckleberry Finn* indicates that black parents and teachers, and their children and students, have complained about books that use the word "nigger" being read aloud in class. Therefore, I recommend that books such as *Huckleberry Finn, The Slave Dancer*, and *To Kill a Mockingbird* be *listed as racist* and excluded from the classroom.

If an educator feels he or she must use *Huckleberry Finn* in the classroom, I would suggest my revised version, *The Adventures of Huckleberry Finn Adapted*, by John H. Wallace. The story is the same, but the words "nigger" and "hell" are eradicated. It no longer depicts blacks as inhuman, dishonest, or unintelligent, and it contains a glossary of Twainisms. Most adolescents will enjoy laughing at Jim and Huck in this adaptation.[7]

6. Documentation on this statement by Marguerite Barnett (possibly from a dissertation) is not currently available. 7. For additional reading on the subject of racial considerations in education, see James A. Banks and Jean D. Grambs, *Black Self-concept: Implications for Education and Social Science* (New York: McGraw-Hill, 1972); Robert F. Biehler, *Psychology Applied to Teaching* (Boston: Houghton Mifflin, 1971); Gary A. Davis and Thomas F. Warren, *Psychology of Education: New Looks* (Lexington, Mass.: Heath, 1974); Marcel L. Goldschmid, *Black Americans and White Racism* (New York: Holt, Rinehart, and Winston, 1970); Donnarae MacCann and Gloria Woodard, *The Black American in Children's Books* (Metuchen, N.J.: Scarecrow, 1972).

The Irony of an "Uncivilized" Friendship

Richard K. Barksdale

Richard K. Barksdale briefly examines the history of the "peculiar institution" of slavery in the United States to help picture the world from which Jim was escaping. He then rejects the argument that *Huck Finn* should be banned as a racist book on the grounds that it ignores Twain's intention in bringing together two outcasts, the young white boy and the older black man. Twain used irony to show the corrupting influence of civilization, Barksdale decides; only when they are beyond its reaches can the two outcasts become friends. Barksdale is the author of *Praisesong of Survival*, a collection of essays on African American authors, and *Langston Hughes*, criticism and interpretation of the poet and his works.

Those who argue that there is a lot of history in fiction have a more plausible argument than those who argue that there is a lot of fiction in history. When Mark Twain wrote his *Adventures of Huckleberry Finn* in the late 1870s and early 1880s describing a series of Mississippi rivertown adventures experienced by a rather ne'er-do-well young man, classified by some as "po' white trash," he set his story in slavery-time Missouri. By virtue of the Missouri Compromise of 1820, that state had joined the Union as a slave state when Maine entered as a free state.

Accordingly, any story having Missouri as its setting prior to 1865 had its setting in a slave state. Thus, whatever history there is in Mark Twain's novel about a rebellious teenager is slave-time history. In fact, the society or "sivilisation" that Huck was attempting to escape was a society or "sivilisation" that had slavery at its core. Especially was this true along the rivers of the South, the channels of trade and

Reprinted from Richard K. Barksdale, "History, Slavery, and Thematic Irony in *Huckleberry Finn*," *Mark Twain Journal*, special issue, vol. 22, no. 2 (Fall 1984), pp. 17–22, by permission of the publisher.

commerce—the Mississippi, the Waccammaw, the Tennessee, the Tombigbee; for as Langston Hughes once wrote, the black man, whether slave or free, had long known rivers and "his soul had grown deep like the rivers."

One gathers a deeper understanding of the meaning of living in a slave society, such as the one Huck and his peers lived in, when one understands that throughout the Americas, from the very beginning, there had always been slavery. This was true of Hispanic America in the sixteenth century, of all of the islands of the Caribbean in the seventeenth century, of the original thirteen British colonies of the North American mainland, and of all the states united into one nation indivisible by the Constitution of 1787. In fact, in 1787 slavery was so pervasive throughout South Carolina and Virginia that whites were in a distinct minority in those two colonies, and this fact gave the founding fathers some cause for concern. Inevitably, as the nation developed, pushing its frontier ever westward, and as slavery in the southern states became an entrenched way of life, the "peculiar institution" began to have a substantive effect on the mores, manners, and values of all of the new nation. Everywhere one looked in the states below the Mason-Dixon line there was a substantial and growing black presence—a huge laboring and servant class—breeding, pulling, hauling, toting, hoeing, threshing, curing, refining, serving and, above all, obeying. By the time of the Huck Finn story, there were over four million, kept in forced bondage by the whip and the immense police power of the plantation owner and his or her overseers and drivers. And, as Justice [Roger] Taney stated in the 1857 *Dred Scott* decision, not one of the four million had any more legal status than an animal, and it was "fixed and universal in the civilized portion of the white race" that there was nothing about a black man ("no rights") that a white man was bound to respect.

The World of the Slave

But there was much more to slavery's story than the impact of the institution on the mores and morals of a fledgling nation. There was the slave himself, herself or itself—the black man, the black woman, and the black child, chained in perpetual ignorance and bound for his or her natural life to a master or to a house or to a plantation field. The world of that slave was restricted to the land or house where he or she worked and to the dismal quarters where he or she lived. Generally, the slave had no choices about anything that affected his or her personal life, and the world beyond his or her master's house and land was a vast *terra incognita* unless the master decreed otherwise. For whatever knowledge came to the slave came only with the express permission and authorization of the master or mistress. Such a system was bound and designed to generate pain, anguish, frustration, and misery for the slave.

From such a background came Mark Twain's Jim. It is true that apologists for the southern way of life did present, for propaganda purposes, a wildly erroneous view that completely distorted slavery—a view that depicted a happy and contented slave living in happy innocence and mutual devotion and affection with a wise and tolerant master or mistress. Such pictures of the bucolic bliss of chattel slavery were products of the romantic imagination, however, and were not in evidence in Twain's Missouri nor in any of the towns, cities, or plantations that bordered the Mississippi in Huck's day. All were, like Jim, slaves in such a grievous state of distress that they became runaways whenever opportunity for successful flight presented itself.

So Jim, nurtured by a callous and cruel system, was naively ignorant of a larger world and, as a runaway, moved about fearfully and without direction or plan. That he survived in his confused freedom long enough to meet Huck was more than a minor miracle. In fact, because of the Fugitive Slave Act of 1850, all the powers of government—local, state, and federal—were ranged against Jim's survival, even in a "free" state. As a runaway slave, he was the preeminent outsider, the existential rebel—the man to be hunted down and punished by all the forces of law and order. Of course, when the hunted black fugitive and outsider meets the disaffected and poor white outsider—one long kept in childlike ignorance of a larger world by slavery's dictum and the other long victimized by his po' white trash status in a capitalist society—Twain, the story-teller, takes over and begins to weave incidents and events into a suspenseful narrative.

Trying to Forget Slavery

It is obvious that Twain's novel about the chance meeting of two runaways, one black and one white, is under attack today because many Americans, guilt-ridden over the racial divisions that continue to plague our society, have difficulty coping with the historical fact of slavery. Blacks, as part of their long and tortuous fight for social and legal justice, would like to blot the memory of centuries of enforced servitude off the record of history. And whites, in large measure, take no joy in remembering slave times; they would rather take patriotic pride in America's written promises of justice and equality for all, regardless of creed, race, or previous condition of servitude. Indeed, slavery times provoke bad memories for both racial groups—memories of the chaos wrought by incestuous concubinage and the birth of half-white half-brothers and half-black white half-sisters, memories of a dehumanising system that reduced grown black men and women to "boys" and "gals" and grown white men and women to groveling hypocrites. Blacks, in particular, would have their children shielded from the ignominious shame of slavery, not only because the memory of slavery exacerbates today's racial problems, but also because their children are racially traumatized by any references to their former inferior status. Thus, they ask that anything that might prove to be racially divisive be banned from all educational programs. Such a ban would include Twain's *Adventures of Huckleberry Finn*, a novel in which the word "nigger," the appellation commonly used for slaves in slavery time, is used 160 times.

ARGUMENTS ABOUT *HUCKLEBERRY FINN*

There are many arguments which can and have been employed to counter those posed by the anti–*Huckleberry Finn* forces. One, of course, is the oft-repeated observation that any race that would ignore its history will be condemned to repeat it. This admonition, if heeded, would prod black Americans to remember slavery, however painful the memory, and urge Jews to recall the Holocaust, however painful the memory. Another countering argument is that patterns of racial discrimination are so deeply interwoven in the fabric of American society that not reading about Huck and Jim would have no effect on lowering racial tensions or removing the sharp racial polarities that exist and will continue to exist in America. The proponents of this position argue that a novel like *Huckleberry Finn* is irrelevant. Whether the book is required reading or not, racial segregation in housing will continue to exist in all of the nation's major cities and throughout suburbia. Racial discrimination will still haunt the market place and employment rosters. Demoralizing statistics about the black family will continue to exist—statistics about the large number of female, single-parent families living below the poverty line, statistics about the large number of young black men in the nation's prisons, and statistics about the large number of teen-age pregnancies. The proponents of this position argue that black America's continuing depressed status is the result of a pattern of discrimination against America's most visible minority that began with the nation's founding. In their view slavery was thus more of a symptom than a root cause of racial prejudice in America.

Some of the more radical supporters of this position even argue that, not only is the reading or non-reading Twain's novel irrelevant, but that a nation that has an achieving majority and a non-achieving but visible minority to victimize and exploit can thereby enjoy national prosperity and good health. The argument advanced in this context is that having such a minority to victimize inflates the psychological self-esteem of the majority and that this self-esteem is essential for the growth and development of a nation. Supporters of this point of view cite the immense success of both republican and imperial Rome in which there was always a large lower class of plebeians, slaves, and conquered colonial subjects to be victimized and thus bolster the self-esteem of an achieving upper class. And, in democratic America, the argument continues, a powerful white majority, its motives shielded by carefully articulated verbal guarantees of democracy and freedom and justice, proceeds to exploit, deny, and exclude America's most visible minority. In other words, the argument suggests, if there were no black minority to be victimized and exploited, white America would zealously strive to find a fit substitute in order to keep the nation on the cutting edge of national progress and achievement. Obviously, in an ethical and social scenario of this kind, slavery and Twain's Jim become not root causes of current racial attitudes but providential symbols of what ought to be.

None of this supersubtle sociological and psychological theorizing, however, can fully alleviate the trauma experienced by a young black teenager when he or she encounters racial discrimination or racial slurs or racial epithets in a racially integrated classroom. Nor can it be expected that the average junior or senior high school English teacher would prepare the black teenager and his or her peers to read a novel like Twain's *Huckleberry Finn* with a full awareness of the far-flung historical and psychological causes and consequences. If a work of fiction demands this much preparation and student-teacher orientation, one may be fully justified in advocating that the work be removed from required reading lists and made an optional reading selection.

Twain's Literary Intention

Unfortunately, the reasoning behind such a recommendation completely ignores, by implication at least, Twain's literary intention when he undertook to tell Huck's story. As has been suggested above, Jim's source, lineage, and status are quite clear; he was a slave who had, in protest over his condition, run away from his mistress. Similarly, Huck, saddled with an improvident, alcoholic father, was a lad without means and a self-proclaimed outcast who, because of his condition, wished to escape "sivilisation." By bringing black runaway Jim into close association with white runaway Huck, Twain obviously desired to explore the ironic implications of such an association in a "sivilisation" riddled by racial division and prejudice. The irony employed here is similar to that used in Pudd'nhead Wilson's story in which Twain recounts the comi-tragic consequences of a situation in which a light-skinned "colored" baby is substituted for a white baby. In the Huck story, however, Twain's ironic conclusion is that two human beings, however different in their backgrounds and "previous condition of servitude," will, if far enough removed from the corrupting influences of "sivilisation," become friends. For Twain, like England's Swift or Rome's Juvenal, believed that the social civilization that man labored so hard to cultivate was itself the great corrupter of man. He believed that from civilization came not only values to preserve and protect but the incentives to divide, control, and inhibit. Twain appears to be asking in his story of Huck and Jim how truly "civilized" is an America which since its beginning has cultivated and nurtured slavery. And he knew, as he observed events in the 1880s, that, although slavery no longer officially existed, blacks were still a large servant and laboring class to be exploited, but kept illiterate, disenfranchised, and socially and culturally oppressed.

So, given the social and cultural conditions that existed in pre–Civil War America, Twain sought to explore the ironic possibilities of the development of an authentic black-white friendship. Under what circumstances could a slave and a white man develop a friendship in slave-time America? Could it occur within the system or would it have to be a clandestine matter hidden from society at large? Twain, the ironist who doubted that social and/or moral benefits would accrue from a civilization beleaguered by greed and prejudice, concluded that, given the nature of slave-time America, a friendship of that kind could develop only outside the normal areas of civil and social discourse. In fact, Twain appears to suggest, with more than an ironic gleam in his eye, that such a friendship could develop only on a socially isolated raft in the middle of the nation's biggest and longest river and thus as far from the shores ruled by law and order as a man could get in middle America. But Twain the ironist did not stop here. He developed, with careful ironic forethought, an interracial friendship between two outcasts who, under civilization's auspices, were normally inveterate enemies. For, during Twain's lifetime and later, it was an observable fact that poor white trash like the Finns had nothing but hatred and disrespect for blacks. Condemned and reviled as economic and social outcasts by "respectable" society, people like the Finns looked for some inferior group on which to vent their social spleen; and in America's social hierarchy, the only class or group considered to be lower than the Finns and their kin were black slaves who, after 1865, became the openly reviled black freedmen.

Thus, Twain's novel, by motive and intention, is really an ironic appraisal of the American racial scene circa 1884. Herein possibly lies the difficulty encountered in trying to teach the novel. Irony, as all students of literature know, involves a deliberate misstatement–a misstatement designed to highlight the longtime adverse effects of a grossly immoral act or a blatantly dishonest deed or an inhumane and unChristian practice. If the ironic statement made by an author in a work of fiction is too subtly wrought, it will not be effectively communicated to the average reader. The continuing controversy about *Adventures of Huckleberry Finn* suggests that the American reading public, in the main, has never fully understood the author's ironic message.

American Society Cannot Fully Comprehend Twain's Irony

It is also probably true that American society—actually the same "sivilisation" castigated by Huck—will never fully comprehend Mark Twain's irony, because one needs to have considerable ethical distance from the object under ironic analysis to appreciate and understand the irony. In other words, students and teachers who are immersed and involved in America's racial problems will never understand the need to develop a disciplined objectivity about those problems before they can appreciate an ironic solution to these problems. Indeed, ironic fiction, whether from the past or present, *is difficult* to teach, especially to young teenagers who usually founder on deliberately over-subtle misstatements.

So, although Jim's roots lie deep in the soil of slavery and American racism and although his is an honest and forthright portrayal of a slave runaway and although young black teenagers are traumatized by reading about the Jims of slavery-time, the great difficulty with *Adventures of Huckleberry Finn* is that it is one of America's best pieces of ironic fiction. To a nation that was and is sharply divided on matters of race, Twain's novel suggests that friendships between black and white can best be forged by the least of us and then only under the worst of circumstances. Undoubtedly, only a reading audience of some maturity and perceptive insight—an audience that can probe for lurking truths under surface facts and figures and events—can grasp the far-reaching implications of the adventures of a white Huck and a black Jim floating down the river of American life. As Francis Bacon once wrote, "Reading maketh the full man"; but not all and sundry in our error-ridden society can sit and sup at fiction's table without occasionally feeling the pain and anguish generated by that error-ridden society.

Mark Twain and African American Voices

Shelley Fisher Fishkin

Commentators generally agree that having the child protagonist Huck speak in his own vernacular was a spectacular innovation, but according to Shelley Fisher Fishkin they have missed a crucial point. Twain expert Fishkin, who is editor of the twenty-nine-volume Oxford edition of Twain's works and president of the Mark Twain Circle of America, asserts that the model for Huck's voice was a black child. She offers evidence of Twain's appreciation of the language of Frederick Douglass and other black speakers, and concludes that giving African American voices a major role helped make the novel both fresh and distinctive.

> The Negro looks at the white man and finds it difficult to believe that the "grays"—a Negro term for white people—can be so absurdly self-deluded over the true interrelatedness of blackness and whiteness.
>
> —Ralph Ellison[1]

The range of models critics cite when they probe the sources of Mark Twain's *Adventures of Huckleberry Finn* is wide. It includes the picaresque novel, the Southwestern humorists, the Northeastern literary comedians, the newspapers Twain contributed to and read, and the tradition of the "boy book" in American popular culture. Twain himself weighed in with a clear statement about the roots of his main character, claiming that Huck Finn was based on Tom Blankenship, a poor-white outcast child Twain remembered from Hannibal, and on Tom's older brother Bence, who once helped a runaway slave.[2] These

1. Ralph Ellison, "Change the Joke and Slip the Yoke," *Partisan Review*, Spring 1958.
2. Twain said, "'Huckleberry Finn' was Tom Blankenship" (*Autobiography*). See also notes on Tom and Bence Blankenship in Dahlia Armon and Walter Blair, "Biographical Directory," in *Huck Finn and Tom Sawyer Among the Indians and other Unfinished Stories*, by Mark Twain.

sources may seem quite different. On one level, however, they are the same: they all give Twain's book a genealogy that is unequivocally white.

Although commentators differ on the question of which models and sources proved most significant, they tend to concur on the question of how *Huckleberry Finn* transformed American literature. Twain's innovation of having a vernacular-speaking child tell his own story *in his own words* was the first stroke of brilliance; Twain's awareness of the power of satire in the service of social criticism was the second. Huck's voice combined with Twain's satiric genius changed the shape of fiction in America.

[I] suggest that Twain himself and the critics have ignored or obscured the African-American roots of his art. Critics, for the most part, have confined their studies of the relationship between Twain's work and African-American traditions to examinations of his depiction of African-American folk beliefs or to analyses of the dialects spoken by his black characters. But by limiting their field of inquiry to the periphery, they have missed the ways in which African-American voices shaped Twain's creative imagination at its core.

A Black Child Helped Inspire Huck Finn's Voice

Compelling evidence indicates that a model for Huck Finn's voice was a black child instead of a white one and that this child's speech sparked in Twain a sense of the possibilities of a vernacular narrator. The record suggests that it may have been yet another black speaker who awakened Twain to the power of satire as a tool of social criticism. This may help us understand why Richard Wright found Twain's work "strangely familiar," and why Langston Hughes, Ralph Ellison, and David Bradley all found Twain so empowering in their own efforts to convert African-American experience into art.[3]

As Ralph Ellison put it in 1970, *"the black man [was] a co-creator of the language that Mark Twain raised to the level of literary eloquence."*[4] But his comment sank like a stone, leaving barely a ripple on the placid surface of American

3. Richard Wright, "Memories of My Grandmother," quoted in Michel Fabre, *Richard Wright: Books & Writers;* Langston Hughes, "Introduction" to Mark Twain, *Pudd'nhead Wilson;* Ralph Ellison, interview with the author, 16 July 1991; David Bradley, "The First 'Nigger' Novel," speech to Annual Meeting of the Mark Twain Memorial and the New England American Studies Association, Hartford, Connecticut, May 1985. 4. Ralph Ellison, "What America Would Be Like Without Blacks," *Time,* 6 April 1970. Italics added.

literary criticism. Neither critics from the center nor critics from the margins challenged the reigning assumption that mainstream literary culture in America is certifiably "white."

[I suggest] that we need to revise our understanding of the nature of the mainstream American literary tradition. The voice we have come to accept as the vernacular voice in American literature—the voice with which Twain captured our national imagination in *Huckleberry Finn,* and that empowered Hemingway, Faulkner, and countless other writers in the twentieth century—is in large measure a voice that is "black."

Mark Twain was unusually attuned to the nuances of cadence, rhythm, syntax, and diction that distinguish one language or dialect from another, and he had a genius for transferring the oral into print. Twain, whose preferred playmates had been black, was what J.L. Dillard might have called "bidialectal"; as an engaging black child he encountered in the early 1870s helped reconnect Twain to the cadences and rhythms of black speakers from Twain's own childhood, he inspired him to liberate a language that lay buried within Twain's own linguistic repertoire and to apprehend its stunning creative potential. Twain, in turn, would help make that language available as a literary option to both white and black writers who came after him. As Ellison put it in 1991, "he made it possible for many of us to find our own voices."[5]

An Enormous Impact on American Literature

Mark Twain helped open American literature to the multicultural polyphony that is its birthright and special strength. He appreciated the creative vitality of African-American voices and exploited their potential in his art. In the process, he helped teach his countrymen new lessons about the lyrical and exuberant energy of vernacular speech, as well as about the potential of satire and irony in the service of truth. Both of these lessons would ultimately make the culture more responsive to the voices of African-American writers in the twentieth century. They would also change its definitions of what "art" ought to look and sound like to be freshly, wholly "American."

5. Ralph Ellison in Fishkin interview, 16 July 1991.

Am I suggesting that the sources and influences that scholars have documented over the last hundred years are not important to our understanding of Twain's career as a whole? No. Southwestern humor, for example, clearly played a key role in shaping Twain's art, particularly in such early works as *Innocents Abroad* and *Roughing It.* But there is something about *Huckleberry Finn* that sets it off from Twain's earlier work and makes it seem less a continuation of the art he had been developing and more of a quantum leap forward; its unrivalled place in both the Twain canon and in the American literary canon reflects this special status.[6] In *Huckleberry Finn* something new happened that would have an enormous impact on the future of American literature. That "something new" has never been adequately accounted for. My suggestion is this: here, more than in any other work, Twain allowed African-American voices to play a major role in the creation of his art. This fact may go a long way toward clarifying what makes this novel so fresh and so distinctive.

Twain's Response to African-American Singing

Twain's responsiveness to African-American speaking voices should come as no surprise to us, for the intense and visceral nature of his response to African-American *singing* voices has been widely documented. After entertaining the Fisk Jubilee Singers in his home in Lucerne, Switzerland, in 1897, Twain wrote,

> Away back in the beginning—to my mind—their music made all other vocal music cheap; and that early notion is emphasized now. It is utterly beautiful, to me; and it moves me infinitely more than any other music can. I think that in the Jubilees and their songs America has produced the perfectest flower of the ages; and I wish it were a foreign product so that

6. Richard Bridgman describes the phenomenon in this way:

> If one accepts provisionally the existence of a change in American prose style, then the next pertinent question is, when did it begin? Recently the date 1884 has been advanced from several quarters, most succinctly by Ernest Hemingway: "All modern American literature comes from one book by Mark Twain called *Huckleberry Finn*. . . ." As early as 1913 H.L. Mencken was championing Mark Twain: "I believe that he was the true father of our national literature, the first genuinely American artist of the blood royal." Later William Faulkner agreed, saying: "In my opinion, Mark Twain was the first truly American writer, and all of us since are his heirs, we are descended from him."
>
> This critical admiration has not extended to Mark Twain's work as a whole nor to his literary theories (such as they were), nor to his practical criticisms. One book alone has drawn the praise. Whatever the merits of Mark Twain's other writing, and whatever the weaknesses of *Huckleberry Finn*, everyone—literary hacks, artists, and critics—agrees that the style of this book has had a major effect on the development of American prose. (Bridgman, *Colloquial Style in America*.)

she would worship it and lavish money on it and go properly crazy over it."[7]

Twain acknowledged his admiration for the beauty and power of these songs and their singers in the publicity blurb he wrote for the Fisk Jubilee Singers on their European tour: "I do not know when anything has so moved me as did the plaintive melodies of the Jubilee Singers." Calling their music "eloquent" (underlining the close connection in his mind between speech and song), Twain wrote, "I heard them sing once, and I would walk seven miles to hear them sing again. You will recognize that this is strong language for me to use, when you remember that I never was fond of pedestrianism."[8]

Katy Leary, a servant of the Clemens family, reports that one evening as a group of guests were sitting in the music room looking out at the moonlight at the home of Charles Dudley Warner, a neighbor in Hartford, Twain "suddenly got

7. Twain preceded this comment with the following description of the Jubilee Singers' visit:

> The other night we had a detachment of the Jubilee Singers—6 I had known in London 24 years ago. Three of the 6 were born in slavery, the others were children of slaves. How charming they were—in spirit, manner, language, pronunciation, enunciation, grammar, phrasing, matter, carriage, clothes—in every detail that goes to make the real lady and gentleman, and welcome guest. We went down to the village hotel and bought our tickets and entered the beer-hall, where a crowd of German and Swiss men and women sat grouped at round tables with their beer mugs in front of them—self-contained and unimpressionable looking people, an indifferent and unposted and disheartened audience—and up at the far end of the room sat the Jubilees in a row. The Singers got up and stood—the talking and glass jingling went on. Then rose and swelled out above those common earthly sounds one of those rich chords the secret of whose making only the Jubilees possess, and a spell fell upon that house. It was fine to see the faces light up with the pleased wonder and surprise of it. No one was indifferent any more; and when the singers finished, the camp was theirs. It was a triumph. It reminded me of Launcelot riding in Sir Kay's armor and astonishing complacent Knights who thought they had struck a soft thing. The Jubilees sang a lot of pieces. Arduous and painstaking cultivation has not diminished or artificialized their music, but on the contrary—to my surprise—has mightily reinforced its eloquence and beauty. (SLC to Joe Twitchell, 22 August 1897, in *Mark Twain's Letters*, ed. Albert Bigelow Paine, vol. 2)

8. The text of Twain's publicity letter for the Jubilee Singers reads as follows:

> Gentlemen: The Jubilee Singers are to appear in London, and I am requested to say in their behalf what I know of them—and I most cheerfully do it. I heard them sing once, and I would walk seven miles to hear them sing again. You will recognize that this is strong language for me to use, when you remember that I never was fond of pedestrianism, and got tired of walking that Sunday afternoon, in twenty minutes, after making up my mind to see for myself and at my own leisure how much ground his grace the Duke of Bedford's property covered.
>
> I think these gentlemen and ladies make eloquent music—and what is as much to the point, they reproduce the true melody of the plantations, and are the only persons I ever heard accomplish this on the public platform. The so-called "negro minstrels" simply mis-represent the thing; I do not think they ever saw a plantation or heard a slave sing.
>
> I was reared in the South, and my father owned slaves, and I do not know when anything has so moved me as did the plaintive melodies of the Jubilee Singers. It was the first time for twenty-five or thirty years that I had heard such songs, or heard them sung in the genuine old way—and it is a way, I think, that white people cannot imitate—and never can, for that matter, for one must have been a slave himself in order to feel what that life was and so convey the pathos of it in the music. Do not fail to hear the Jubilee Singers. I am very well satisfied that you will not regret it. Yours faithfully, Saml. L. Clemens. Mark Twain. (SLC to Tom Hood and George Routledge and Sons, 10 March 1873, Hartford, reprinted in Gustavus D. Pike, *The Singing Campaign for Ten Thousand Pounds; or, The Jubilee Singers in Great Britain.*)

right up without any warning" and began to sing "negro Spirituals." He sang "low and sweet," Leary recalled, and "became kind of lost in it." When he came to the end of the song, "to the Glory Halleluiah, he gave a great shout—just like the negroes do—he shouted out the Glory, Glory, Halleluiah!" Those who were there said that "none of them would forget it as long as they lived."[9]

As his voice projected in song black voices from his childhood, Twain's bearing would become strangely transformed. Drawing on accounts by guests who were present, Justin Kaplan describes an evening at Twain's Hartford home in 1874:

> After dinner, with a log fire blazing in the red-curtained drawing room, he sang "Swing Low, Sweet Chariot," "Golden Slippers," "Go Down, Moses". . . . He swayed gently as he stood; his voice was low and soft, a whisper of wind in the trees; his eyes were closed, and he smiled strangely. Through the sadness and exultation of these songs which he had known through boyhood, he transported himself far from the circle of polite letters and from the New England snowscape, and he found it difficult to go back.[10]

Twain could often be found singing his favorite African-American spirituals when he was farthest from home—in Liverpool in 1873, as well as in Florence in 1904, the night his wife, Livy, died.[11] William Dean Howells recalled the "fervor" and "passion" with which Twain's "quavering tenor" sang these songs during his last visit to Twain's home in Redding, Connecticut, shortly before Twain's death.[12] Twain identified with these songs in ways that went to the core of his being; they spoke uniquely to a part of himself that no other art could touch.

Impressed by Black Speakers

African-American speaking voices played much the same role, on a subliminal level, in Twain's consciousness.[13] Twain never expressed his admiration for the power of

9. Katy Leary, quoted in Mary Lawton, *A Lifetime with Mark Twain: The Memories of Kate Leary, for Thirty Years His Faithful and Devoted Servant.* 10. Justin Kaplan, *Mr. Clemens and Mark Twain.* 11. Kaplan, *Mr. Clemens and Mark Twain.* 12. William Dean Howells, *My Mark Twain,* 99. 13. As a number of critics have noted, there are important links between speaking and singing voices in African-American culture. Henry Louis Gates, Jr., for example, explains the decision to include a cassette tape with the *Norton Anthology of Afro-American Literature* as follows:

> Because of the strong oral and vernacular base of so very much of our literature, we included a cassette tape along with our anthology. . . . . This means that each period section includes both the printed and spoken text of oral and musical selections of black vernacular culture: sermons, blues, spirituals, rhythm and blues, poets reading their own "dialect" poems, speeches–whatever! Imagine an anthology that includes Bessie Smith and Billie Holiday singing the blues, Langston Hughes reading "[I've] Known Rivers," Sterling Brown

African-American speaking voices as publicly as he expressed his admiration for the Fisk Jubilee Singers, but many such voices . . . made deep impressions on him during the years preceding *Huckleberry Finn.* During his childhood, Twain had stood in awe of the storytelling powers of a slave named Uncle Dan'l, whom he remembered from summers spent on his uncle's farm in Florida, Missouri. In his autobiography, when Twain described "the white and black children grouped on the hearth" listening to Uncle Dan'l's folk tales, he recalled "the creepy joy which quivered through me when the time for the ghost story of the 'Golden Arm' was reached—and the sense of regret, too, which came over me for it was always the last story of the evening."[14]

In the late 1860s and 1870s, Twain was impressed by the narrative skills of black speakers like Frederick Douglass and Mary Ann Cord (a servant at the Clemenses' summer home in Elmira, New York). In 1869, the "simple language" in which Douglass told a story in the course of social conversation struck Twain as so remarkably "effective" that he described it in detail in a letter to his future wife:

> Had a talk with Fred Douglas [sic], to-day, who seemed exceedingly glad to see me—& I certainly was glad to see *him*, for I do so admire his "spunk." He told the history of his child's expulsion from Miss Tracy's school, & his simple language was very effective. Miss Tracy said the pupils did not want a colored child among them—which he did not believe, & challenged the proof. She put it at once to a vote of the school, and asked "How many of you are willing to have this colored child be with you?" And they *all* held up their hands! Douglas added: "The children's hearts were right." There was pathos in the way he said it. I would like to hear him make a speech.[15]

> reading "Ma Rainey," James Weldon Johnson, "The Creation". . . . We will change fundamentally not only the way our literature is taught, but the way in which any literary tradition is even conceived. . . . In our anthology we wanted to incorporate performance and the black and human voice. (Gates, Jr., "The Master's Pieces: On Canon Formation and Afro-American Tradition," in Dominick LaCapra, ed., *The Bounds of Race: Perspectives on Hegemony and Resistance.*)

As Gates notes elsewhere, "the nature of black music is the nature of black speech and vice versa" (Gates, Jr., "Dis and Dat: Dialect and the Descent," in his *Figures in Black: Words, Signs, and the "Racial" Self*). 14. *Mark Twain's Autobiography*, ed. Albert Bigelow Paine, vol. 1. Twain often told a story he had heard at the hearth, "The Golden Arm," when he gave lectures and readings. As his cousin Tabitha Quarles recalled, every night at the Quarles farm, where Twain spent his summer, the children would gather "around the fire place and [hear] the darkies tell their ghost stories. Sam just repeated those tales Uncle Dan'l and Uncle Ned told and folks said he was smart" (Anon., "Mark Twain's Cousin, His Favorite, Tabitha Quarles," in *The Twainian*, July/August 1952). Twain's older brother Orion thought Twain may have confused Uncle Dan'l with Ned, one of the Clemenses' own slaves from Hannibal (*Mark Twain's Letters*, ed. Paine, vol. 2) Tabitha Quarles's comments suggest that both men were important storytellers in Twain's youth. 15. SLC to Olivia L. Langdon, 15 and 16 December 1869, *Letters, vol. 3: 1869*, ed. Victor Fischer and Michael B. Frank.

And in 1874, the "vigorous eloquence" with which former slave Mary Ann Cord told the story of her reunion with her son after the Civil War inspired Twain's first contribution to the esteemed *Atlantic Monthly;* a quarter-century later, Twain would still recall her stunning "gift of strong & simple speech."[16*] Twain wrote that he found the story she told a "curiously strong piece of *literary work* to come unpremeditated from lips untrained in the literary art," showing his awareness of the close relationship between speaking voices and "literature." "The untrained tongue is usually wandering, wordy & vague," Twain wrote; "but this is clear, compact & coherent—yes, & vivid also, & perfectly simple & unconscious."[17*] Throughout his career as a lecturer and as a writer, Twain aspired to have the effect upon his listeners and readers that speakers like Frederick Douglass and Mary Ann Cord had upon *him.*

Ernest Hemingway declared, "All modern American literature comes from one book by Mark Twain called *Huckleberry Finn.*"[18] William Faulkner called Twain "the father of American literature."[19] The African-American roots of Twain's art, however, have never been fully recognized or explored. In 1987 Toni Morrison issued a call for critics to examine "literature for the impact Afro-American presence has had on the structure of the work, the linguistic practice, and fictional enterprise in which it is engaged."[20] *Was Huck Black? Mark Twain and African-American Voices* is a response. My goal is to foreground the role previously neglected African-American voices played in shaping Mark Twain's art in *Huckleberry Finn.* Given that book's centrality in our culture, the points I make implicitly illuminate, as well, how African-American voices have shaped our sense of what is distinctively "American" about American literature.

16. Photocopy of manuscript of Mark Twain, "A Family Sketch," Mark Twain Papers. Original in Mark Twain Collection, James S. Copley Library, La Jolla, Ca. Quoted with permission. *Mark Twain's previously unpublished words quoted here and throughout are copyright © 1993 by Edward J. Willi and Manufacturers Hanover Trust Company as Trustees of the Mark Twain Foundation, which reserves all reproduction or dramatization rights in every medium. Quotation is made with the permission of the University of California Press and Robert H. Hirst, General Editor of the Mark Twain Papers. Each quotation is identified by an asterisk (*). 17. Typescript of Mark Twain's notebook 35, May–Oct. 1895, Mark Twain Papers. Quoted with permission. Emphasis added. 18. Ernest Hemingway, *Green Hills of Africa.* 19. William Faulkner, quoted in Robert A. Jelliffe, ed., *Faulkner at Nagano.* 20. Toni Morrison, "Unspeakable Things Unspoken: The Afro-American Presence in American Literature," *Michigan Quarterly Review,* Winter 1989.

Blackface Minstrels Influenced Many Aspects of *Huck Finn*

Eric Lott

Mark Twain loved blackface minstrel shows, reports Eric Lott, author of *Love and Theft: Blackface Minstrelsy and the American Working Class.* Minstrelsy provided *Huck Finn* with both strengths and weaknesses, he asserts, reflecting the insecurity of whites during the industrial revolution, when they both identified with and violently rejected blacks. The most emotional moments of the novel recall the sentimental racialism of blackface shows, Lott notes, especially as expressed in songs such as those by Stephen Foster.

Soon after leaving Hannibal for New York in 1853, Sam Clemens wrote home to his mother: "I reckon I had better black my face, for in these Eastern States niggers are considerably better than white people."[1] As the youth who would be Mark Twain wrote these words, Christy's Minstrels were at the peak of their extraordinary eight-year run (1846–1854) at New York City's Mechanics' Hall, and many other blackface troupes battled them for public attention. Meanwhile, the whole new phenomenon of the "Tom show"—dramatic blackface productions of Harriet Beecher Stowe's *Uncle Tom's Cabin*, published the year before—was emerging to (briefly) displace and reorient the minstrel tradition; by 1854 there were several such shows running in New York alone. Probably the prominence of blackface in New York only clinched Clemens's love of minstrelsy, which extended back to his Hannibal childhood.

Blackface minstrelsy—"the genuine nigger show, the extravagant nigger show," Twain calls it in the autobiography

1. Mark Twain, *Mark Twain's Letters*, ed. Edgar Marquess Branch et al. (Berkeley: University of California Press, 1988), 4.

he dictated in his last years—had burst upon the unwitting town in the early 1840s as a "glad and stunning surprise."[2] Usually involving a small band of white men armed with banjo, fiddle, tambourine, and bone castanets and arrayed in blackface makeup and ludicrous dress, the minstrel show, from the 1830s to the early years of the twentieth century, offered white travesties and imitations of black humor, dance, speech, and music. It most often opened with assorted songs, breakdowns, and gags, followed by an "olio" portion of novelty acts such as malapropistic "stump speeches" or parodic "lectures," and concluded with a burlesque skit set in the South. In his *Autobiography* Twain averred: "If I could have the nigger show back again in its pristine purity and perfection I should have but little further use for opera." This quite unguarded attraction to "blacking up" perhaps made it inevitable that in a letter to his mother Twain would reach for the blackface mask to finesse his response to racial difference in the northern city. For the rest of his life, Twain's imaginative encounters with race would be unavoidably bound up with blackface minstrelsy.

If Sam Clemens's class- and race-conscious recoil from free blacks sounds a lot like Huck Finn's Pap—"And to see the cool way of that nigger—why, he wouldn't a give me the road if I hadn't shoved him out o' the way"—it also reminds us that such consciousness, as in minstrelsy, often acknowledged the lure to *be* black ("I reckon I had better black my face"), to inhabit the cool, virility, humility, abandon, degradation, or *gaite de coeur* that were the prime components of white fantasies of black manhood. Pap himself, in Twain's sly depiction of his rage against the black professor, is actually as black as the hated "mulatter," since he is, as Huck says, "just all mud" after a drunken night lying in the gutter. These subterranean links between black and lower-class white men called forth in the minstrel show, as in Mark Twain's work, interracial recognitions and identifications no less than the imperative to disavow them. Certainly nineteenth-century blackface acts sought to deny the idea that blacks and whites shared a common humanity. Their racist gibes and pastoral gambols asserted that slavery was amusing, right, and natural; their racial portrayals turned blacks into simps, dupes, and docile tunesmiths. . . .

2. Mark Twain, *The Autobiography of Mark Twain*, ed. Charles Neider (New York: Harper and Row, 1959), 63–64.

Hostility and Identification

Exhibited before tradesmen, teamsters, and shopkeepers (and, in the 1850s and after, their female counterparts) in northern entertainment venues such as New York City's Mechanics' Hall, minstrel shows were in part the cultural flank of a generalized working-class hostility to blacks. This hostility was evinced in public slurs and violent acts—the casual racial policing that produced innumerable brawls and forced indignities, as well as the organized racial panic that fomented New York's terrible 1834 antiabolitionist race riots.

Yet the minstrel show very often twinned black and white, equating as much as differentiating them. The sources of this equation lay in exactly the same social conditions that gave rise to racist violence. One glimpses in the violence a severe white insecurity about the status of whiteness. To be lower class and white in the early nineteenth century, as the industrial revolution began to grind into high gear, was to be subject to remorseless assaults on one's independence and livelihood. The terms and conditions of work were steadily and alarmingly deteriorating; the status and character of white manhood struck masculinist workingmen as increasingly like that of women and blacks. The term "wage slave" came into being to denote this social drift, implying a defiant, "manly" outrage about the common condition of slaves and workingmen, as well as a primacy of concern for the status of white wage workers. Blackface minstrelsy was founded on this social antinomy. On one hand it basked in what one historian has called the "wages of whiteness"; on the other it revelled in the identifications between white men and slaves.[3]. . .

Working-class antislavery feeling was intermittently strong in the antebellum years and may have aided blackface minstrelsy's turn toward a liberating sentimentalism in the late 1840s.[4] Stephen Foster's "Old Folks at Home" (1851) or "My Old Kentucky Home, Good-Night!" (1853), sung from behind the blackface mask, unquestionably evoked sympa-

3. David Roediger, *The Wages of Whiteness: Race and the Making of the American Working Class* (London: Verso, 1991). 4. John B. Jentz, "The Anti-Slavery Constituency in Jacksonian New York City," *Civil War History* 27.2 (1981): 101–122; Williston Lofton, "Abolition and Labor," *Journal of Negro History* 33.3 (1948): 249–283; Joseph G. Rayback, "The American Workingman and the Antislavery Crusade," *Journal of Economic History* 3.2 (1943): 152–163; Eric Foner, "Abolitionism and the Labor Movement in Ante-Bellum America," *Politics and Ideology in the Age of the Civil War* (New York: Oxford University Press, 1980), 57–76; Herbert Shapiro, "Labor and Antislavery: Reflections on the Literature," *Nature, Society, and Thought* 2.4 (1989): 471–490.

thy for separated slave families and generally implied the feeling humanity of slaves, though in doing so it relied on the old racial stereotypes. As Ralph Ellison has remarked, even when the intentions of minstrel performers were least palatable, still "these fellows had to go and listen, they had to open their ears to (black) speech even if their purpose was to make it comic."[5] The complex and active exchanges of white self and black Other in blackface performance, however derisive, opened the color line to effacement in the very moment of its construction.[6]

Twain's Response to Blackface Minstrelsy

Twain's own response to blackface minstrelsy illustrates the ambivalence of lower-class white racial feeling, which suffuses his greatest novelistic treatments of race and slavery. Said Twain [in his *Autobiography*] of the minstrel show:

> The minstrels appeared with coal-black hands and faces and their clothing was a loud and extravagant burlesque of the clothing worn by the plantation slave of the time; not that the rags of the poor slave were burlesqued, for that would not have been possible; burlesque could have added nothing in the way of extravagance to the sorrowful accumulation of rags and patches which constituted his costume; it was the form and color of his dress that was burlesqued.

Twain proceeds here with some caution and not a little sympathy for the slave; he senses, perhaps uncomfortably, that the pleasures of stage burlesque have been wrought out of the quotidian violence of slavery. He even observes that blackface minstrels had "buttons as big as a blacking box," collapsing blackface masquerade, the means of its artifice, and an echo of one of its literal models—Negro bootblacks—in a single self-conscious figure. But Twain easily abandons such self-consciousness, as his reference to the slave's "costume," a clearly aestheticizing gesture, might lead us to expect:

> The minstrel used a very broad negro dialect; he used it competently and with easy facility and it was funny—delightfully and satisfyingly funny.... [Minstrels'] lips were thickened and lengthened with bright red paint to such a degree that their mouths resembled slices cut in a ripe watermelon.... The minstrel troupes had good voices and both their solos and their choruses were a delight to me as long as the negro show continued in existence.

5. Interview with Ralph Ellison, quoted in Shelley Fisher Fishkin, *Was Huck Black?: Mark Twain and African-American Voices* (New York: Oxford University Press, 1993), 90. 6. For more on the minstrel show, see Eric Lott, *Love and Theft: Blackface Minstrelsy and the American Working Class* (New York: Oxford University Press, 1993).

Twain is undeniably attracted to and celebratory of black culture. Yet just what that culture *is* to him is not altogether easy to make out, distorted and filtered as it is by white fantasy, desire, and delight. When views like Twain's do not simply fall into ridicule they are certainly the patronizing flip-side of it, suggesting Twain's ability to lose sight of the sorry circumstances that underlie his mirth and his continued and unexamined interest in racial exoticism. Ralph Ellison once observed that *Huckleberry Finn*'s Jim rarely emerges from behind the minstrel mask; Twain's remarks on the minstrel show lend a great deal of force to that observation.[7]. . .

Huck Finn and Blackface Minstrels

Blackface minstrelsy indeed underwrote one of the nineteenth century's most powerful antiracist novels—a tribute to the political fractures of minstrelsy and *Huckleberry Finn* both. This is no simple matter of minstrel-show "trappings" or "residues" in Twain's novel (as we often hurry to say), an issue of unfortunate, merely historical formal qualities in the portrayal of Jim disrupting Twain's liberal thematic intentions. The text is shot through with blackface thinking. Written as well as situated in the minstrel show's boom years, *Huckleberry Finn,* as Anthony J. Berret has argued, relies on comic dialogues between Huck and Jim (much of the humor at Jim's expense), many and various novelty acts (the king and the duke's scams, the circus, and so forth), and riotous burlesques of social and cultural matters (Emmeline Grangerford's sentimental poetry, the final setting-free of an already-free Jim). The whole book may thus conform to a tripartite minstrel-show structure of comic dialogues, olio, and southern burlesque.[8] And circumstances surrounding *Huckleberry Finn*'s writing only clarify its indebtedness to the minstrel tradition.

In 1882 Twain got the idea for a lecture tour (which he termed a circus or menagerie) to include himself, William Dean Howells, Thomas Bailey Aldrich, George Washington Cable, and Joel Chandler Harris. This authorial circus seems hardly more than the variety acts of a minstrel show, and the reading tour that came out of the idea, featuring

7. Ralph Ellison, *Shadow and Act* (1964; rpt. New York: Vintage, 1972), 50. 8. Anthony J. Berret, "*Huckleberry Finn* and the Minstrel Show," *American Studies* 27.2 (1986): 37–49.

Cable's straight man and Twain's clown, was in a sense precisely one, since both authors read the roles of black characters onstage, Cable even singing black songs.[9] This was the tour during which Twain first read parts of *Huckleberry Finn,* significantly the "King Sollermun" and "How come a Frenchman doan' talk like a man?" passages, whose blackface resonances are very clear. These passages may in fact have been written to be so performed after *Huckleberry Finn* was already completed.[10] The political complexity of this affair is compounded by Cable's having published, mid-tour, "The Freedman's Case in Equity," a forthright attack on southern racism that appeared in the same issue of *Century Magazine* that ran an excerpt from *Huckleberry Finn.* Somehow the authors' views did not arrest the blackface tones of their readings, nor Twain' s naming of one of his selections "Can't Learn a Nigger to Argue," a title he changed only when Cable requested it.[11] These events no doubt put a highly ambiguous spin on *Huckleberry Finn,* but they indicate as well that the contradiction between the book's overt politics and its indebtedness to the minstrel show was less cumbrous in the nineteenth century. Even the most enlightened nineteenth-century political thinkers, for example, adhered to "romantic racialism," as historian George Fredrickson has termed it, which celebrated the supposedly greater emotional depth and spiritual resources of black people even as it postulated innate differences between the races, just as the minstrel show seemed to do.[12] *Huckleberry Finn*'s limitations can surely be laid at the minstrel show's doorstep, but its strengths are oddly imbricated with strains of thought and feeling that inspired blackface performance.

We are thus led to a rather scandalous conclusion. The liberatory coupling of Huck and Jim *and* the gruesome blackface sources of Jim's character are the unseparate and equal results of minstrelsy's influence on the work of Mark Twain. Writers who have rightly denounced the minstrel-show aura of *Huckleberry Finn* miss the extent to which even

9. Paul Fatout, *Mark Twain on the Lecture Circuit* (Carbondale and Edwardsville: Southern Illinois University Press, 1960), 204–231. 10. Fredrick Woodard and Donnarae MacCann, "*Huckleberry Finn* and the Traditions of Blackface Minstrelsy," *Interracial Books for Children Bulletin* 15 (1984): 5. 11. Guy Cardwell, *Twins of Genius* (East Lansing: Michigan State College Press, 1953), 105; Steven Mailloux, *Rhetorical Power* (Ithaca: Cornell University Press, 1989), 57–99; Forrest Robinson, *In Bad Faith: The Dynamics of Deception in Mark Twain's America* (Cambridge: Harvard University Press, 1986), 111–211. 12. George M. Fredrickson, *The Black Image in the White Mind: The Debate on Afro-American Character and Destiny 1817–1914* (New York: Harper and Row, 1971), 101–102.

the best moments have a blackface cast.[13] True enough Twain's lapses are easy to spot, and we ought to remark a few of these. There is, for instance. the slave down on the Phelps farm who at the end of *Huckleberry Finn* tends to Jim in his reenslavement. Named Nat in what one can only assume is jocular homage to Nat Turner, this character is so reminiscent of Jim's portrayal at the novel's beginning that he undermines the steady commitment Jim exhibits in the final chapters; the blackface aspersions against him taint Jim as well. Possessed of what Huck/Twain calls a "good-natured, chuckleheaded face," obsessed with fending off the witches he says have been haunting him, Nat is a sort of hysterical paranoiac. . . . Nat observes that Jim sings out when he first sees Huck and Tom, and says so; but the boys flatly deny having heard it, pushing Nat to resort to mystical explanations. "'Oh, it's de dad-blame' witches, sah, en I wisht I was dead. I do. Dey's awluz at it, sah, en dey do mos' kill me, dey sk'yers me so.'" Even if we remark that Nat is forced to this conclusion by the boys' denial, his squirms are rendered with infantilizing exactitude. Shortly after, amid one of Tom's stratagems in the digressive freeing of Jim, some hounds rush into the hut and Nat is again afrighted: "you'll say I's a fool, but if I didn't b'lieve I see most a million dogs, er devils, er some'n, I wisht I may die right heah in dese tracks. I did, mos' sholy." Tom offers to make Nat a witch pie to ward them off, to which Nat responds: "Will you do it, honey?—will you? I'll wusshup de groun' und' yo' foot, I will!" Twain may have intended us to pick up on Tom's callousness in fanning the flames of Nat's fear: we note, for instance, that Nat has never heard of the now-implanted idea of a witch pie, and indeed that Nat promises not to disregard Tom' s request that he let alone the witch preparations, "not f'r ten hund'd thous'n' billion dollars"—a sum that would probably free Nat from his fetters. But the very uncertainty of Twain's intentions, together with his seemingly happy blackface depiction of Nat's self-abasement, undercuts all but racist meanings from the scene.

At the same time, moments very like this one may reveal more sympathetic dimensions. At the beginning of *Huckle-*

13. Woodard and MacCann, "*Huckleberry Finn* and the Traditions of Blackface Minstrelsy"; Woodard and MacCann, "Minstrel Shackles and Nineteenth-Century 'Liberality' in *Huckleberry Finn*," in James S. Leonard, Thomas A. Tenney, and Thadious M. Davis, eds., *Satire or Evasion? Black Perspectives on Huckleberry Finn* (Durham and London: Duke University Press, 1991), 141–153; Bernard Bell, "Twain's 'Nigger' Jim: The Tragic Face Behind the Minstrel Mask," *Mark Twain Journal* 23.1 (1985): 10–17.

berry Finn Tom Sawyer can't help playing a trick on Jim while he sleeps; he puts his hat on a branch above his head. Jim believes he's been bewitched and put in a trance and ridden by witches. Huck says Jim tells demonstrably self-serving tales of his adventures:

> Jim was monstrous proud about it, and he got so he wouldn't hardly notice the other niggers. Niggers would come miles to hear Jim tell about it, and he was more looked up to than any nigger in that country. Strange niggers would stand with their mouths open and look him all over, same as if he was a wonder. . . . Jim was most ruined, for a servant, because he got so stuck up on account of having seen the devil and been rode by witches.

In one sense this is standard "darky" fare. Huck even supplies the proper white exasperation with such charlatanism. Yet as several scholars have shown, this moment of apparent blackface foolishness is in fact an occasion in which Jim seizes rhetorical and perhaps actual power. Despite Huck's rather harsh judgment of Jim's self-investment, the fact is that he becomes a "wonder" within the black community and is "most ruined" for a servant—unsuited for slavery—in the wake of his tales. The superstition to which we are encouraged by Huck to condescend has actual and potentially subverting results in the world of the novel. One notes that Jim's actual words are not rendered here, which in the orthographic hierarchy of white dialect writing might have had the effect of reducing their impact. This is a moment when Jim, as he does in other ways throughout *Huckleberry Finn*, uses tricks and deceits to his advantage.[14] We may call this a kind of blackface antiracism, of whose political duplicity and indeed variability Twain was not always the complete master.

Twain's Use of Black Lore

This may even be a moment, as Shelley Fisher Fishkin has argued, that reveals Twain's intimacy with black life. For beliefs and stories such as Jim's were present and alive within black culture, which coded terrifying "night rides" by patrolling whites or Ku Klux Klan brigades as those of ghouls and spirits. Tales of such night rides, says Gladys-Marie Fry,

14. David L. Smith, "Huck, Jim, and American Racial Discourse," in James S. Leonard et al., eds. *Satire or Evasion?*, 103–120; James M. Cox, "A Hard Book to Take," in Robert Sattelmeyer and J. Donald Crowley, eds., *One Hundred Years of Huckleberry Finn* (Columbia: University of Missouri Press, 1985), 386–403.

duly suffered and survived by resilient blacks, allowed the heroic exploits of a subject people free expression.[15] Yet Twain leaves his white readers to divine for themselves the pressing uses of such tales as Jim tells, and in doing so steps again into the uncharmed circle of blackface—for it is, after all, Twain who is deploying black lore for his own ambiguous uses. Ambiguity arises also in scenes where racialist assumptions seem to be under the novelist's scrutinizing gaze. Soon after Huck and Tom arrive on the Phelps farm, with Jim still to be located, Tom suddenly realizes that the dinners the boys see regularly transported to a certain hut seem suspicious:

> "Looky here, Huck, what fools we are, to not think of it before! I bet I know where Jim is."
>
> "No! Where?"
>
> "In that hut down by the ash-hopper. Why, looky here. When we was at dinner, didn't you see a nigger man go in there with some vittles?"
>
> "Yes."
>
> "What did you think the vittles was for?"
>
> "For a dog."
>
> "So'd I. Well, it wasn t for a dog."
>
> "Why?"
>
> "Because part of it was watermelon."
>
> "So it was—I noticed it. Well, it does beat all, that I never thought about a dog not eating watermelon. It shows how a body can see and don't see at the same time."

Working on the assumption that, as Tom puts it, "Watermelon shows man," Huck and Tom detect Jim's whereabouts. This is a craftily constructed scene, one that makes some of Twain's largest political points. Huck's recognition that one can see and not see simultaneously is perhaps the aptest self-description in his whole twisted history of antislavery antiabolitionism. The scene pointedly distinguishes man from dog. And yet the means of this distinction is the clichéd watermelon reference, as though that stereotypical food in particular were the one to best locate Jim. It is true that Tom's words only suggest that dogs do not eat watermelon, not that black people do; and even if this latter is implied, it is Tom and Huck, not Twain, speaking. But Twain is joking around here even in the midst of one of his most earnest moral observations. I think we are justified in concluding that the closer Twain got to black cultural practices

15. Gladys-Marie Fry, *Night Riders in Black Folk History* (1975; rpt., Athens: University of Georgia Press, 1991), 9–10.

and to racially subversive meanings the more, paradoxically, his blackface debts multiplied. Blackface was something like the device or code or signifying system through which Twain worked out his least self-conscious and most sophisticated impulses regarding race in the United States. Jim's triumphs and Twain's ironies have to be as elaborately deciphered as Huck's future through Jim's hair-ball, so self-evident are their minstrel roots.

What is more, scenes we always take as Twain's most enlightened strokes suggest a surprising complicity with the minstrel show. Jim's emotionalism, and the fugitives' several joyous reunions on the raft, call on the romantic racialism that underwrote minstrelsy's sentimental strain—its broken-family nostalgia and long-suffered separations. Stephen Foster's "Old Folks at Home" (1851), for instance, depends for its effect on the pathos culled from black families forced to split up. . . . Foster's "Oh! Susanna" (1848) exploits the poignance of black attempts to reunite. . . .

Revealing the Contradictions of White Racial Feelings

Twain anticipated Antonio Gramsci's remarks on "national-popular" literature—that it emerges out of extant popular materials rather than artificially refined or imposed ideas.[16] Twain took up the American dilemma not by avoiding popular racial representations but by inhabiting them so forcefully that he produced an immanent criticism of them. It is not just that Huck more or less fulfills Twain's intention of making nonsense of America' s racial strictures (including those of Twain's readers) by living up to them the best anyone can; Twain himself pushed his blackface devices so far that they turned back on themselves, revealing the contradictory character of white racial feeling.[17] It is this simultaneous inhabitance and critique that makes *Huckleberry Finn* so scabrous, unassimilable, and perhaps unteachable to our own time. I don't think Twain chose to work within the popular racial codes of his day out of calculation, as a way of exploiting racist entertainment for antiracist uses, though that often turns out to be *Huckleberry Finn*'s effect. He did it with an odd relish, out of a sense of inwardness and intimacy

16. Antonio Gramsci, *Selections from Cultural Writings*, ed. David Forgacs and Geoffrey Nowell-Smith, trans. William Boelhower (London: Lawrence and Wishart, 1985), 207, 209–211. 17. On immanent criticism see Theodor Adorno, "Cultural Criticism and Society," *Prisms*, trans. Samuel and Shierry Weber (Cambridge: MIT Press, 1967), 32.

with the mass audience who shared his love of minstrelsy—the "mighty mass of the uncultivated" he said he wanted to reach with his novel (sold door to door by canvassing agents) and with whom he felt the greatest kinship.[18] It is worth noting here Twain's own willingness in effect to put on the blackface mask. After dinner one night at an 1874 Twain dinner party in Hartford, Twain dropped into his version of several slave spirituals, which had begun to be disseminated by black university singing groups in the early 1870s. Later, an overimbibed Twain mimicked a black man at a hoedown, dancing black dances for his guests in his drawing room.[19] Out of this sensibility came writing based on Twain's immersion in lower- or working-class racial feeling: writing that still resists attempts to tame down or clean up its engagements with race and class in America, and that is as partial, flawed, and disturbing as it is penetrating, emblematic, and current.

18. Justin Kaplan, *Mr. Clemens and Mark Twain* (New York: Simon and Schuster, 1966), 270. 19. Ibid., 174.

Huckleberry Finn Versus *Uncle Tom's Cabin*

Jane Smiley

When she reread *Huck Finn* for the first time since junior high school, Pulitzer Prize-winning novelist Jane Smiley was stunned to discover how overrated she found it. Mark Twain's lack of respect for Jim as a human being weakens the book's antiracist slant, she charges. Twain was unable to produce a work as uncompromisingly antislavery as Harriet Beecher Stowe's *Uncle Tom's Cabin*, which Smiley suggests should be read instead of *Huckleberry Finn*. Smiley is the author of several novels and novellas, including *Moo* and *A Thousand Acres.*

So I broke my leg. Doesn't matter how. . . . At any rate, like numerous broken-legged intellectuals before me, I found the prospect of three months in bed in the dining room rather seductive from a book-reading point of view, and I eagerly got started. Great novels piled up on my table, and right at the top was *The Adventures of Huckleberry Finn*, which, I'm embarrassed to admit, I hadn't read since junior high school. The novel took me a couple of days (it was longer than I had remembered), and I closed the cover stunned. Yes, stunned. Not, by any means, by the artistry of the book but by the notion that this is the novel all American literature grows out of, that this is a great novel, that this is even a serious novel.

Critics Decide *Huckleberry Finn* Is a Great Novel

Although Huck had his fans at publication, his real elevation into the pantheon was worked out early in the Propaganda Era, between 1948 and 1955, by Lionel Trilling, Leslie Fiedler, T.S. Eliot, Joseph Wood Krutch, and some lesser lights, in the introductions to American and British editions of the novel and in such journals as *Partisan Review* and *The New York Times Book Review.* The requirements of Huck's installation rapidly revealed themselves: the failure of the last twelve chapters (in which Huck finds Jim imprisoned on the Phelps plantation and Tom Sawyer is reintroduced and elaborates a cruel and unnecessary scheme for Jim's liberation) had to be diminished, accounted for, or forgiven; after that, the novel's special qualities had to be placed in the context first of other American novels (to their detriment) and then of world literature. The best bets here seemed to be Twain's style and the river setting, and the critics invested accordingly: Eliot, who had never read the novel as a boy, traded on his own childhood beside the big river, elevating Huck to the Boy, and the Mississippi to the River God, therein finding the sort of mythic resonance that he admired. Trilling liked the river god idea, too, though he didn't bother to capitalize it. He also thought that Twain, through Huck's lying, told truths, one of them being (I kid you not) that "something . . . had gone out of American life after the [Civil War], some simplicity, some innocence, some peace." What Twain himself was proudest of in the novel—his style—Trilling was glad to dub "not less than definitive in American literature. The prose of *Huckleberry Finn* established for written prose the virtues of American colloquial speech. . . . He is the master of the style that escapes the fixity of the printed page, that sounds in our ears with the immediacy of the heard voice, the very voice of unpretentious truth." The last requirement was some quality that would link Huck to other, though "lesser," American novels such as Herman Melville's *Moby-Dick,* that would possess some profound insight into the American character. Leslie Fiedler obligingly provided it when he read homoerotic attraction into the relationship between Huck and Jim, pointing out the similarity of this to such other white man–dark man friendships as those between Ishmael and Queequeg in *Moby-Dick* and Natty Bumppo and Chingachgook in James Fenimore Cooper's *Last of the Mohicans.*

The canonization proceeded apace: great novel (Trilling, 1950), greatest novel (Eliot, 1950), world-class novel (Lauriat Lane Jr., 1955). Sensible naysayers, such as Leo Marx, were lost in the shuffle of propaganda. But, in fact, *The Adventures of Huckleberry Finn* has little to offer in the way of greatness. There is more to be learned about the American character *from* its canonization than *through* its canonization.

Twain's Problems with Huck

Let me hasten to point out that, like most others, I don't hold any grudges against Huck himself. He's just a boy trying to survive. The villain here is Mark Twain, who knew how to give Huck a voice but didn't know how to give him a novel. Twain was clearly aware of the story's difficulties. Not finished with having revisited his boyhood in *Tom Sawyer*, Twain conceived of a sequel and began composition while still working on *Tom Sawyer*'s page proofs. Four hundred pages into it, having just passed Cairo and exhausted most of his memories of Hannibal and the upper Mississippi, Twain put the manuscript aside for three years. He was facing a problem every novelist is familiar with: his original conception was beginning to conflict with the implications of the actual story. It is at this point in the story that Huck and Jim realize two things: they have become close friends, and they have missed the Ohio River and drifted into what for Jim must be the most frightening territory of all—down the river, the very place Miss Watson was going to sell him to begin with. Jim's putative savior, Huck, has led him as far astray as a slave can go, and the farther they go, the worse it is going to be for him. Because the Ohio was not Twain's territory, the fulfillment of Jim's wish would necessarily lead the novel away from the artistic integrity that Twain certainly sensed his first four hundred pages possessed. He found himself writing not a boy's novel, like *Tom Sawyer*, but a man's novel, about real moral dilemmas and growth. The patina of nostalgia for a time and place, Missouri in the 1840s (not unlike former President Ronald Reagan's nostalgia for his own boyhood, when "Americans got along"), had been transformed into actual longing for a timeless place of friendship and freedom, safe and hidden, on the big river. But the raft had floated Huck and Jim, and their author with them, into the truly dark heart of the American soul and of American history: slave country.

Twain came back to the novel and worked on it twice again, once to rewrite the chapters containing the feud between the Grangerfords and the Shepherdsons, and later to introduce the Duke and the Dauphin. It is with the feud that the novel begins to fail, because from here on the episodes are mere distractions from the true subject of the work: Huck's affection for and responsibility to Jim. The signs of this failure are everywhere, as Jim is pushed to the side of the narrative, hiding on the raft and confined to it, while Huck follows the Duke and the Dauphin onshore to the scenes of much simpler and much less philosophically taxing moral dilemmas, such as fraud. Twain was by nature an improviser, and he was pleased enough with these improvisations to continue. When the Duke and the Dauphin finally betray Jim by selling him for forty dollars, Huck is shocked, but the fact is neither he nor Twain has come up with a plan that would have saved Jim in the end. Tom Sawyer does that.

Considerable critical ink has flowed over the years in an attempt to integrate the Tom Sawyer chapters with the rest of the book, but it has flowed in vain. As Leo Marx points out, and as most readers sense intuitively, once Tom reappears, "[m]ost of those traits which made [Huck] so appealing a hero now disappear. . . . It should be added at once that Jim doesn't mind too much. The fact is that he has undergone a similar transformation. On the raft he was an individual, man enough to denounce Huck when Huck made him the victim of a practical joke. In the closing episode, however, we lose sight of Jim in the maze of farcical invention." And the last twelve chapters are boring, a sure sign that an author has lost the battle between plot and theme and is just filling in the blanks.

The Real Problem: A Lack of Respect

As with all bad endings, the problem really lies at the beginning, and at the beginning of *The Adventures of Huckleberry Finn* neither Huck nor Twain takes Jim's desire for freedom at all seriously; that is, they do not accord it the respect that a man's passion deserves. The sign of this is that not only do the two never cross the Mississippi to Illinois, a free state, but they hardly even consider it. In both *Tom Sawyer* and *Huckleberry Finn*, the Jackson's Island scenes show that such a crossing, even in secret, is both possible and routine, and even though it would present legal difficulties for an escaped slave, these would certainly pose no more hardship than locating the mouth of the Ohio and then finding passage up it. It is true that there could have been slave catchers in pursuit (though the novel ostensibly takes place in the 1840s and the Fugitive Slave Act was not passed until 1850), but Twain's moral failure, once Huck and Jim link up, is never even to account for their choice to go down the river rather than across it. What this reveals is that for all his lip service to real attachment between white boy and black man, Twain really saw Jim as no more than Huck's sidekick, homoerotic or otherwise. All the claims that are routinely made for the book's humanitarian power are, in the end, simply absurd. Jim is never autonomous, never has a vote, always finds his purposes subordinate to Huck's, and, like every good sidekick, he never minds. He grows ever more passive and also more affectionate as Huck and the Duke and the Dauphin and Tom (and Twain) make ever more use of him for their own purposes. But this use they make of him is not supplementary; it is integral to Twain's whole conception of the novel. Twain thinks that Huck's affection is a good enough reward for Jim.

The sort of meretricious critical reasoning that has raised Huck's paltry good intentions to a "strategy of subversion" (David L. Smith) and a "convincing indictment of slavery" (Eliot) precisely mirrors the same sort of meretricious reasoning that white people use to convince themselves that they are not "racist." If Huck *feels* positive toward Jim, and *loves* him, and *thinks* of him as a man, then that's enough. He doesn't actually have to act in accordance with his feelings. White Americans always think racism is a feeling, and they reject it or they embrace it. To most Americans, it seems more honorable and nicer to reject it, so they do, but they almost invariably fail to understand that how they *feel* means very little to black Americans, who understand racism as a way of structuring American culture, American politics, and the American economy. To invest *The Adventures of Huckleberry Finn* with "greatness" is to underwrite a very simplistic and evasive theory of what racism is and to promulgate it, philosophically, in schools and the media as well as in academic journals. Surely the discomfort of many readers, black and white, and the censorship battles that have dogged *Huck Finn* in the last twenty years are understandable in this context. No matter how often the critics "place in context" Huck's use of the word "nigger," they can never excuse or fully hide the deeper racism of the novel—the way Twain and Huck use Jim because they really don't care enough about his desire for freedom to let that desire change their plans. And to give credit to Huck suggests that the only racial insight Americans of the nineteenth or twentieth century are capable of is a recognition of the obvious—that blacks, slave and free, are human.

Uncle Tom's Cabin

Ernest Hemingway, thinking of himself, as always, once said that all American literature grew out of *Huck Finn*. It undoubtedly would have been better for American literature, and American culture, if our literature had grown out of one of the best-selling novels of all time, another American work of the nineteenth century, *Uncle Tom's Cabin,* which for its portrayal of an array of thoughtful, autonomous, and passionate black characters leaves *Huck Finn* far behind. *Uncle Tom's Cabin* was published in 1852, when Twain was seventeen, still living in Hannibal and contributing to his brother's newspapers, still sympathizing with the South, nine years before his abortive career in the Confederate Army. *Uncle Tom's Cabin* was the most popular novel of its era, universally controversial. In 1863, when Harriet Beecher Stowe visited the White House, Abraham Lincoln condescended to remark to her, "So this is the little lady who made this great war."

The story, familiar to most nineteenth-century Americans, either through the novel or through the many stage adaptations that sentimentalized Stowe's work, may be sketched briefly: A Kentucky slave, Tom, is sold to pay off a debt to a slave trader, who takes him to New Orleans. On the boat trip downriver, Tom is purchased by the wealthy Augustine St. Clare at the behest of his daughter, Eva. After Eva's death, and then St. Clare's, Tom is sold again, this time to Simon Legree, whose remote plantation is the site of every form of cruelty and degradation. . . .

Stowe's Brilliant Analysis Plus Wisdom of Feeling

The power of *Uncle Tom's Cabin* is the power of brilliant analysis married to great wisdom of feeling. Stowe never forgets the logical end of any relationship in which one person is the subject and the other is the object. No matter how the two people feel, or what their intentions are, the logic of the relationship is inherently tragic and traps both parties until the false subject/object relationship is ended. Stowe's most oft-repeated and potent representation of this inexorable logic is the forcible separation of family members, especially of mothers from children. Eliza, faced with the sale of her child, Harry, escapes across the breaking ice of the Ohio River. Lucy, whose ten-month-old is sold behind her back, kills herself. Prue, who has been used for breeding, must listen to her last child cry itself to death because her mistress won't let her save it; she falls into alcoholism and thievery and is finally whipped to death. Cassy, prefiguring a choice made by one of the characters in Toni Morrison's *Beloved*, kills her last child so that it won't grow up in slavery. All of these women have been promised something by their owners—love, education, the privilege and joy of raising their children—but, owing to slavery, all of these promises have been broken. The grief and despair these women display is no doubt what T.S. Eliot was thinking of when he superciliously labeled *Uncle Tom's Cabin* "sensationalist propaganda," but, in fact, few critics in the nineteenth century ever accused Stowe of making up or even exaggerating such stories. One group of former slaves who were asked to comment on Stowe's depiction of slave life said that she had failed to portray the very worst, and Stowe herself was afraid that if she told some of what she had heard from escaped slaves and other informants during her eighteen years in Cincinnati, the book would be too dark to find any readership at all.

Stowe's analysis does not stop with the slave owners and traders, or with the slaves themselves. She understands perfectly that slavery is an economic system embedded in America as a whole, and she comments ironically on Christian bankers in New York whose financial dealings result in the sale of slaves, on Northern politicians who promote the capture of escaped slaves for the sake of the public good, on ministers of churches who give the system a Christian stamp of approval. One of Stowe's most skillful techniques is her method of weaving a discussion of slavery into the dialogue of her characters. . . .

Stowe also understands that the real root of slavery is that it is profitable as well as customary. Augustine and his brother live with slavery because it is the system they know and because they haven't the imagination to live without it. Simon Legree embraces slavery because he can make money from it and because it gives him even more absolute power over his workers than he could find in the North or in England.

Twain Cannot Face the Realities of Slavery

The very heart of nineteenth-century American experience and literature, the nature and meaning of slavery, is finally what Twain cannot face in *The Adventures of Huckleberry Finn.* As Jim and Huck drift down Twain's beloved river, the author finds himself nearing what must have been a crucial personal nexus: how to reconcile the felt memory of boyhood with the cruel implications of the social system within which that boyhood was lived. He had avoided this problem for the most part in *Tom Sawyer:* slaves hardly impinge on the lives of Tom and the other boys. But once Twain allows Jim a voice, this voice must speak in counterpoint to Huck's voice and must raise issues that cannot easily be resolved, either personally or culturally. Harriet Beecher Stowe, New Englander, daughter of Puritans and thinkers, active in the abolitionist movement and in the effort to aid and educate escaped slaves, had no such personal conflict when she sat down to write *Uncle Tom's Cabin.* Nothing about slavery was attractive to her either as a New Englander or as a resident of Cincinnati for almost twenty years. Her lack of conflict is apparent in the clarity of both the style and substance of the novel.

Why, then, we may ask, did *Uncle Tom's Cabin,* for all its power and popularity, fail to spawn American literature? Fail, even, to work as a model for how to draw passionate, autonomous, and interesting black literary characters? Fail to keep the focus of the American literary imagination on the central dilemma of the American experience: race? Part of the reason is certainly that the public conversation about race and slavery that had been a feature of antebellum American life fell silent after the Civil War. Perhaps the answer is to be found in *The Adventures of Huckleberry Finn:* everyone opted for the ultimate distraction, lighting out for the territory. And the reason is to be found in *Uncle Tom's Cabin:* that's where the money was. . . .

The Real Loss

The real loss is not to our literature but to our culture and ourselves, because we have lost the subject of how the various social groups who may not escape to the wilderness are to get along in society; and, in the case of *Uncle Tom's Cabin,* the hard-nosed, unsentimental dialogue about race that we should have been having since before the Civil War. Obviously, *Uncle Tom's Cabin* is no more the last word on race relations than *The Brothers Karamazov* or *David Copperfield* is on any number of characteristically Russian or English themes and social questions. Some of Stowe's ideas about inherent racial characteristics (whites: cold, heartless; blacks: naturally religious and warm) are bad and have been exploded. One of her solutions to the American racial conflicts that she foresaw, a colony in Africa, she later repudiated. Nevertheless, her views about many issues were brilliant, and her heart was wise. She gained the respect and friendship of many men and women of goodwill, black and white, such as Frederick Douglass, the civil-rights activist Mary Church Terrill, the writer and social activist James Weldon Johnson, and W.E.B. Du Bois. What she did was find a way to talk about slavery and family, power and law, life and death, good and evil, North and South. She truly believed that all Americans together had to find a solution to the problem of slavery in which all were implicated. When her voice, a courageously public voice—as demonstrated by the public arguments about slavery that rage throughout *Uncle Tom's Cabin*—fell silent in our culture and was replaced by the secretive voice of Huck Finn, who acknowledges Jim only when they are alone on the raft together out in the middle of the big river, racism fell out of the public world and into the private one, where whites think it really is but blacks know it really isn't.

TEACHING *HUCK FINN* IS A POLITICAL ACT

Should *Huckleberry Finn* be taught in the schools? The critics of the Propaganda Era laid the groundwork for the universal inclusion of the book in school curriculums by declaring it great. Although they predated the current generation of politicized English professors, this was clearly a political act, because the entry of *Huck Finn* into classrooms sets the terms of the discussion of racism and American history, and sets them very low: all you have to do to be a hero is acknowledge that your poor sidekick is human; you don't actually have to act in the interests of his humanity. Arguments about censorship have been regularly turned into nonsense by appeals to Huck's "greatness." Moreover, so much critical thinking has gone into defending Huck so that he *can* be great, so that American literature can be found different from and maybe better than Russian or English or

French literature, that the very integrity of the critical enterprise has been called into question. That most readers intuitively reject the last twelve chapters of the novel on the grounds of tedium or triviality is clear from the fact that so many critics have turned themselves inside out to defend them. Is it so mysterious that criticism has failed in our time after being so robust only a generation ago? Those who cannot be persuaded that *The Adventures of Huckleberry Finn* is a great novel have to draw *some* conclusion.

I would rather my children read *Uncle Torn's Cabin*, even though it is far more vivid in its depiction of cruelty than *Huck Finn*, and this is because Stowe's novel is clearly and unmistakably a tragedy. No whitewash, no secrets, but evil, suffering, imagination, endurance, and redemption—just like life. Like little Eva, who eagerly but fearfully listens to the stories of the slaves that her family tries to keep from her, our children want to know what is going on, what has gone on, and what we intend to do about it. If "great" literature has any purpose, it is to help us face up to our responsibilities instead of enabling us to avoid them once again by lighting out for the territory.

Chapter 4

The Problematic Ending of *Huckleberry Finn*

A Bitterly Comic Inversion of Tragic Truth

Joyce A. Rowe

The ludicrous ending of *Huckleberry Finn*, in its farcical repetition of the major themes of the book, is a bitter burlesque of a happy ending, writes Joyce A. Rowe. In Rowe's view, Twain's bogus finale is a comic inversion that mocks America's view of its special destiny as well as the failure of Huck's journey. In fact, she maintains, Huck represents the dilemma of an America caught between reality and desire, able to travel between the two worlds but unable to bring them together. Just as Huck's journey with Jim ends, so does America's chance to create the unfettered social possibility Huck and Jim temporarily created on their raft. Rowe is the author of *Equivocal Endings in Classic American Novels*, from which this viewpoint is excerpted.

If Karl Marx's dictum that all great events and characters of world history occur twice, first as tragedy, then as farce, can be imagined as having an analogue within a fictional history, the farcical ending of [*Huckleberry Finn*] might be seen as a case in point. For nowhere in the book is Twain's extensive use of parallel passages that contrast in tone more marked than in the relation between its beginning and ending. Through a kind of black parody, the major themes of the story (evasion, disguise, imprisonment, escape and rebirth) as well as many minor motifs, established in the first section of the book (up to the escape from Jackson's Island) are recapitulated here in a ludicrous *dénouement* which does nothing so much as reinforce one's sense of those barbarous conditions of social existence to which Huck has borne witness all along.

As the modest vernacular style of the preceding portions of the book supports the weight of a tragic truth—the implicit failure of the journey—so the ending presents us with its bitterly comic inversion. It is as if Mark Twain were saying: Only in a society of willing victims and fools could such a bogus ending be believed. And further, that America's view of itself, of its special destiny among nations, is itself only another con-game out of historical romance. If you are foolish enough to live by such fictions, then you will believe that Miss Watson's deathbed conversion creates a happy ending, and be equally successful in conning yourself into ignoring every cruel absurdity that Tom invents to orchestrate it. Mark Twain's burlesque of literary romance and boy's adventure is only the screen for a deeper attack on an American society that has failed to realize its own promise of moral and social rebirth.[1] . . .

An Altered Concept of Humanity

The authentic feeling which has arisen between Huck and Jim, based upon mutual respect for one another's integrity, dies on the Phelps Farm. As opposed to all the weak, corrupt, and fairly insane fathers we have seen on shore, Jim has been the ideal—nurturer, friend, protector, and moral tutor in one. But once at the farm their personal bond is obliterated from Huck's consciousness as he, Jim, and Tom conform their relations to the pattern of their days at Miss Watson's. However, although the Phelps Farm is akin to life at Miss Watson's, these chapters afford no simple drama of return. For Jim, allowed some comforts at the beginning of his imprisonment here, is eventually reduced to a condition of misery and exploitation far worse than anything he endured at the outset of the story. If at Miss Watson's he was a clever but superstitious slave, here he assumes the role, for Huck and Tom as well as for us, of an abused gull. His childlike awe of Tom and continued trust in Huck only deepen the humiliation to which Twain subjects him.

What is striking about the main parallel actions of the beginning and ending—kidnapping and imprisonment of

1. Cf. Bernard DeVoto, *Mark Twain at Work*, p. 92. Based on his reading of Twain's unpublished papers, DeVoto believed that he was ignorant of the change of tone in the ending and its effect on the reader; that he wrote "in response to an inner drive, consequently exercised little voluntary control over and [was] unable to criticize what he had written." Many later critics have contested this description of Twain's artistry; see especially, Walter Blair, *Mark Twain and Huck Finn* (Berkeley, Univ. of Calif. Press, 1960); although Blair, too, is confounded by the tone of the ending.

Huck by a con-man (his father), kidnapping and imprisonment of Jim by the duke and king—is that the course of the journey has so altered our conception of the reciprocal humanity of Jim and Huck that we are repelled here, as we would not necessarily have been in the first chapter, by seeing Jim used as a prop in a boys' game. In other words, Jim here occupies the same position and is in potentially the same danger as Huck was *vis à vis* his father. One was depicted in realistic vernacular terms. The other, utilizing Jim's shore persona of ignorant 'darky,' is played for a joke. But now the joke only heightens the inhumanity of treating a human being as if he were a counter in a game. Moreover, the journey has educated us to see that this inhumanity toward Jim is only a more extreme version of the exploitative relations that pervade every other shore episode—the Shepherdson-Grangerford feud, where killing enhances male vanity and pride; the Arkansas lynch mob, where Boggs's death serves the crowd's appetite for drama; the Wilkses' funeral 'orgies,' where Anglophile snobbery enables the con-men to prey on the pretensions and greed of an entire town. All of these incidents are funny as well as horrific, and each evokes a measure of sympathy for the folly of the protagonists. The distinction of the ending is that its antics are neither funny nor engaging but merely grotesque. That, I believe, is its point. At the end of the journey the fictional comforts of verisimilitude entirely break down, and with them any possibility of an emotionally consistent world. Instead, 'reality' is perceived to be nothing but a violent and dangerous masquerade. Tom's 'fun' ends in a nightmare posse of local farmers eager to kill him in order to protect the Phelpses' investment in Jim's return to his putative master.

The Enslavement of Everyone

Much has been written about Jim's slavery, especially in relation to the ending.[2] And, indeed, the increasing harshness of Jim's treatment, as well as his own regression, suggests an historical parallel to the worsening conditions for blacks as the nineteenth century wore on. However, the larger issue of the book is the mental and moral enslavement which is the lot of everyone in this society: so while Jim's condition

2. On the failure of Reconstruction as the satiric motive for this episode, see Richard and Rita Gollin, "*Huck Finn* and the Time of the Evasion," *Modern Language Studies,* 9, ii (Spring, 1979), pp. 5–15.

underlines the hypocritical inhumanity of a particular era, it cannot be separated, except by degree, from those more comprehensive cultural failings that the Thirteenth Amendment did not abolish. Jim is the necessary extreme—at once the most complete social and legal victim and yet the freest to live naturally within himself. Cast out by the society that exploits him, he is left alone to define his own moral life, and in so doing to serve as a measure for Huck's. If his slavery becomes one term in a series of related images of enslavement, this is not to deny the dramatic impact of his condition. Nothing is so damning to the visionary ideal which America proposes for itself as its actual treatment of racial minorities, beginning with blacks and Indians. But this is also why Jim's aborted escape into free territory (which has been of concern to many readers) is a false issue in terms of the subject matter of the book—as if Mark Twain in 1876 had set out to recapitulate *Uncle Tom's Cabin*. Rather, Jim's enslavement and subsequent humiliation bespeak Twain's overwhelming revulsion (behind the comic mask) from all manifestations of shore life. Jim provides an image of the infernal conditions which lie in wait for Huck should he actually give up his identity and become Tom Sawyer.

For in assimilating himself with Tom, Huck becomes the traducer of that self which had flourished on the river under the tutelage of Jim. In effect, he becomes one of the ghosts he has always feared, one of those intimations of another self which threatens the integrity of the nascent ego. So he stands by while Jim, trusting in his presence, submits himself to Tom's ambitious cruelties, while Tom crows triumphantly that "it was the best fun he ever had in his life . . . and if he only could see his way to it we would keep it up all the rest of our lives and leave Jim to our children to get out; for he believed Jim would come to like it better and better the more he got used to it." The Huck who responds to Aunt Sally's query about the fictitious steamboat accident—"Good gracious! Anybody hurt?" "No'm. Killed a nigger." "Well, it's lucky; because sometimes people do get hurt."—is a figure who has so instinctively resumed the false skin of his shore 'conscience' at the appearance of his shore 'home' that even before he finds out who he is ("It was like being born again, I was so glad to find out who I was") there is little prospect that here he could ever be anyone but Tom Sawyer.

On shore Huck has always disbelieved his own powers, but here his awe and admiration of Tom make him nearly as impotent as Jim. In fact, once they accept Tom's direction, Huck and Jim become as dependent upon him for the resolution of their common fate as Tom himself is on "the best authorities." In each case, the subject's piety enhances the satire. Just as Tom is the fool of his literary 'principles,' so Huck and Jim become his fools. The nadir of this benighted subservience is surely the sight we are given of Jim temporarily freed in order to collect another prop for his imprisonment. With Tom supervising, Jim and Huck roll a heavy grindstone back to the cabin for Jim to chisel on it the mournful inscriptions that stimulate Tom's tears.

Because Mark Twain prevents Huck from acknowledging the cruelty of Tom Sawyer's games, Huck is denied the option of consciously rejecting Tom as a social model and, therefore, of entertaining any alternative shore identity for himself. With his social self given over to Tom's dominion, and Tom standing as metaphor for the cast of mind of an entire society, Huck has no choice, if he is to break free of the Tom in himself, but to reject 'civilization' in toto. The bitterness here derives from Mark Twain's insistence that there is no exit from this hellish maze because cultural forms not only distort moral intentions but the shape of consciousness itself—the sense we carry in us of who and what we are.[3]. . .

The sense of the entire episode as a kind of blasphemy, at least a blasting, of the mutual world Jim and Huck have created is intensified by the juxtaposition, just before this, of Huck's memory of Jim on the river—perhaps the most compelling image in the book. It is a visual recollection in which Huck's characteristically quiet idiom expands to capture something of the rhythm and tone of the Jubilee singing which Mark Twain is said to have enjoyed.[4]

> . . . and I see Jim before me, all the time, in the day, and in the nighttime, sometimes moonlight, sometimes storms, and we a-floating along, talking, and singing, and laughing . . .

The passage continues with Huck's recollection of scenes, encapsulating the flow of their entire river journey and

3. Walter Blair records that throughout the writing of *Huckleberry Finn*, Mark Twain was reading W.E.H. Lecky's *History of European Morals*. Blair found in Twain's marginalia and notebooks a wavering between the two major views of man that Lecky discusses: i.e., motivated by intuitive powers of goodness or driven by exterior forces and selfish interests. Just before Mark Twain wrote the concluding parts "he delivered a paper in which he championed determinism and selfish motivation." Furthermore, Twain's marginalia show that he recognized that moral influences and perceptions begin in infancy: "We never get a chance to find out whether we have any that are innate or not." *Mark Twain and Huck Finn* (Berkeley, Univ. of Calif. Press, 1960), p. viii, p. 138. 4. DeVoto, *Mark Twain's America*, p. 40

galvanizing him into his climactic decision to go to Hell and rescue Jim. The irony is that once on shore, at the gates of Hell, Huck must become a ghost of himself—divest himself of his 'natural' parts. What these metaphoric terms mean is that there is no correlative shore life which can give his river imagery social texture or meaning. There is no possibility of Huck taking his wisdom back into society.

In retrospect, we can see that self-division was always the functional principle of Huck's character. He can't stand being "sivilized," but loneliness drives him back to Tom Sawyer and his robber games. As Richard Poirier points out, "Tom Sawyer's games are intimately related . . . to the respectable aspects of adult society." The necessary condition for membership in Tom's gang is that Huck return to the Widow Douglas. The metaphoric suggestion is that "'respectable' society as represented by the Widow is equivalent to a 'band of robbers'."[5]

It is his connection to Jim that enables Huck to express the antithetical side of his own nature. Alone, it is doubtful whether he would have gone so far as to leave Jackson's Island on a raft. It would have been more characteristic of him to remain a few yards off-shore, hiding in the woods, watching the river boats go by, and sneaking back at night for contact with Tom. For Huck's choices, even once on the river, are never final ones. The anxiety associated with his socialized shore "conscience," as well as his instinctive submission to the power of circumstance to determine the outcome of events, perhaps explains the quality of reprise in the decision of Chapter 31 to commit himself to Jim's rescue, when we might have thought this issue had been settled for him once before.

Unlike Jim, who is an absolute outsider and whose peril is the catalyst for Huck's going into action, the boy has the power to utilize verbal disguise, to dress himself in the fictions which complement his conventional appearance. His pathos is that although able to travel between two worlds, he is unable to achieve any internal mediation between the commitments and values which divide them. As he embodies the two opposing principles of received morality and natural law

5. Richard Poirier, *A World Elsewhere* (New York, Oxford University Press, 1966), p. 182. See also Tony Tanner, "The Literary Children of James and Clemens," *Nineteenth Century Fiction,* XVI (Dec., 1961), pp. 205–18. "Huck's loneliness is the measure of the extent of his involvement" in society. "Huck is searching for something society doesn't have to offer, and the enforced alternatives are capitulation or escape" (p. 212).

which dominate the book's structure, so Huck is representative of the problem of America itself—forever caught between the forms that history has actually taken there, and the desire for what might have been, for that freedom of social possibility which, for a moment, Jim and Huck together seem to create in the wilderness of the raft.

A Psychoanalytic Study of the Ending of *Huckleberry Finn*

José Barchilon and Joel S. Kovel

Taking a psychoanalytic view of the ending of *Huck Finn*, José Barchilon and Joel S. Kovel see the final chapters as a rebirth—an unconscious struggle toward freedom. Jim's prison is the womb from which all three conspirators—Jim, Huck, and Tom—are trying to escape. At the same time, Barchilon and Kovel believe, the story of Moses offers subliminal support to a mythical view of Huck. As they combine these two ideas, the authors conclude that Huck finds a satisfactory substitute mother—the river—who will sustain him as he turns away from "sivilization" in the last lines of the book. Argentine author Barchilon has written in Spanish on collective communication; Kovel is the author of several books on therapy, philosophy, and racism.

The last section of [*Huckleberry Finn*] has been attacked, even by some of the book's staunchest supporters. For example, Bernard DeVoto wrote in *Mark Twain at Work* (2):* "And now, without any awareness that he was muddying the waters of great fiction, he plunges into a trivial extravaganza on a theme he had exhausted years before. In the whole reach of the English novel there is no more abrupt or more chilling descent."

Huck, Jim, and Tom Are Reborn

Seen in the light of the unconscious struggle toward freedom, however, these last chapters acquire their artistic jus-

* Numbers in parentheses refer to entries in the Bibliography at the end of this essay.

Reprinted from José Barchilon and Joel S. Kovel, "*Huckleberry Finn:* A Psychoanalytic Study," *Journal of the American Psychoanalytic Association*, vol. 14, no. 4, pp. 799–808, by permission of International Universities Press, Inc.

tification:[1] Twain cannot be true to Huck Finn unless he makes the boy bungle his attempt at mature action. Once the escape theme gets under way the book becomes a game, the humor becomes wilder and less restrained, even farcical, the sense of profound despair which creeps in when he first arrives at the Phelps farm to contemplate the enormity of his task recedes further into the depths, Jim becomes a plaything again and for the first and only time elation appears and the action is accelerated by a quasi-hypomanic tempo. The tale has undergone a full cycle, the characters are restored to life, and the dream ends. Huck has indeed changed, even grown, but he is still recognizable—and still a child.

The first stage of Huck's return to the world occurs when he re-encounters Tom Sawyer. Through Tom and his fantasies, Huck can partially express his own aggressive destructive impulses and yet return to a passive style of behavior. The boys agree to free Jim together and to maintain their false identities (Tom all the while knowing what Huck doesn't: that it is really a game, that Jim is free already). When they discover just where Jim is imprisoned, we begin to see evidence of anxiety over the forthcoming task. Tom has outlined his plan—which, of course, has superseded Huck's simple scheme for freedom and reunion—and Huck ironically comments: "I see in a minute it was worth fifteen of mine for style, and would make Jim just as free a man as mine would, and maybe get us all killed besides. So I was

1. The situation is analogous to that of the patient in the later stages of analysis who has liberated himself and grown to the extent that he can offer deep material freely. But it is also reminiscent of the techniques of the theater of the absurd which dilutes the significant elements in a mass of primary-process thoughts, feelings, and actions. Since anything goes, anything is permissible; the deep unconscious needs little disguise. Here we are perhaps witnessing the effect of Twain's caveat at the beginning of the novel, when he warned us against finding in it either motive, plot or moral; isn't that also a way of saying that it is absurd? Alfred Jarry had to wait for another twelve years before performing his "absurd" "King Ubu" in Paris. In spite of the superficial rationalization that it was a skit written by him as a schoolboy, Jarry scandalized as he hoped he would, while Twain made his "absurdity" palatable (8). Trilling compares this finale to those of Molière and found its comical qualities quite apt (14).

Nor is that the only place where our analysis of the unconscious elements agrees with Trilling's penetrating literary criticism of the moral and psychosocial factors in *Huckleberry Finn*. For him, the bond between Huck and Jim is a moral one; on the raft they "make a community of saints" to parallel our community of orphaned babies. And after Huck humbled himself to Jim, Trilling says, "this incident is the beginning of the moral testing and development which a character so morally sensitive as Huck's must inevitably undergo." Finally, he sees Huck as solving his problem, "not by doing right but by doing wrong." This insight illustrates the resonances which exist between the many levels of the story, its manifest contents, its artistic meaning, its social message, its superficial psychological consistency, and the deep unconscious nuclear conflicts and solutions. Thus the story tells how Huck did "wrong" which morally is right; preconsciously it feels right too, since it satisfies Huck's need to save the friend whom he has a need to destroy and humiliate (as does his society), even as it fits unconsciously with his love for Jim who in part represents a hated yet longed-for mother.

satisfied, and said we would waltz in on it." A little later Huck makes a suggestion which reveals the functional identity between Jim's liberation and his own escape—or separation—from his father: "how'll it do to saw him out, the way I done before I was murdered that time?" To which Tom replies, "I bet we can find a way that's twice as long. There ain't no hurry; le's keep on looking around."

The entire hilarious escape sequence has the structure of a symptom. The hard-won and deep relationship with Jim, and the urgent need to free him and to undertake action in his behalf, are experiences in which hitherto deeply repressed conflicts become close to conscious realization; the anxiety is a measure of this, and the means of escape become therefore neurotically determined actions constructed to master the tension. Neurotic acting out does not fully succeed in this, however, and tension persists, necessitating repetition after repetition of elaborate and absurd schemes, until it becomes plain that what interests the boys is not so much the end of liberation as the means of attaining it.

Infantile Impulse Undermines Mature Goals

Embedded in these rituals can be found both the wish-impulse and its defense. The very rigidity and wild impracticality of the plans are the best defense against success. As if this were not enough, delay and procrastination are built into every step. The creation of a tunnel to Jim's hut-prison is unnecessary, difficult at best, impractical and dangerous to boot; but Tom must compound the problem by attempting to do it with case knives and imagining that it will require thirty-seven years for the job. On top of all this, they punish themselves every step of the way: they eat sawdust and get a colossal stomachache; they blister their hands unmercifully while trying to dig the tunnel; they drag huge rocks over the ground, never seem to sleep, and in general make the task as arduous as possible. Tom is not even satisfied with returning to the house via a normal route, but must climb up the lightning rod, only to fall three times (and "most busted his brains out") before he finally succeeds. The greatest indignities are reserved for the long-suffering Jim; but one may imagine that the boys obtained their full share of vicarious involvement in his tribulations.

While the mature aim of liberation is thoroughly undermined by these defensive maneuvers, the entire gamut of infantile impulse is represented and gratified by the same devices.

The tunnel, for example, is not only a means of delay but transforms the hut into a womb symbol in which Jim's chains become an umbilical cord. It would be easy to remove this chain from the bedstead to which it is attached, but that would not preserve the symbol; instead the bedstead must be sawed off and Tom even weighs the idea of sawing off Jim's leg. This itself is not a simple aggressive fantasy, but also becomes another castrative procedure by which the infantility in Jim is established yet again. At this level of meaning, the eating of sawdust can become the enactment of an oral-incorporative fantasy by means of which the two boys unite with Jim. Later they bring Jim "food" in the form of a "witches pie," which even contains a useless rope ladder made from one of Aunt Sally's bed sheets. "He's got to have a rope ladder," says Tom, "they all do"—an assertion which still makes sense if the rope ladder is conceived of as an umbilical cord. "We let on it took nine months to make it," says Huck. The sense of intra-uterine life comes through strongly all during their plans, reinforced, for example, by the changes of identity and the sending of "nonnamous" letters, one of which is even called "the grand bulge," to the adults to tip them off about the impending escape, or shall we say delivery.

The unconscious birthlike elements underlying the actual escape continuously reshape the more superficial fantasies; according to the romantic tradition of escape—which is Tom's avowed model—at least one of the boys should have been posted as a sentry, but seemingly without reason the model is abandoned. A final touch is the use of an effigy of mother which is put into Jim's bed to be left behind after the trio escapes. Of this Tom says, "And it's usual for the prisoner's mother to change clothes with him, and she stays in, and he slides out in her clothes."[2] Thus the deep inner need which underlies all these rituals has so altered the essential nature of the escape that what began as a liberation on the basis of mature attachment ends a birth of three helpless babes.

A Hidden Message

The function and general meaning of this game are quite understandable and obvious, but a more specific message may be hiding in this absurd-appearing fantasy. The manifest content says that Jim's mother (presumably a Negro woman) must be

2. This is similar to the abundance of realistic or pseudorealistic details in fairy tales. They are necessary elements which give plausibility to the fantastic (1).

left behind after he escapes. But since the latent wishes have transformed the prison into a common womb out of which the three abandoned infants must crawl out as one, it would follow that Huck and Tom are expressing a typical unconscious fantasy of Southern children: to possess the warmth, nurture, and instinctual gratifications offered by a Negro mammy. This Southern dream fits well with the rest of the story: the assumption that Jim and Huck are brothers, their voyage on the Mississippi, and the fact that Tom and Huck have every reason to be dissatisfied with the absence of their real white parents, as well as with the inhibitory qualities of their surrogate ones. But there is also some direct evidence, such as it is, to support our reconstruction. Right after Tom tells Huck that he must "hook that yaller girl's frock" to impersonate a Negro girl servant, a most peculiar argument arises. First, Huck objects on the grounds that stealing the girl's only dress is bound to create difficulties, but he relents eventually and the following exchange takes place:

"[Huck:] 'All right, I ain't saying nothing; I'm the servant-girl. Who's Jim's mother?'

"[Tom:] 'I'm his mother. I'll hook a gown from Aunt Sally.'

" 'Well, then, you'll have to stay in the cabin when me and Jim leaves.'

"Not much. I'll stuff Jim's clothes full of straw and lay it on his bed to represent his mother in disguise, and Jim'll take the nigger woman's gown off of me and wear it, and we'll all evade together." (All three disguised as girls—while the mother effigy will wear a man's clothes.)

These rapid shifts in identity from boys to girls or mother figures speak clearly in the language of dreams; the logic and condensations are those of the primary process—Tom says in one sentence that he will wear Aunt Sally's dress and five lines further the same dress has become the "nigger woman's gown." We must assume that the unconscious urge come what may to introduce on the scene a Negro mother to be born to, or a young Negro girl to identify with, was so peremptory that it dispensed with the need for secondary elaborations.[3]

3. Those who believe that Twain became careless in the last chapter will dismiss this error as a slip of the pen. Some well-meaning editors have corrected the "nigger woman Aunt Sally gown error" but curiously enough Twain never did, even in the subsequent, cleaned-out editions. We prefer to think that as Twain's humor became wilder and farcical, he fell in with the accelerated tempo and felt that the reader would be carried away so that "errors" of this kind would not be noticed; moreover, the ability to understand if anything were noticed would be inhibited by his promise to shoot anyone trying to find meaning in his plot. In this, he could have been imitating Melville who, in *Moby Dick*, ended the chapter describing the sperm whale's penis with the misspelled word: archbishoprick.

The logic of the whole fantasy decrees that the escape shall fail; Tom gets wounded; Huck is nabbed by old Silas Phelps when he goes to find a doctor for Tom; and Jim gives himself up voluntarily to help the doctor care for Tom. They are caught and returned to the adult world through their very attempts to care for each other, for, in the terms of the novel and society such a mode of relationship—the community of childhood—is not compatible with an independent existence.

The Relationship of the Moses Myth to the Story of Huck

We may now be in a better position to elaborate on the relationship of the archetypal Moses to the boy, Finn. The myth, by its subliminal existence in the memory of most of us, facilitates the task of the reader as we mentioned earlier. We assume, as does Kubie (9) in another context, that the readers' system preconscious is constantly and rapidly responding to stimuli from the story; it "shakes them together" (*cogitare*) and "selects" what it can bind together (*intelligere*) (11). These activities of the ego (probably involving id and superego as well) are automatic, relatively conflict free, and, as Hartmann puts it, "the logical place for these automatisms . . . is the preconscious" (6, 7). Thus we visualize the ego as constantly integrating facts, possibilities, and seeming contradictions into explanations or "theories" (7) about the behavior of the characters. These "theories," if they have congruence, form the basis for that feeling of "consistency and validity" (12), not to speak of the pleasure, which the story conveys to us. The presence of the myth of Moses in the background of our consciousness offers an already accepted, ritualized, symbolic realization for the personal mainsprings in Huck's life.[4] Instead of perceiving these highly personal elements as alien to us, we feel as if we already knew them, first because they may resonate with our own experiences, private fantasies, and unconscious, and next because knowledge of the saga catalyzes rather rapidly the transmutation of Huck into a variant of the Moses archetype.

So, the myth stands midway between the personal unconscious of the characters and reader on the one hand and the

4. Myths are accepted but not really understood; their heroes are "symbols" expressing in a language acceptable to the unconscious of individuals those deeply human features which their society was powerless to understand in terms of science or reason alone. Really, society is mostly afraid to understand.

derivatives described in the manifest story. It facilitates the acceptance and preconscious understanding of those idiosyncratic and unconscious elements. But many lesser novels or a simple case history would have sufficed for that task. *Huckleberry Finn* is a great novel, one possessing originality. Fiedler calls Huck "the first Existentialist hero" and says, "There are mythic qualities in Ahab and even Dimmesdale, but Huck *is* a myth" (3). Lionel Trilling calls it "an almost perfect work" and agrees with Hemingway that "all modern American literature comes from . . . *Huckleberry Finn*" (14).

This literary originality corresponds, we believe, to a similar originality in the relationship of unconscious determinants to conscious derivatives. In other words, *Huckleberry Finn* offers us much more than parallel and accurate derivatives of the inner struggles of a latter-day Moses. It tells us *why* and *how* Huckleberry Finn had to become a Moses. Upon reading the novel, the threadbare myth begins to gain life and color, the relationship of Huck to Moses now appears as a two-way street, the myth borrowing from the novel as much if not more than the novel did from the myth. This reciprocal relationship of the myth and its retelling in a new version, what some have called the Eternal Return, is basic to the whole of literature. It is the area, it seems to us, in which originality or the lack of it resides and could be studied. The story of Huck pours new life and strength in an old and tired legend; we become aware of the vast possibilities: how many of the determinants of Huck's behavior can apply to Moses or, for that matter, to all those who try to break out of a similar type of "aloneness" by saving someone more miserable than themselves—to all those who try to unshackle themselves from the bonds of their own psyche by freeing slaves from iniquitous social orders.[5] How many liberators were such orphans? Had such weak fathers, etc., etc., etc.?

This artistic and creative aspect of the novel is one to which analysts do not pay enough attention, according to literary critics, since their formulations fit equally well the neurosis, the creative masterpiece or the dime novel. That criticism ignores the importance of understanding the common substrate to thinking processes in neuroses, normality,

5. One cannot help but wonder whether we are not hearing here the first vague and obscure sounding of whatever made Freud ask, "Is it possible that Moses was not a Hebrew slave, the black or 'noble savages' of the day, but an Egyptian, the unhappy 'sivilized white men' of yore?" (4).

and creativity. But it may be that originality in art as well as in science should be judged by criteria common to originality rather than to thinking processes: is it really new? Does it account better for known facts, has it enlarged our horizons (9, 10)?

In that case, the core of *Huckleberry Finn*'s originality lies in the fact that it has bound together old, well-known facts and offered us a new understanding of how they fit together. Even if Twain knew nothing of how unconscious factors actually fit together, he nevertheless transcribed accurately what he *felt* to be true against powerful urges to make his novel more rational, traditional, but also more commonplace. Thus, Twain has achieved here what so many attempt but so few succeed in doing. What Jean Giraudoux graphically illustrated when he wittily entitled one of his plays *Amphitryon 38* (5)—a succinct way of saying: I know that 37 of my predecessors have sung to you the plight of Amphitryon, the husband of Alcmene, legal father of Hercules and luckless rival of Zeus, but what they told you was only good for the knowledge and ken of their day. In the light of new facts we are in need of a theory which will encompass more of the known phenomena, so let *me* tell you, this 38th time, how it *really* was. . . .

We must now return to the conclusion of Jim's, Huck's, and Tom's adventures. Their game of escape finished, the boys assume their proper identities and Jim is told that he has been freed. Even now the fantasy returns in one final utterance of Tom's: "le's all three slide out of here one of these nights and get an outfit, and go for howling adventures amongst the Injuns, over in the territory, for a couple of weeks or two." Huck initially agrees with this plan, but soon changes his mind and makes his final statement: "I . . . ain't a-going to [write] no more. But I reckon I got to light out for the territory ahead of the rest, because Aunt Sally she's going to adopt me and sivilize me, and I can't stand it. I been there before."

He is released for this through the knowledge of his father's death and the full acquisition of his 6,000 dollars. This liberates him from all binding links with his past, and is an undoing of his former deprivation. But the final statement also represents a solidification in Huck, an end to the turmoils of early adolescence, and the formation of a more stable and adaptive identity. He will become a wanderer on the

American frontier. In this he has combined something of his rootless father with the last phase of the life of Moses, the prophet and leader who could not enter the Promised Land. Though he could not grow into the full adult image of his Biblical progenitor, their fates have this in common: for both, the mother, once lost, is never wholly regained.

Nonetheless, in this last identity, Huck has finally found a substitute mother who can meet his needs and whom he can tolerate without ambivalence. In turning away from "sivilization," with all of its unbearable cruelties and contradictions, he elects at the same time to relate directly to nature. This shall now be the mother. She has been present all the time as the river god which sustained and swept him along; now he shall give over his life to her. Only by wandering in nature can his dilemma of separation and reunion, birth and death, attachment to or flight from objects find a self-contained resolution; only there can the rhythms of life thwart the influence, not altogether spent, of a past haunted by the Angel of Death.[6]

Bibliography

1. Barchilon, Jacques. Uses of the fairy tale in the eighteenth century. In: *Studies on Voltaire and the Eighteenth Century,* 24:111–138. Geneva, Transactions of the First International Congress on the Enlightenment, 1963.
2. DeVoto, B.A. *Mark Twain at Work.* Cambridge: Harvard University Press, 1942.
3. Fiedler, L.E. Huckleberry Finn: Faust in the Eden of childhood. In: *Love and Death in the American Novel.* Cleveland: World Publishing Company, 1960, pp. 553–591.
4. Freud, S. Moses and monotheism (1939). *Standard Edition,* 23:1–137. London: Hogarth Press, 1964.
5. Giraudoux, J. *Amphitryon 38* (1929). New York: Random House, 1938.
6. Hartmann, H. Technical implications of ego psychology. *Psychoanal. Quart.,* 20:31–43, 1951.

6. Alfred De Vigny's Moses, tired of all his wandering around the frontier of the Promised Land, says to God: "Laissez-moi m'endormir du sommeil de la terre" ["Let me rest the sleep of the Earth"] (15). Professor Henry Nash Smith, guardian of the Twain Papers, after hearing this paper in October 1965, validated, so to speak, this finding by telling us that Twain's favorite poem was "The Burial of Moses" by Cecil F. Alexander (13). We hope to be forgiven for this infraction of our basic rule to shun any material not contained in the novel.

7. Hartmann, H. & Loewenstein, R.M. Notes on the superego. *The Psychanalytic Study of the Child,* 17:42–81. New York: International Universities Press, 1962.
8. Jarry, A. Ubu Roi. In: *Tout Ubu.* Paris: Librairie General Francaise, 1962, p. 12.
9. Kubie, L.S. *Neurotic Distortion of the Creative Process.* Lawrence: University of Kansas Press, 1958, pp. 32-50.
10. Nicole, C. *Biologie de l'Invention.* Paris: Alcan, 1932.
11. Partridge, E. Origins: *A Short Etymological Dictionary of Modern English.* New York: Macmillan, 1963.
12. Rapaport, D. *The Structure of Psychoanalytic Theory* [*Psychological Issues,* Monogr. 6]. New York: International Universities Press, 1960, p. 14.
13. Smith, H.N. *Personal communication,* 1965.
14. Trilling, L. Huckleberry Finn. In: *The Liberal Imagination.* New York: Doubleday, 1950, pp. 104–117.
15. Vigny, A. "Moise" from "Poèmes Antiques et Modernes," ed. H. Clouard. In: *Anthologie de la Litterature Française.* New York: Oxford, 1960, p. 44.

A Savage Indictment of "the Best Authorities"

Carson Gibb

Although the last nine chapters of *Huck Finn* may seem to be a failed attempt to indulge in fun, Carson Gibb finds in them a deliberate attack on education, social position, and wealth. When Tom turns to these "best authorities" to coerce Jim and Huck into risking Jim's life to indulge his desire for fantasy, Gibb sees an attack not on Tom but on the world that created him. That world, Gibb charges, considers the escape from boredom to be its highest purpose. Gibb, formerly an instructor in English at Lafayette College in Easton, Pennsylvania, and the University of Baltimore, now researches the early settlers of colonial Maryland at the Maryland State Archives.

The last nine chapters of *The Adventures of Huckleberry Finn* have been deplored almost as generally as the whole book has been praised. According to Andrew Lang, "The story . . . ends by lapsing into burlesque, when Tom Sawyer insists on freeing the slave whom he knows to be free already, in a manner accordant with 'the best authorities.'" Newton Arvin speaks of "the dreary elaboration of Tom Sawyer's rescue of Jim."[1] Brander Matthews uses the rescue as an example of "passages where the interest falls off."[2] Dixon Wecter calls this part "shallows of burlesque and extravaganza."[3] And Lionel Trilling sums up: "In form and style *Huckleberry Finn* is an almost perfect work. Only one mistake has ever been charged against it, that it concludes with Tom Sawyer's elaborate, too elaborate, game of Jim's escape. Certainly this episode is too long—in the original draft it was much

1. See *Mark Twain: Selected Criticism*, ed., Arthur L. Scott (Dallas, 1955), p. 40 & p. 233. 2. Harper's Classics edition of *The Adventures of Huckleberry Finn* (New York, 1948), p. xvii 3. "Mark Twain," *Literary History of the United States*, ed., Spiller, Thorp, Johnson & Canby (New York, 1948), II, p. 933

Reprinted from Carson Gibb, "The Best Authorities," *College English*, December 1960. Reprinted courtesy of the National Council of Teachers of English.

longer—and certainly it is a falling off, as most anything would have to be, from the incidents on the river."[4]

The usual explanation is that this is an egregious example of Twain's defective taste and inability to criticize his own work. Wecter and Trilling offer additional explanations, which are much alike. Trilling says that the ending is a "device . . . needed to permit Huck to return to his anonymity, to give up the role of hero, to fall into the background which he prefers." Wecter says, "The story thus closes on the farcical note with which the Hannibal cycle has begun, in the whitewashing episode."

The judgment is hardly disputable. But the explanations are apt to leave one wondering why a man who (though "unequal" and "never keen at self-criticism") could write "an almost perfect work" should nod so violently that the last fifth of that work uniformly depresses critics. Was Twain perhaps doing something more than mechanically ending a book or a cycle, something more than indulging his predilection for fun?

Is the rescue really fun? It is fun when Tom and Huck raid the A-rabs, swear dark oaths, and trick Jim. But is this sort of foolery the same after Huck has assisted mountebanks and swindlers, out-maneuvered murderers, witnessed the butchery of a feud, and learned how filthy it is to trick Jim? Is it fun to confront A-rabs when the A-rabs are not a Sunday school class (primer) but men armed with rifles? When the booty is not "some doughnuts and jam . . . a rag doll . . . a hymnbook and a tract" but Jim? Tom may still think it is fun when he gets a bullet in his leg—he shows real pluck. But Huck discovers it was not really much fun when he sees how "grieved" Aunt Sally is:

> I wished I could do something for her, but I couldn't, only to swear that I wouldn't never do nothing to grieve her any more. And the third time I waked up at dawn, and slid down, and she was there yet, and her candle was most out, and her old grey head was resting on her hands, and she was asleep.

If it is not fun, or at least not merely fun, what is it? It is the pranks of two boys—one accustomed to danger, the other intoxicated by fantasy—who believe niggers and people are two different things. When lying to Aunt Sally about how he happened to arrive as he did, Huck tells her he was in a steamboat accident, and she reacts with characteristic humaneness:

4. Rinehart edition of *The Adventures of Huckleberry Finn* (New York, 1948), p. xv–xvi

"Good gracious! anybody hurt?"

"No'm. Killed a nigger."

"Well, it's lucky; because sometimes people do get hurt."

And she rattles on about a Baptist who had been "crippled" by an explosion in a boat Uncle Silas was aboard. Neither Aunt Sally nor any other decent person would reproach a boy for having his fun at a nigger's expense. Tom and Huck's attitude toward niggers is standard—the attitude of the rich and the poor, of the prim and the disreputable, even of the niggers themselves. And all the fun of the prolonged emancipation of Jim depends on this attitude, just as Huck's accounts of Colonel Sherburn's murder of Boggs and the Grangerford-Shepherdson butchery depend on Southern chivalry. The point is the same: custom brutalizes.

The Best Authorities

But if Twain wished to end the book with a burst of spleen, why did he aim it at two likable youngsters? Huck does his best to free Jim—his best, that is, without challenging Tom's established superiority. Huck never forgets that Tom has the support of "the best authorities"; even when alone on the river, Huck never faced a difficult situation without wishing Tom were with him and wondering what he would do. Tom's grip on him is so strong that Huck, loving Jim as he now does, can only feebly protest against Tom's fantasies and humbly offer his own common sense—which, of course, Tom always demolishes with scorn. Not even love can make Huck, the outcast, doubt Tom, who has book-learning, respectability, wealth—all the best authorities. Tom alone is *responsible* for playing with Jim's life in order to indulge in fantasy. And Tom knows all the while Jim is legally free.

Compared with Huck, Tom looks shabby. Still, he is all good nature, and when his fantasy suddenly turns real, his courage does not falter. Absurd and outrageous as his behavior is, Tom comes off well; he is as good as it is possible for one of his breeding to be. Tom is not under attack, but the world that created him is.

Not long before Tom appears, Huck becomes conscious of how sinful he has been in "stealing a poor old woman's nigger that hadn't ever done me no harm." First he tries to excuse himself.

> Well, I tried the best I could to kinder soften it up somehow for myself by saying I was brung up wicked, and so I warn't so much to blame; but something inside of me kept saying, "There was the Sunday-school, you could 'a' gone to it; and if you'd 'a' done it they'd 'a' learnt you there that people that acts as I'd been acting about that nigger goes to everlasting fire."

Since he had a choice, he cannot blame circumstances for his sinful conduct. Then he finds he is so steeped in sin that he cannot pray, and decides to cleanse himself by writing a letter telling Miss Watson where Jim is. The act has the effect he hoped for: he feels he can pray. But before praying, he starts "thinking—thinking how good it was all this happened so, and how near I come to being lost and going to hell. And went on thinking. And got to thinking over our trip down the river; and I see Jim before me all the time." And all he can remember is how grateful, generous, and forgiving Jim always was. He notices the letter.

> "All right, then, I'll go to hell"—and tore it up.
>
> It was awful thoughts and awful words, but they was said. And I let them stay said; and never thought no more about reforming. I shoved the whole thing out of my head, and said I would take up wickedness again, which was in my line, being brung up to it, and the other warn't. And for a starter I would go to work and steal Jim out of slavery again.

Huck's heart is too black for even the church—the best of all possible authorities—to cleanse. Custom brutalizes and perverts. It could not be plainer.

Tom Pretends to Be on the Devil's Side

Huck is not too depressed by his new commitment to sin to be delighted when Tom turns up a little later. As soon as he has convinced Tom he is not a ghost and Tom has planned how to fool Aunt Sally, Huck blurts out his intention to free Jim. Tom is surprised, but he sizes up the situation and says:

> "I'll *help* you steal him!"
>
> Well, I let go all holts then, like I was shot. It was the most astonishing speech I ever heard—and I'm bound to say Tom Sawyer fell considerable in my estimation. Only I couldn't believe it. Tom Sawyer a *nigger-stealer!*
>
> "Oh, shucks!" I says; "you're joking."
>
> "I ain't joking, either."
>
> "Well, then," I says, "joking or no joking. . . ."

Ignorant that Tom *is* joking in a way different from what he supposes, Huck is not to be convinced by any number of words that Tom could be guilty of anything more heinous than concealing his knowledge of an attempt to steal a nigger. But before long, by committing himself to the theft, Tom succeeds in convincing Huck that he too is on the side of the Devil.

> Well, one thing was dead sure, and that was that Tom Sawyer was in earnest, and was actuly going to help steal that nigger out of slavery. That was the thing that was too many for me. Here was a boy that was respectable and well brung up; . . . and yet here he was, without any more pride, or rightness, or feeling, than to stoop to this business, and make himself a shame, and his family a shame, before everybody. I *couldn't* understand it no way at all.

To tell Huck the truth would spoil the game; so Tom simply asserts his authority, which has behind it all the best authorities—in fiction and in life. Tom will do many outrageous things, but he wouldn't really steal a nigger. So he must grasp this unique opportunity to pretend to steal one; he must use Huck and Jim for his amusement.

Here on this farm peopled by obedient Huck and Jim, gullible Aunt Sally and Uncle Silas, and proportionally simple-minded niggers, Tom—the comparative sophisticate—uses his opportunity like a truly civilized man. As soon as he has sized up the situation, he is dissatisfied.

> "Why, drat it, Huck, it's the stupidest arrangement I ever see. You got to invent *all* the difficulties. Well, we can't help it; we've got to do the best we can with the materials we've got. Anyhow, there's one thing—there's more honor in getting him out through a lot of difficulties and dangers, where there warn't one of them furnished by the people who it was their duty to furnish them, and you had to contrive them all out of your own head."

Having displayed his ability to observe accurately and make reasonable deductions by locating Jim, Tom proceeds spectacularly "to invent *all* the difficulties" consistent with the principles laid down by such best authorities as "Baron Trenck," Casanova, "Benvenuto Chelleeny," and Henry IV. He does not make so much of *honor* as would a Grangerford, a Shepherdson, or a Hotspur, but he disdains the ignoble expedient of raising Jim's bed and slipping the chain off in favor of sawing off the bed leg, and at one moment he is prepared to amputate Jim's leg for the sake of honor. This, of course, is only the beginning of his invention of fantastic difficulties. A truly sophisticated mind.

The Sophisticate's High Purpose: To Escape Boredom

Tom's purpose is the epitome of civilized man's purposes: to escape boredom (damn the cost!) by inventing high adventure. In a few years he will be ready to attack Mount Everest, take off for the moon, or fight a war over something of no concern to him. His shrewdness in finding and seizing the opportunity for adventure is remarkable; his shrewdness in calculating just how long he can extend his game without having it spoiled is even more so. He is able to foresee what steps Uncle Silas will take to find Jim's owner and how long they will take, and therefore, to manipulate the complex preparations so they are complete at exactly the right moment. When Tom's purpose is evident, so is the expedience of his actions.

Once he has plunged into his fantasy, Tom's reasoning and behavior are the *reductio ad absurdum* of the adult precepts and practices—the best authorities—that have stamped him. Once it is granted that fiction and history are properly a means of escape from the boredom of every day, that absurdity is justified by appeal to precedent ("the regulations") and authority, and that a nigger is not a human being, his behavior is reasonable and understandable. Now that he is in a world in which common sense is irrelevant, he logically abandons it. Though Jim could easily be let out through the door, Tom determines to dig him out. Huck accepts this absurdity on Tom's authority and reminds Tom of "them old crippled picks and things" in the lean-to against Jim's prison. Tom "turns on me, looking pitying enough to make a body cry."

> "Well then," I says, "if we don't want the picks and shovels, what do we want?"
>
> "A couple of case knives." . . .
>
> "Confound it, it's foolish, Tom."
>
> "It don't make no difference how foolish it is, it's the *right* way—and it's the regular way. And there ain't no *other* way."

When it becomes obvious, even to Tom, that the case knives will not do, he disgustedly adopts the picks and shovels.

> "I'll tell you. It ain't right, and it ain't moral, and I wouldn't like it to get out; but there ain't only just the one way: we got to dig him out with the picks, and *let on* it's case knives."

And he refuses to explain further or call the picks and shovels anything but "case knives." "He was always just that particular," comments Huck. "Full of principle." Always the man of principle, Tom never admits the folly of a plan; he simply calls things by other names.

Sustaining the Joke

For a while the combination of Tom's fancy, his half-consciousness of his own absurdity, and Huck's salty common sense is comically satiric. It is hard not to laugh at Tom even when he is explaining why it might be a good idea to cut off Jim's leg.

> "Well some of the best authorities has done it. They couldn't get the chain off, so they just cut their hand off and shoved. And a leg would be better still. But we got to let that go. There ain't necessity enough in this case, and, besides, Jim's a nigger and wouldn't understand the reasons for it, and how it's the custom in Europe; so we'll let it go."

Even if the reference to Jim's subhuman status recalls what is at stake in this game, there is no anger. And when Tom's fancy is no longer funny, Huck's objections and comments sustain the joke. While they are planning to dig Jim out, Tom tells Huck that it took one of the prisoners thirty-seven years to dig his way out of the "Castle Deef" and that at the end he found himself in China. Huck says, "'*Jim* don't know nobody in China.'" When, on account of his scraped and blistered hands, Tom cannot climb the lightning rod back to the bedroom, he asks Huck, "'Can't you think of no way?' 'Yes,' I says, 'but I reckon it ain't regular. Come up the stairs, and let on it's a lightning-rod.' So he done it." Huck has caught on to the game, and were his common sense not dulled by admiration of Tom, his attitude toward the whole game would be like Jim's toward the plan for him "to keep a journal on the shirt with his blood, and all that. . . . Jim he couldn't see no sense in the most of it, but he allowed we was white folks and knowed better than him; so he was satisfied, and said he would do it all just as Tom said."

Later, when he has described Jim's coat of arms, Tom gives up explaining, for the simple reason that he has not the slightest idea what a coat of arms signifies. But as he knows the words, he is still an authority.

Bringing in the grindstone (which Jim has to be temporarily freed to accomplish) ends the part of the rescue that is substantially independent of the real challenge—to alarm and outwit Jim's captors. The possibilities of Tom's fantasy in a vacuum are exhausted; the humor and wit—and satire—of Tom's schemes and Huck's and Jim's reactions have been worked for (at least) all they are worth.

Tom is probably becoming bored again, and is certainly apprehensive that word will arrive that Jim is free before he and Huck can free him. So he creates new excitement by writing "nonnamous letters." In stealing their equipment—a shirt, sheets, spoons, a candlestick, and six candles—the boys have risked discovery by Aunt Sally and have had some narrow escapes. Now they deliberately alarm Aunt Sally, Uncle Silas, and the neighbors. With the intrusion of the world of adults comes new emphasis on the plight Tom and Huck have put Jim into during the three weeks of their game.

> . . . you never see a cabin as blithesome as Jim's was when they'd [the snakes] all swarm out for music and swarm for him. Jim didn't like the spiders, and the spiders didn't like Jim; and so they'd lay for him, and make it mighty warm for him. And he said that between the rats and the snakes and the grindstone there warn't no room in bed for him skasely; and when there was, a body couldn't sleep, it was so lively; and it was always lively, he said, because *they* never all slept at one time, but took turn about. . . . He said if he ever got out this time he wouldn't ever be a prisoner again, not for a salary.

"Blithesome," indeed, but as Tom or Huck might say, "Only a nigger."

Tom Is Exonerated

Tom's fantasy ends in delirium, as the doctor, with Jim's help, extracts the bullet from his leg, and Jim is led back into chains. Later, Tom demonstrates his decency by giving "Jim forty dollars for being prisoner for us so patient, and doing it up so good, and Jim was pleased most to death," and construes the forty-dollar present as proof that "'signs is signs.'" And when Huck learns that Jim was free all along and that Tom knew it, he feels only relief and delight that Tom did not really have a heart as black as his: "I couldn't ever understand before, until that minute and that talk, how he *could* help a body set a nigger free with his bringing up."

So Tom is exonerated. In a world where the Devil's party steals niggers out of slavery and the Lord's party puts them in chains, Tom Sawyer—Miss Watson to the contrary notwithstanding—remains among the elect. For all his mischief and adventures, real and fancied, Tom is the creature of the best authorities. Histories, novels, schools, churches, respectable guardians—they have begot, borne, and nurtured him. He is their folly—occasionally glorious—blindness, astuteness, double-thinking, perverted logic, brutality, superficiality; their genius for making the simple complicated, the lucid obscure, the good evil.

From Huck and Jim's point of view he *is* the best authority. Before his voyage down the river with Jim—a long time ago, it seems—Huck thought he would rather go to hell with Tom than to heaven with Miss Watson. This was a juvenile thought. When Huck is faced with a real choice between heaven and hell, against all he has been taught, against his better judgment and conscience, he must choose hell—hell without Tom, but with the Duke and the Dauphin, Pap, Jim, and all the other outcasts. Having damned himself, Huck is still concerned as much for Tom's welfare as for Jim's. He is still obedient to and respectful of Tom as the authority he is, and he does not want to see that authority fall. The denouement is a complete relief: Tom has proved to him that civilization is exactly what he thought it was. Huck has more than Aunt Sally's benevolent oppression in mind when he closes his book:

> But I reckon I got to light out for the territory ahead of the rest, because Aunt Sally she's going to adopt me and sivilize me, and I can't stand it. I been there before.

A Beautifully Crafted Ending

Richard Hill

Critics who love all of *Huck Finn* except the ending are missing the point, according to Richard Hill, author of the following essay. The burlesque elements deplored by some are quite appropriate for boys of Tom and Huck's age, he points out. Hill also rejects the notion that Huck and Jim fall out of character and lose autonomy in the face of Tom's dangerous plots; in fact, he says, both Huck and Jim are more powerful than they are given credit for being, and each reserves—and exercises—the right to refuse or alter Tom's plans when they go too far. Hill finds subtle clues to demonstrate that Huck is amiable but not a pushover, and that Jim cannily manipulates the situation when necessary.

As a concept, "The Weak Ending of *Huckleberry Finn*" is a given for most modern critics. Hamlin Hill and Walter Blair sum up the popular outlook nicely: "Every once in a while someone offers a new justification for the last chapters . . . but the very fact that this insistence is necessary suggests an uneasiness which the ending causes. . . . Whatever alibis can be offered for it reduce both Huck and Jim in stature."[1] This idea of reduced stature will be discussed in depth later; of far greater interest initially is the assumption that any defense of the ending is a "justification" or an "alibi," as if the lawful opinion were set in stone and only a few apostates stood against it. Such fierce conviction would certainly have puzzled earlier generations of critics. Although many dismissed the book as profane or merely sensational, not one singled out the ending for the utter disdain so common over the past

1. Hamlin Hill and Walter Blair, "The Composition of Huckleberry Finn," in *The Art of Huckleberry Finn* (San Francisco: Chandler, 1969)

Reprinted from Richard Hill, "Overreaching: Critical Agendas and the Ending of *Adventures of Huckleberry Finn*," *Texas Studies in Literature and Language*, vol. 33, no. 4, Winter 1991, pp. 492–513, by permission of the author and the University of Texas Press.

forty years. Of the dozens of 1885–1900 essays I have examined, only one critic, T.S. Perry, disliked the ending in particular.[2] The majority of early reviewers (discounting those who dismissed the book on moral grounds) seem to follow Brander Matthews's wholehearted approval: "The romantic side of Tom Sawyer is shown in most delightfully humorous fashion in the account of his difficult devices to aid in the easy escape of Jim, a runaway negro."[3]. . .

Attacks on the Ending

The first fully realized attack on the ending of *Huckleberry Finn* came from Leo Marx. . . . For Marx, the whole account of the boys' vast labors under the noses of the Phelpses fails as burlesque: it is "out of keeping," and "the slapstick tone jars with the underlying seriousness of the voyage."[4] But Marx's indignant, "What is [this bad burlesque] doing here?" can be answered simply enough by most twelve-year-old readers. The Tom/Huck/Aunt Sally dynamic continues the same manner of boy versus mother/older sister burlesque that Twain has presented throughout the novel, including passages in the "serious" Grangerford and Wilks chapters. This particular component of the story demonstrates beautifully the wide gulf between how old women and young boys view the natural world, especially that part of it composed of insects, rats, and snakes. . . . Huck's bland narrative puzzlement at her escalating panic is hilarious even after several readings, yet the wild humor of her confusion is tempered with a fine pathos when her sentimental qualities are played against her vexations.

What is also going on here is a beautifully crafted comedic buildup underscored with Huck's tension as he sees Tom's plans inching slowly into dangerous territory. Unfortunately, Marx and his disciples seem to find, in Mencken's words, "humor and sound sense essentially antagonistic";[5] and more unfortunately, as DeVoto pointed out decades before, "the colorblind are unqualified critics of painting . . . [and] the solemn have been granted authority about humor."[6]

2. Thomas Sargeant Perry's reservation about the ending is rather mild by modern critical standards: "It is possible to feel, however, that the fun in the long account of Tom Sawyer's artificial imitation of escapes from prison is somewhat forced" (review of *Adventures of Huckleberry Finn, Century Magazine* 30 [May 1885]). 3. Brander Matthews, review of *Adventures of Huckleberry Finn, Saturday Review* (London) 59 (31 January 1885), 153–54 4. Leo Marx, "Mr. Eliot, Mr. Trilling, and *Huckleberry Finn," American Scholar* 22 (Autumn 1953) 5. H.L. Mencken, "The Burden of Humor," *The Smart Set* 38 (February 1913) 6. Bernard DeVoto, *Mark Twain's America* (Cambridge: Houghton Mifflin, 1932)

Marx finds "much more serious ground for dissatisfaction . . ." in his notion that Huck and Jim become "comic characters" in the ending. Though Huck has matured socially, over the course of the first thirty-one chapters, to a degree in keeping with Marx's expectations, the critic feels that Huck "regresses to the subordinate role." The "traits which made him so appealing a hero now disappear"; he "submits in awe to Tom's notion of what is amusing [and] makes himself a party to sport which aggravates Jim's misery."

Many critics have advanced this idea, but does Huck really fall out of character in the ending? Certainly he is in awe of Tom: "What a head for just a boy to have! If I had Tom Sawyer's head I wouldn't trade it off to be a duke, nor mate of a steamboat, nor clown in a circus, nor nothing I can think of." This is no new attitude on Huck's part; such admiration is well distributed throughout the book . . . —and as James M. Cox points out, he wants to be like Tom whenever he can, or whenever he is not "living on too thin a margin to afford Tom's luxurious romances."[7]. . .

A Plausible Fourteen-Year-Old Boy

Bruce Michelson agrees with the popular view that Huck's "passivity in these closing chapters, his reversion . . . ought to trouble us"; nonetheless, he resists Marx's critical urge to strengthen Huck's character when he points out that to make Huck disdain Tom and suddenly act like the mature man "we might want him to be" would be "cheating indeed," for "Huck has come as far on his moral journey as a plausible boy of that time could."[8]

Readers concerned with Jim's plight (especially those critics who are more worried about it than either Huck or Jim seem to be) might be disappointed in Huck when he takes time off from the rescue to go fishing, or to steal watermelons, or to plug up rat holes. They may chafe when Huck obeys Uncle Silas's order to go home, which leaves Jim stuck with Tom in the heat of the manhunt, or when Huck obeys Aunt Sally's wish that he not leave that night. But each of these childish acts (or refusals to act) is true to the fact that Huck is, after all, a fourteen-year-old boy who, as Alfred Kazin points out, "must steal from the adult world the power,

7. James M. Cox, "Remarks on the Sad Initiation of Huckleberry Finn," *Sewanee Review* 62 [July–September 1954] 8. Bruce Michelson, "Huck and the Games of the World," *American Literary Realism* 13 (Spring 1980)

but also the fun, he needs to keep feeling like a boy."[9] Huck is also a fourteen-year-old boy who is feeling relatively safe for the first time in months. Tom Sawyer is on the job, so Huck can afford to relax. . . .

But perhaps we still owe it to Huck to rehabilitate his reputation after all the slander. First of all, he has always been amiably inclined to let strong-minded associates have their own way as long as doing so promotes general harmony. He did it with Pap and later with the king and duke, so why not with Tom? Huck is in character when he says, "I see in a minute [Tom's plan] was worth fifteen of mine for style, and would make Jim just as free a man as mine would, and maybe get us all killed besides. So I was satisfied and said we would waltz in on it." The implication that Huck has final approval of the plan[10] is an important piece in a mosaic of evidence that, despite his admiration for Tom, Huck at least theoretically retains control of the operation. While allowing Tom room to "spread himself" (since, after all, the whole thing is supposed to take only "about a week"), Huck reserves the right to end the elaborations if anything goes wrong. Far from being, as Marx sees it, "submissive and gullible" and "completely under Tom's sway," Huck contradicts Tom (even sarcastically at times) and challenges him on several occasions when the situation warrants.[11] As Alan Gribben, one of the few critics who disagree that "Huck Finn is completely, absolutely in thralldom to Tom's bidding," points out:

> an unjaundiced reading of the texts [both *Tom Sawyer* and *Huckleberry Finn*] confirms quite the reverse: that Huck resists Tom at virtually every turn in their many colloquies. It is true that Tom usually wins his point, relying in extreme cases on his printed "authorities"—but he never gains Huck's acquiescence and cooperation until he has rephrased his argument in terms that suit Huck's notions of practicality and reason.[12]

9. Alfred Kazin, Afterword to *Adventures of Huckleberry Finn* (New York: Bantam, 1981) 10. The other implication of this passage—that Huck has some sort of death wish—is best left for interested psychoanalytic critics. See, for example, Forrest G. Robinson's "Silences in *Adventures of Huckleberry Finn*," *Nineteenth-Century Fiction* 37 (June 1982): 50–74. 11. Examples of Huck's standing up to Tom and even contradicting him sarcastically are found throughout the final chapters: "'Tom, if it ain't unregular and irreligious to sejest it,'" I says. "'If a pick's the handiest thing . . . I don't give a dead rat what the authorities thinks about it nuther.'" Thomas A. Gullason cites several others (arguments over the moat, the rope ladder, and sawing Jim's leg off) in his study, "The 'Fatal' Ending of *Huckleberry Finn*," *American Literature* 29 (March 1957): 89–90. 12. Allan-Gribben, "'I Did Wish Tom Sawyer Was There': Boy Book Elements in *Tom Sawyer* and *Huckleberry Finn*," in *One Hundred Years of Huckleberry Finn: The Boy, His Book, and American Culture*, ed. Robert Sattelmeyer and J. Donald Crowley (Columbia: University of Missouri Press, 1985), 169. Gribben also points out the importance of Tom's influence throughout the novel and is one of the few critics willing to view *Huckleberry Finn* as essentially a "boy's book."

. . . As Michelson points out: "The book would certainly be tidier if Huck's boyishness were utterly gone at the end, but Mark Twain did not sacrifice his best character for the sake of tidiness, and we should be thankful for that."

Jim Is Subtle and Intelligent

But what of Jim? Does his character really degenerate into that of an "end man at a minstrel show" or "submissive stage-Negro," as Marx and so many other critics have asserted? Marx feels that in the final chapters Jim suffers nothing less than a de-evolution from humanity:

> On the raft he was an individual, man enough to denounce Huck when Huck made him the victim of a practical joke. In the closing episode, however, we lose sight of Jim in the maze of farcical invention. He ceases to be a man. . . . This creature who bleeds ink and feels no pain is something less than human.

Marx scorns the fact that "Jim doesn't seem to mind [the evasion] too much," for he attributes it to Jim's "dehumanizing transformation" and the "discordant farcical tone" of the ending. Henry Nash Smith also speaks of Jim's being "reduced to the level of farce,"[13] but I assert that Jim is smarter, more human, and much more pragmatic—both before and after the evasion episodes—than Marx or Smith have noticed.

David L. Smith sums up the general understanding of Jim's pre-Phelps character as "compassionate, shrewd, thoughtful, self-sacrificing, and wise," and he goes deeper when he notes that Jim exploits common attitudes about "superstitious Negro behavior" to his advantage. As proof, Smith cites the early scenes in which Jim uses Tom's prank nickel to raise his status in the slave community and notes Jim's triumph in "wily and understated economic bartering" with Huck over the counterfeit quarter and the hair ball.[14]

Though he does not mention it in his essay, David Smith's conclusion that Jim "clearly possesses a subtlety and intelligence which "the '[stage] Negro' allegedly lacks" leads into a still deeper observation. In the river scene where Huck decides that he must go no further in the "crime" of helping a slave escape,[15] he paddles off in the canoe, ostensibly to find

13. Henry Nash Smith, *Mark Twain: The Development of a Writer* (New York: Atheneum, 1974) 14. David L. Smith, "Huck, Jim, and American Racial Discourse," *Mark Twain Journal* 22 (Fall 1984) 15. Unfortunately for Marx's thesis that Huck's moral growth is unswerving until the last chapters, the decision to turn Jim over to the authorities *follows* his repentance of the joke he played on Jim and his supposed awakening to Jim's inviolable humanity.

out whether they are near Cairo but really to turn in Jim. Henry Nash Smith notes in his discussion of raft dynamics that Jim "seems to guess what is passing through Huck's mind and does what he can to invoke the force of friendship and gratitude." This perceptive observation can be gainfully expanded if we imagine Jim's feeling of impotence as he perceives the white boy's inner turmoil. What amazing presence of mind he shows as he adroitly manipulates Huck's feelings: "Pooty soon I'll be a-shout'n' for joy, en I'll say, it's all on accounts o' Huck; I's a free man, en I couldn't even ben free ef it hadn't ben for Huck; Huck done it. Jim won't ever forgit you, Huck: you's de bes fren' Jim's ever had; en you's de *only* fren' ole Jim's got now." This psychologically aware inducement, probably suggested to Jim by Huck's new willingness to treat him as a human and even "humble himself before a nigger," takes "the tuck" out of the boy. As Huck wavers in his decision (his inner turmoil made evident to the hypersensitive runaway slave by a slowing down in his canoe paddling), Jim increases the pressure with: "Dah you goes, de ole true Huck; de on'y white genlman dat ever kep' his promise to ole Jim."

This passage demonstrates that Jim is able to employ both sides of the adult-child nature that his slave role has forced upon him. He is the wise adult, skilled at using child psychology on a boy, and at the same time, he is a powerless child (slave) who has learned the hard way to use subterfuge, not brawn, to manipulate the giant (white) creatures who rule him. Straightforward intellectual argument will not do: in a child, arguing is "smart alecky"; in a slave, it is "upity." When in doubt, Jim must sublimate his intelligence and manhood into a seeming childlike passivity while he controls the situation as best he can.

This reading would probably seem reasonable to most of the critics with whom I have disagreed; however, whereas Marx, Henry Nash Smith, and others feel strongly that Jim abdicates his "manhood" in the ending that they so despise, I would argue that none of Jim's courage, intelligence, and humanity disappear once he is "Tom's prisoner." If anything, the final chapters prove him more shrewd and/or noble than ever. His first act upon capture is to expose the king and duke, an action that demonstrates an inclination toward revenge not found in passive two-dimensional characters. Jim is hardly submissive here, as we can see when we contrast his attitude toward retribution with that of Huck, who is willing to continue playing the cowed child to those monsters even when he has nothing to lose: "I wanted to stop Jim's mouth till these fellows could get away. I didn't want no trouble with their kind."

Jim's first opportunity to prove that he has lost none of his shrewdness and intelligence comes when he is surprised by Tom and Huck in his hut. He quickly comprehends Tom's plan to fool the witch-haunted old turnkey, and he plays his part in the ruse perfectly. Certainly Jim needs cheering up in this chapter, but his situation is not so bleak as some commentators would have us believe. He knows that his captors are relying on a false handbill to locate his "owner," which will give him valuable time. And the prospects for escape look promising, for he is not exactly in a maximum security situation. Meanwhile, he is "looking hearty and healthy"; he is well-fed, prayed over, and supplied with plenty of pipes and tobacco. He knows, too, that Huck is close by and has reason to hope the boy will help him if he can.

But suddenly a whole new world of possibilities opens up. Here is not only Huck, miraculously ensconced in the family of his captors but Tom Sawyer as well—the brilliant and awesome Tom Sawyer, hero nonpareil of St. Petersburg, telling him: "If you hear any digging going on nights, it's us; we're going to set you free." Small wonder that Jim, like Huck, relaxes a bit in these final chapters; after what he has been through, he is, while still anxious to escape, naturally prone to optimism and disinclined to question Huck or Tom. . . .

[But] Jim has the courage to find fault when Tom begins to "spread himself." The official prisoner complains about the coat of arms, the inscriptions, the rats, the spiders—and he positively rebels at rattlesnakes: "I's willin to tackle mos' anything 'at ain't onreasonable, but ef you en Huck fetches a rattlesnake in heah for me to tame, I's gwyne to *leave,* dat's *shore.*" Jim is all assertive adult here, and Tom promptly retreats with, "Well, then let it go, let it go," which suggests, first, that Tom dominates his "subordinates" much less than some critics charge and, second, that Jim is in a more powerful position than Marx and others care to note. Jim, like Huck, has reserved the right to call off Tom's elaborate over-management whenever the need arises.

In short, Jim's will and mind have by no means been stolen from him by a capricious author or a cruel boy. So long as things "ain't onreasonable," it is in Jim's best interest to stick with Tom. He knows that phase two of the escape—the world beyond the Phelps farm—will be infinitely more difficult without Tom's resources. . . .

Jim's Nobility and Humanity

As to the supposed loss of Jim's noble character in the ending of the book, his nobility is nowhere more evident than in the climax of the escape. Whereas earlier Jim has given of himself in small ways, such as standing extra watches on the raft, in the final chapters he forfeits what is probably his last chance for freedom in order to help the old doctor operate on Tom. Moreover, when he is driven back to the farm with blows, loaded down with chains, and threatened with hanging, he refuses to say a word to implicate his accomplices, even though at this point he might well be harboring a justifiable resentment against Tom.

A slightly less noble, but no less interesting interpretation of Jim's character is also possible; we can, if we look closely, see more besides a full measure of humanity in Jim when Twain gives him the final "nub" in the story. Jim's timing in revealing to Huck that Pap was the dead man in the floating house suggests more, not less, shrewdness than anything in the earlier chapters. Many critics believe that Jim's being set free by Miss Watson makes the story anticlimactic, but it was *Jim* who withheld the most important anticlimactic secret from the hero of the book: "Doan' you 'member de house dat was float'n down de river, en dey wuz a man in dah, kivered up, en I went in en unkivered him and didn't let you come in? Well, den, you kin git yo' money when you wants it, kase dat wuz him."

With this, Jim's last speech in the novel, we must consider the idea that the entire journey—from Jackson's Island on, with all its terrors and heartaches—has been completely unnecessary so far as Huck is concerned. If Jim had told him that Pap was dead, Huck could have gone back, recovered his money, and lived the truly free life from which Pap, and Pap alone, had always kept him. So why did Jim not mention it until now? One very pragmatic reason is that if Huck were free to go back, where would that leave Jim? One could argue that Jim did not tell because he wished, in a fatherly way, to protect Huck from the sadness of losing his real father, but Jim promptly reveals the "gashly" truth when there is no more danger of his being abandoned. Until then, the desperate runaway slave clearly *needed* that white boy and "dasn't tell."

The argument that only an emasculated parody of Jim would abide Tom's not telling him he was free is weaker in this light. After all, Jim had his own interesting little secret. But whether we see nobility or shrewdness as Jim's outstanding trait, he is, in the last scene of the book, free at last and aware of the fact. He has been paid forty dollars for three weeks' work, and Tom is no doubt planning to buy him a steamboat ticket home to see his wife and children. This is simply no time for a wise adult like Jim to show irritation.

A product of "raised consciousness" Hollywood or a mass-market paperback version of the story would of course present us with a Jim who speaks perfect English, instructs Tom and Huck in relative morality, outwits his captors at every turn, and single-handedly exposes Southern slavery in all its hypocrisy. But even with the full modern treatment, he would be no more of a man—a "compassionate, shrewd, thoughtful, self-sacrificing, and wise" man—than the Jim that Twain portrayed in the ending of *Huckleberry Finn.* Jim neither loses his humanity nor becomes a "stage Negro" in the final section; to claim either point without reservation is to ignore evidence.

Tom's Silly but Noble Romanticism

If we are willing to look beyond the critical cliché of the "bad ending of *Huckleberry Finn,"* we can see a clear rationale for Huck's and Jim's conduct therein. But surely Tom Sawyer, the oft-cited villain of the final section, deserves some censure—or does he? . . .

It is certainly true that Tom oversteps the bounds of prudence; he becomes drunk on romanticism and endangers Jim and Huck unnecessarily with the "nonnamous letters.". . .

Tom Sawyer is a fine representative of those infatuated with false romanticism whom Twain liked to parody, and as such he makes a good symbol (if one is looking for symbols) for yet another aspect of the river society (carried over from *Life on the Mississippi)* that is an important subtext of *Huckleberry Finn.* But Tom is more than a symbol and more than a straw man. Twain makes his first literary boy-child, whom he may indeed distrust on one level, a sometimes brilliant and always brave lad. . . . Tom respects Jim's feelings, and despite the pressure of his romantic delusions, he is willing to compromise on most of his schemes. During the planning stages of the evasion, Tom also keeps Huck from stealing from the slaves unnecessarily and shows that he is less than totally self-centered when he mends Uncle Silas's rat holes without taking credit. In the escape he insists on being the last one out, so it is he who is shot. Rather than inhibit the escape (probably realizing that a claim that Jim was free might not be believed in the heat of capture), he is willing to suffer rather than seek a doctor.

Tom, like Twain, is not easily pigeon-holed; he is silly, yet noble as well. He is, in a sense, an updated Don Quixote: exasperating, yet sympathetic. If he is the symbol of "the decadent-romantic South" or "the spirit of the Gilded Age," or some sort of psychopath (or manifestation of Samuel Clemens's psychological problems) as some critics tend to see him, he is also full of the heroic pioneer spirit, the give-me-liberty-or-give-me-death, I-only-regret-I-have-one-life-to-give-for-my-country, damn-the-torpedoes-full-speed-ahead American Right Stuff. It is well that he has this aspect to balance the soft spots in his character: without it he would be as flat and boring as all the other two-dimensional "social" symbols in literature. . . .

If we take Tom as the Iago of the novel, he is an antagonist on the order of Milton's Satan or Thackeray's Becky Sharp. We cannot help but like him, even if we despise some of his actions—though Tom, . . . is hardly in Satan's or Becky's league as a candidate for despising.

CHRONOLOGY

For names and dates of more of Twain's works, see Works by Mark Twain.

1835

November 30—Samuel Langhorne Clemens (who will become Mark Twain) is born in Florida, Missouri.

1838

Frederick Douglass escapes from slavery. Race riots and lynchings have been increasing for three years. The Underground Railroad, which helps slaves escape, is established.

1839

The Clemens family moves to Hannibal, Missouri, on the Mississippi River.

1843

Sojourner Truth, a freed slave who saw most of her thirteen children sold as slaves, speaks out against slavery around the country.

1847

March—Sam's father, John Marshall Clemens, dies.

1850

September—Congress adopts the Compromise of 1850 in an attempt to prevent the dissolution of the Union over the issue of slavery.

1851

January—Sam begins working on Hannibal's *Western Union.*

1852

Harriet Beecher Stowe's *Uncle Tom's Cabin* is published.

1854

Abraham Lincoln calls for the gradual emancipation of slaves.

1856

October 18—Sam's first letter signed "Thomas Jefferson Snodgrass" appears in the Keokuk, Iowa, *Daily Post.*

1857

Sam begins training as a riverboat pilot.

1858

June 13—The steamer *Philadelphia* explodes; victims include Sam's brother Henry, who dies six days later.

1859

April 9—Sam Clemens receives his pilot's license.

June—The Comstock silver lode is discovered in Nevada.

1860

November 6—Abraham Lincoln is elected president.

December 20—South Carolina votes to secede from the Union.

1861

April 14—Fort Sumter, South Carolina, is captured by Confederate forces.

April 15—Lincoln declares a state of "insurrection." The American Civil War begins.

June—Ten more states have seceded to join South Carolina in the Confederacy; Sam sees brief service with the Confederate Marion Rangers ("The Campaign That Failed").

1863

January 1—Lincoln signs the Emancipation Proclamation.

February 3—Sam first uses "Mark Twain" byline.

November 20—Lincoln delivers the Gettysburg Address.

1865

March 4—Lincoln is sworn in for his second term as president.

April 9—Confederate general Robert E. Lee surrenders to Union general Ulysses S. Grant at Appomattox Courthouse, Virginia, bringing the Civil War to an end.

April 14—Lincoln is assassinated.

November 18—"The Celebrated Jumping Frog of Calaveras County" is printed in the New York *Saturday Press.* Relief at the end of the war has many Americans looking for light-hearted fare; the "Frog" is an immediate success.

1867

June 8—As travel correspondent for the San Francisco *Alta California,* Twain sails on the *Quaker City* for a tour of the Mediterranean and the Holy Land. This tour will become the basis of *The Innocents Abroad.*

December 27—Twain meets Olivia ("Livy") Langdon.

1869

February 4—Sam becomes engaged to Livy.

1870

February 2—Sam marries Livy.

November 7—Their first child, Langdon Clemens, is born.

1872

March 19—Olivia Susan (Susy) Clemens is born.

June 2—Langdon Clemens (Sam and Livy's only son) dies.

1874

June 8—Clara Clemens is born.

1876

The Adventures of Tom Sawyer is published.

1880

July 26—Jean Clemens is born.

1884

Twain campaigns for Grover Cleveland for president.

1885

The Adventures of Huckleberry Finn (Tom Sawyer's Companion) is published.

Fall—Twain publishes the memoirs of Ulysses S. Grant.

1890

Twain begins investing in the Paige typesetting machine.

1891

March 4—The International Copyright Act Twain and Charles Dickens lobbied for is passed, protecting foreign authors from piracy at the hands of American publishers. (Twain, who has suffered piracy from publishers around the world, hopes other countries will follow suit.)

1893

A stock market crash in June leads to a national financial panic; by the end of the year, the country is in what is being called the worst depression in its history.

1894

April 18—With the failure of his publishing company and other financial difficulties, Twain is bankrupt.

1895

July—Twain begins world lecture tour to pay off debts.

1896

August 18—Susy Clemens dies.

1898

The Twains' last debts are paid off in late 1898 or early 1899. In winning the Spanish-American War, the United States establishes itself as a world power. The Anti-Imperialist League objects to the growing drive to claim American colonies. Twain, reformer Jane Addams, philosopher William James, industrialist Andrew Carnegie, labor leader Samuel Gompers, and thirty thousand other members of the league object to U.S. conquests to build an empire.

1901

February—*To the Person Sitting in Darkness* is published (the publisher is the Anti-Imperialist League of New York).

1904

June 5—Livy Clemens dies.

1909

December 24—Jean Clemens dies.

1910

April 21—Mark Twain dies.

For Further Research

Biographies

Guy Cardwell, *The Man Who Was Mark Twain.* New Haven, CT: Yale University Press, 1991.

Clara Clemens, *My Father, Mark Twain.* New York: Harper & Brothers, 1931.

Cyril Clemens, *Young Sam Clemens.* Portland, ME: Leon Tebbetts, 1942.

Everett Emerson, *The Authentic Mark Twain: A Literary Biography of Samuel Clemens.* Philadelphia: University of Pennsylvania Press, 1984.

Delancey Ferguson, *Mark Twain, Man and Legend.* New York: Russell and Russell, 1965.

Andrew Jay Hoffman, *Inventing Mark Twain: The Lives of Samuel Langhorne Clemens.* New York: William Morrow, 1997.

William Dean Howells, *My Mark Twain: Reminiscences and Criticisms.* New York: Harper & Brothers, 1910.

Justin Kaplan, *Mark Twain and His World.* New York: Simon and Schuster, 1974.

—, *Mr. Clemens and Mark Twain: A Biography.* Simon and Schuster, 1966.

John Lauber, *The Making of Mark Twain: A Biography.* New York: American Heritage Press, 1985.

Stephen Butler Leacock, *Mark Twain.* New York: Haskell House, 1974.

Charles Neider, *Mark Twain.* New York: Horizon, 1967.

Albert Bigelow Paine, *Mark Twain: A Biography: The Personal and Literary Life of Samuel Langhorne Clemens.* 3 vols. New York: Harper & Brothers, 1912.

George Sanderlin, *Mark Twain: As Others Saw Him.* New York: Coward, McCann & Geoghegan, 1978.

Henry Nash Smith, *Mark Twain: The Development of a Writer.* Cambridge, MA: Harvard University Press, 1962.

Jeffrey Steinbrink, *Getting to Be Mark Twain.* Berkeley and Los Angeles: University of California Press, 1991.

Edward Wagenknecht, *Mark Twain: The Man and His Work.* New Haven, CT: Yale University Press, 1935.

Dixon Wecter, *Sam Clemens of Hannibal.* Boston: Houghton Mifflin, 1952.

Analysis and Criticism

Harold Beaver, *Huckleberry Finn.* London: Allen & Unwin, 1987.

Walter Blair, *Mark Twain and Huck Finn.* Berkeley and Los Angeles: University of California Press, 1960.

Louis J. Budd, ed., *New Essays on* Adventures of Huckleberry Finn. New York: Cambridge University Press, 1985.

George C. Carrington, *The Dramatic Unity of* Huckleberry Finn. Columbus: Ohio State University Press, 1976.

Thadious M. Davis, ed., *Black Writers on* Adventures of Huckleberry Finn: *A Hundred Years Later.* Special edition of *Mark Twain Journal*, vol. 22, no. 2, Fall 1984.

Shelley Fisher Fishkin, *Was Huck Black? Mark Twain and African-American Voices.* New York: Oxford University Press, 1993.

John C. Gerber, comp., *The Merrill Studies* in Huckleberry Finn. Columbus, OH: Merrill, 1971.

Andrew Jay Hoffman, *Twain's Heroes, Twain's Worlds.* Philadelphia: University of Pennsylvania Press, 1988.

M. Thomas Inge, ed., *Huck Finn Among the Critics: A Centennial Selection.* Frederick, MD: University Publications of America, 1985.

James S. Leonard, Thomas A. Tenney, and Thadious M. Davis, eds., *Satire or Evasion? Black Perspectives on* Huckleberry Finn. Durham, NC: Duke University Press, 1992.

Tom Quirk, *Coming to Grips with* Huckleberry Finn: *Essays on a Book, a Boy, and a Man.* Columbia: University of Missouri Press, 1993.

Roger Blaine Salomon, *Mark Twain and the Image of History.* New Haven, CT: Yale University Press, 1961.

Robert Sattelmeyer and J. Donald Crowley, eds., *One Hundred Years of* Huckleberry Finn: *The Boy, His Book, and American Culture.* Columbia: University of Missouri Press, 1985.

Claude M. Simpson, ed., *Twentieth Century Interpretations of* Adventures of Huckleberry Finn: *A Collection of Critical Essays.* Englewood Cliffs, NJ: Prentice-Hall, 1968.

Arthur Lawrence Vogelback, *The Publication and Reception of* Huckleberry Finn *in America.* Durham, NC: Duke University Press, 1939.

Literary or Historical Background

Walter Blair, ed., *Mark Twain's Hannibal, Huck & Tom.* Berkeley and Los Angeles: University of California Press, 1969.

Carl Bode, ed., *American Life in the 1840s.* Garden City, NY: Anchor, 1967.

John M. Dobson, *Politics in the Gilded Age.* New York: Praeger, 1972.

Frank Otto Gattell and John M. McFaul, eds., *Jacksonian America, 1815–1840.* Englewood Cliffs, NJ: Prentice-Hall, 1970.

Arthur M. Schlesinger Jr., *The Age of Jackson.* Boston: Little, Brown, 1953.

The World Wide Web

Websites are notoriously ephemeral, but new information is posted often, so a good search engine will help track down the latest postings. At this writing, interesting information about Twain and *Huckleberry Finn* can be found at these websites:

etext.lib.virginia.edu/twain (posted by the Electronic Text Center at the University of Virginia, and likely to remain available)

web.mit.edu/linguistics/www/forum/twainweb.html (includes archives of messages posted to the Mark Twain Forum)

marktwain.miningco.com (includes links to e-texts, reviews, and a variety of useful information)

Works by Mark Twain

Since many volumes and many different editions and combinations of Mark Twain's work have been made available over the years (and previously unpublished material still appears occasionally), the following is not a complete listing. Short stories and essays are generally included only when they have been collected into books; dates are for first U.S. publication.

The Celebrated Jumping Frog of Calaveras County and Other Sketches (1867)

The Innocents Abroad, or The New Pilgrims' Progress (1869)

Mark Twain's (Burlesque) Autobiography and First Romance (1871)

Roughing It (1872)

The Gilded Age: A Tale of To-day (with Charles Dudley Warner) (1873)

Mark Twain's Sketches (1874)

Sketches, New and Old (1875)

The Adventures of Tom Sawyer (1876)

Ah Sin (with Bret Harte) (1877)

A True Story and the Recent Carnival of Crime (*The Facts Concerning the Recent Carnival of Crime in Connecticut)* (1877)

Punch, Brothers, Punch! and Other Sketches (1877)

A Tramp Abroad (1880)

"1601" or Conversation at the Social Fireside as It Was in the Time of the Tudors (1880)

The Prince and the Pauper (1882)

The Stolen White Elephant, Etc. (1882)

Life on the Mississippi (1883)

The Adventures of Huckleberry Finn (Tom Sawyer's Comrade) (1885)

Mark Twain's Library of Humor. Edited by Samuel Langhorne Clemens, William Dean Howells, and Charles Hopkins Clark. (Contains works by Twain, "Anonymous," and forty-six other authors) (1888)

A Connecticut Yankee in King Arthur's Court (1889)

The Man That Corrupted Hadleyburg (1890)

The American Claimant (1892)

Merry Tales (1892)

The £1,000,000 Bank-note and Other New Stories (1893)

The Niagara Book (by W.D. Howells, Mark Twain, Prof. Nathaniel S. Shaler, and others) (1893)

The Tragedy of Pudd'nhead Wilson and the Comedy of Those Extraordinary Twins (by 1899 called *Pudd'nhead*

Wilson and Those Extraordinary Twins) (1894)

Tom Sawyer Abroad ("by Huck Finn, edited by Mark Twain") (1894)

The Personal Recollections of Joan of Arc (1896)

Tom Sawyer Abroad, Tom Sawyer Detective, and Other Stories (1896)

How to Tell a Story and Other Essays (1897)

Following the Equator (1897)

The Man That Corrupted Hadleyburg and Other Stories and Essays (1900)

To the Person Sitting in Darkness (1901)

A Double Barrelled Detective Story (1902)

My Debut as a Literary Person with Other Essays and Stories (1903)

The Jumping Frog in English, Then in French, Then Clawed Back into a Civilized Language Once More by Patient Unremunerated Toil (1903)

Extracts from Adam's Diary, Translated from the Original MS (1904)

A Dog's Tale (1904)

King Leopold's Soliloquy: A Defense of His Congo Rule (1905)

Editorial Wild Oats (1905)

Eve's Diary, Translated from the Original MS (1906)

What Is Man? (1906)

The $30,000 Bequest and Other Stories (1906)

Christian Science (1907)

A Horse's Tale (1907)

Extract from Captain Stormfield's Visit to Heaven (1909)

Is Shakespeare Dead? From My Autobiography (1909)

Published Posthumously

Mark Twain's Speeches. Compiled by F.A. Nast. Introduction by W.D. Howells. (1910)

Death Disk (1915)

The Mysterious Stranger (1916)

Mark Twain's Letters. Edited by Albert Bigelow Paine. (1917)

Who Was Sarah Findlay? With a Suggested Solution of the Mystery by J.M. Barrie (1917)

The Curious Republic of Gondour and Other Whimsical Sketches (by Samuel L. Clemens) (1919)

Mark Twain, Able Yachtsman, Interviews Himself on Why Lipton Failed to Lift the Cup (1920)

The Writings of Mark Twain. 37 vols. Edited by Albert Bigelow Paine. (Includes *Mark Twain's Autobiography*, 2 vols., 1924.) (1922–1925)

The Adventures of Thomas Jefferson Snodgrass. Edited by Charles Honce. (1928)

A Champagne Cocktail and a Catastrophe: Two Acting Charades (1930)

Mark Twain's Notebook. Edited by Albert Bigelow Paine. (1935)

Letters from the Sandwich Islands Written for the Sacramento Union *by Mark Twain.* Edited by G. Ezra Dane. (1938)

Mark Twain in Eruption: Hitherto Unpublished Pages About Men and Events. Edited by Bernard De Voto. (1940)

Mark Twain's Travels with Mr. Brown. Edited by G. Ezra Dane. (1940)

Mark Twain's Letters to Will Bowen: "My First & Oldest & Dearest Friend." Edited by Theodore Hornberger. (1941)

Mark Twain's Letters in the Muscatine Journal. Edited by Edgar M. Branch. (1942)

The Letters of Quintus Curtius Snodgrass (1946)

The Love Letters of Mark Twain. Edited by Dixon Wecter. (1949)

Mark Twain to Mrs. Fairbanks. Edited by Dixon Wecter. (1949)

Mark Twain to Uncle Remus. (Joel Chandler Harris) Edited by Thomas H. English. (1953)

Mark Twain of the Enterprise. Edited by Henry Nash Smith with Frederick Anderson. (1957)

The Autobiography of Mark Twain. Edited by Charles Neider. (Quotations from the *Autobiography* in the present work were taken from this version.) (1959)

Mark Twain–Howells Letters: The Correspondence of Samuel L. Clemens and William Dean Howells, 1872–1910. 2 vols. Edited by Henry Nash Smith and William M. Gibson. (Cover says "1869–1910.") (1960)

Mark Twain's Letters to Mary. Edited by Lewis Leary. (1961)

Letters from the Earth. Edited by Bernard De Voto. (1962)

Early Tales and Sketches, vol. 1 (1851–1864). Edited by Edgar Marquess Branch and Robert H. First with Harriet Elinor Smith. (1979)

The Outrageous Mark Twain: Some Lesser-Known but Extra-ordinary Works, with "Reflections on Religion" Now in Book Form for the First Time. Edited by Charles Neider. (1987)

Mark Twain's Aquarium: The Samuel Clemens Angelfish Correspondence, 1905–1910. Edited by John Cooley. (1991)

The Adventures of Huckleberry Finn. With new text; foreword and addendum by Victor Doyno, introduction by Justin Kaplan. Includes omissions and variations from the recently discovered first half of Twain's manuscript. (1996)

INDEX